INNER LIVES

PAULA C. JOHNSON

INNER LIVES

Voices of African American Women in Prison

With a Foreword by Joyce A. Logan
and an Afterword by Angela J. Davis

New York University Press • *New York and London*

NEW YORK UNIVERSITY PRESS
New York and London
www.nyupress.org

First published in paperback in 2004.

Library of Congress Cataloging-in-Publication Data
Johnson, Paula C.
Inner lives : voices of African American women in prison /
Paula C. Johnson ; with a foreword by Joyce A. Logan.
p. cm.
Includes bibliographical references and index.
ISBN 0-8147-4254-8 (cloth : alk paper) —
ISBN 0-8147-4255-6 (pbk : alk paper)
1. Women prisoners—United States—Biography.
2. Women prisoners—United States—Interviews.
3. African American prisoners—United States—Biography.
4. African American prisoners—United States—Interviews.
5. Discrimination in criminal justice administration—
United States.   I. Title.
HV9468 .J65 2002
365'.43'08996073—dc21   2002014118

New York University Press books are printed on acid-free paper,
and their binding materials are chosen for strength and durability.

Manufactured in the United States of America

c 10 9 8 7 6 5 4 3 2
p 10 9 8 7 6 5 4 3 2 1

Contents

Foreword

Joyce A . Logan

WHEN I WAS ASKED to write the foreword to *Inner Lives: Voices of African American Women in Prison*, I was humbled and overwhelmed by the request. Never in my wildest dreams did I ever imagine that I would meet and have an opportunity to work with and assist a law professor in such an endeavor as a book about African American women in prison. Although I was a "writ writer" in prison, even obtaining a reversal of a conviction for a fellow inmate, as I began writing this introduction I worried that my words would not be adequate for such a distinguished publication. Part of my resolve since my release, however, has been to try to live up to the expectations and encouragement of newfound friends and acquaintances. Professor Paula Johnson has motivated me to reach even higher.

All of us who are featured in the pages of this book have had our lives transformed because of our incarceration, our removal from society. We were taken from our families, friends, and communities and placed in environments that were strained and artificial. But, as the stories contained in *Inner Lives: Voices of African American Women in Prison* illustrate, we remain your daughters, sisters, mothers, aunts, and nieces. We have been separated, but we are not gone. We may be distant, but we are a part of you. We may be absent, but we are very much present.

This book poignantly conveys this message from African American female prisoners and former prisoners. Being locked up does not eliminate our need to believe that we have something to offer and contribute to others. It does not end our need to be productive. It does not destroy our need to feel connected to something good and positive.

When I was a young person growing up in Dallas, Texas, education was not emphasized. Though my parents punished me for skipping school, I somehow did not grasp just how critical education was to a person's success in life. I have since learned that education does not occur just in formal classrooms. Self-education for me began in the county jail as I refused to accept what I viewed as an unjust sentence. To save myself, I sought out the law library, reading cases and learning how to do research, looking for a way to get my sentence reduced. Even though I was never able to accomplish this goal, fighting, reading, and helping others in their legal struggles kept me alive in prison. Being able to help people gave me a sense of self-worth that I had never felt in the free world.

The stories shared in this book will educate people in all walks of life who have never been personally touched by someone who has been incarcerated. Our voices speak loudly of our upbringing, families, crimes, and imprisonment. But most resounding are our words of hope and anticipation, the excitement of a brighter future.

While my transition to freedom has been challenging, it has proven to be a most rewarding and satisfying part of my life. The strength and courage that we as African American women maintain in prison allow us to tackle the new situations and technologies that we encounter upon our return home. The endurance and patience that African American women must learn in prison carries us through our anxiety and our fears of readapting to society. The lessons that we learn, and hopefully will teach upon our return to society, are ones of faith, determination, and humanity. We are the history, the present, and the future. That is the message that I see in this book—one I hope you will embrace.

Preface

I HAVE BEEN intimately involved in the criminal justice system on the grassroots and professional level for twenty years. As a former prosecutor, I worked closely with women and children who had been physically and sexually abused. In battered women's and emergency shelters, I worked closely with women who were beaten, homeless, jobless, hungry, and alone. They sought safety and refuge for their children and for themselves, and relief from the strife in their lives. For survival, they sometimes became perpetrators of crimes.

Despite my years of involvement on criminal justice issues related to women's lives, the intensity of my meetings with African American women in prison was repeatedly humbling. Ultimately, what impressed me about the women I interviewed for *Inner Lives* was their refusal to remain permanently in despair. The women with whom I spoke were more honest than many people in the "free world" about their personal flaws, naiveté, wrongdoing, and responsibility for harms they caused or contributed to. Even when I was despairing about the magnitude of the difficulties and disadvantages that the women experienced, I was buoyed by their refusal to concede their humanity under such dispiriting odds and conditions. I recognized, however, that the women's perseverance often came at a high price for themselves, their children, other family members, friends, victims, and others affected by their actions.

My desire to communicate my belief in the value of Black women's lives impelled me to begin this project. At times, I identified with Deborah Gray White, who sometimes found the work on her historical account of twentieth-century Black women's struggles in defense of themselves to be captured in the title of her book, *Too Heavy a Load*.[1] Throughout it all I also have learned something more about perseverance. I share with the women who participated in *Inner Lives* a vision of U.S. society that is more dedicated to prevention and wellness than to retribution. Their visions impelled me to complete this work. Foremost, then, I thank all the women who participated in this book project and who constantly reminded me of its importance.

Acknowledgments

IN ADDITION TO all of those who participated in *Inner Lives*, including those whose narratives are featured in the book and those whose experiences are reflected in the data summaries, I thank many others who helped to make this book a reality. I thank the numerous administrators and staff members at Departments of Correction and women's correctional institutions in Arkansas, Connecticut, Florida, Louisiana, Nevada, New Jersey, New York, and Ohio for granting permission to interview participants in facilities in these states. With apologies to those whom I may forget to mention, I especially thank Heather Ziemba, Connecticut; Linda Guidroz, Sheidra Traveler, and Helen Travers, Louisiana; Christine Bodo, Loy Hayes, and Jerry Alexander, Nevada; Charlotte Blackwell, New Jersey; Elaine Lord, Theresa McNair, and Delores Thornton, New York; and Norman Rose, Maralene Sines, Joe Andrews, and Valerie Aden, Ohio, for their pivotal assistance in making this project possible.

Several people helped me during the preparatory stages of this book. During my visit at the University of Arizona College of Law, Professor Barbara Atwood and now-Dean Toni Massaro made helpful suggestions on my book proposal and expressed much enthusiasm for the project. They also shared their infectious love for Arizona, a place that provided the physical and psychic space for further honing this project. I also valued the assistance of the staff at the Center for Contemporary Photography at the University of Arizona who allowed me to pore over their photography collections.

Many thanks go to the Syracuse University community. First, special thanks to Dean Daan Braveman of Syracuse University College of Law. I have been very fortunate to work with him, first as a colleague and then as our dean. For this project, he provided generous financial and moral support. Associate Deans Arlene Kanter and Leslie Bender, too, were ardent believers in this project and provided meaningful assistance. I also thank my faculty colleagues, the staff, and students at S.U. College of Law. Throughout this project, any one of them would stop me to inquire, "How's the book coming?" Their words of interest and encouragement helped see this project to completion. Also, I thank my "sistaprofs"—Africana women professors at S.U.—for their belief in my work.

I have benefited from excellent and enthusiastic research assistance over the course of this project from Nellie Abdallah, Tylyn Bozeman, Laura Clemens, Julinda Dawkins, Susan Grimes, Kathleen Guinses, Kirstin Keel, and Martine Voltaire. Our secretarial staff also provided expert skill and advice in completion of the manuscript. I particularly thank Theresa Coulter for remaining flexible, and for typing, proofreading, and making important editorial suggestions on the text.

I thank Ellen Barry, Jon Getz, Abbe Jolles, Bonnie Kerness, Andrea D. Lyon, Deborah Waire Post, Monica Pratt, Beth E. Richie, Dorothy Roberts, Katheryn Russell, Sister Patricia Schlosser, Brenda V. Smith, Gail Smith, Cheryl Wattley, and Cathy McDaniels Wilson for sharing their time, knowledge and constructive suggestions for the book. Everett Green provided an early opportunity for me to present this work and receive valuable feedback at his colloquium at the New School for Social Research, New York. I also received important feedback from my colleagues in the Clinical Legal Education Section of the American Association of Law Schools, where I also presented the work.

Of course, without a publisher, the book would not find the public and the public would not find the book. Here I am grateful to Niko Pfund, former editor in chief of NYU Press and now at Oxford University Press, for his profound excitement upon receiving my book proposal, leading to my relationship with NYU Press. I am also grateful to Steve Maikowski, current editor in chief at NYU Press, and Alison Waldenberg, my editor for *Inner Lives*, for their care and commitment to this project.

My friends also sustained me throughout this project, especially Althea Henry, Roxanne Hill, Michelle Johnson, Elena Levy, and Masani

Tyler. Theodora H. Brown-Greene provided friendship and legal counsel, and Michelle Johnson and Dana Davis were also early believers.

My family supported me throughout completion of the book. My parents, Wanza N. Johnson and Ed Beasley, nurtured me and encouraged all of my educational goals. My partner, Delores M. Walters, supported me in innumerable ways so that I could complete this book. And I thank all of my extended family for their love and encouragement.

Finally, I thank all of those whose work preceded mine and who continue to raise critical questions and seek effective responses to the social dilemmas in our society.

Yet the question remains, What is different about Black women? What makes them worthy of separate and distinct study? All women, in all times and places, have been concerned about family, education, and religion. Black women are no exception. Yet Black women are different, and the source of their difference is best reflected through examination of their inner lives. How can we really come to know and understand their culture of struggle and resistance? The best means is to record and listen to their own personal voices. Here, among the images, are the words of Black women, completing the picture, so to speak.

—Darlene Clark Hine, *The Faces of Our Past: Images of Black Women from Colonial Times to the Present*

Introduction

I would always be the song struggling to be heard.
                                        —Maya Angelou, "The Reunion"

Dear Professor Johnson,
    I pray that you're doing well. I have been thinking a lot
about my life since the interview. I felt nervous and did my
best to answer your questions, but now I feel that there were
more details I should have mentioned. It's sort of hard for me
to trust people, so I was hesitant about some of the things I
said. But after getting back to my cell and contemplating the
day, I felt like there was more I wanted to say so that you can
have a clearer picture of the makings of who I am today and
what I was before this experience. . . . Where do I begin?
    My childhood was surrounded by violence. My father
was always fighting with my mom, especially when he got
drunk. Growing up, my mother always beat me a lot. She
used anything she got her hands on. I was very withdrawn as
a child. I was never talked to, only talked at and never asked
how I felt about anything.
    I loved music, especially gospel. I sang in the church
choir, played in both the elementary school band (recorder)
and in high school (clarinet). I taught myself how to play the
organ, piano, guitar, bass, and violin. Music just always made
me feel better about things. I also liked looking at things
through a microscope and experimenting. Science, biology,
chemistry, and similar subjects interested me. Studying them
helped me take my mind off my environment.
    Through all my childhood experiences, I still tried to treat
people the way I hoped they would treat me. I have risked my

life on many occasions to save someone's life. These were people I did not even know most of the time. For example, when I
was about twelve years old I saw an old man getting mugged
and the guy was about to stab him after already cutting off his
pants pocket. I started yelling and ran to help the old man,
which stopped the man from sticking the knife in him. In November 1985, I was walking down [the street] and saw the
building on fire. I went into the burning building and woke
up everybody. The hallway didn't even have lights in it but I
ran all the way up to the top floor. The newspaper wrote
about the fire but no one knew it was me who woke those
people up.

So, although I committed a terrible crime, it doesn't really
describe the type of person I am on the inside. There were
times when I witnessed people getting shot or stabbed and
stood by them and tried to stop their bleeding until the paramedics came. I'm not trying to sound like a hero, but I have
done a lot more good in my life than wrong. Most of the time
prisoners are only defined/judged by their crime and nothing
else matters.

My experiences in prison have been like living in hell, especially for the first seven years. It has also been a very productive experience because I have learned so much about who
I really am. . . . While enduring hardships, I learned just how
strong I was and the importance of staying focused on long
term and short term goals. I took courses from five different
schools at one time. Some of the courses took two to three
years to complete and one took eight years. I felt proud of myself. For the first time in my life, I never gave up when things
were not going well.

So, as you put everything together for your project I pray
that you will put together the whole picture about who I am.

I received the above letter from Cynthia, an African American woman
whom I had interviewed two weeks earlier in a maximum-security
prison in New Jersey. She is serving a life sentence for murder. Our interview was rather lengthy by prison visit standards and we discussed
a great deal. Still, it was clear that there was more on Cynthia's mind, as
she struggled to communicate the depths of her feelings about her life

prior to incarceration and during her prison experience. The letter she sent to me after our visit indicated that our conversation remained on her mind and prompted continued reflections on her life. She also stated that she thought it essential that I understand the most difficult experiences of her life, as well as the internal changes that she underwent during incarceration. She wrote about her acquired self-awareness and perseverance and stated: "I never thought that I would even be able to express the things I'm saying in this letter, so I came a long way."

Cynthia is one of numerous African American women whom I interviewed about their lives and experiences in U.S. prisons and jails. As an African American woman, she is a member of the largest percentage of incarcerated women in the United States. Further, as an incarcerated African American woman, she is also among the most invisible members of American society. African American women's voices, such as Cynthia's, are rarely heard on crucial concerns about social policy, criminality, and the administration of the criminal justice system in the United States. Instead, these women are often absent from academic and social policy discussions relating to their lives.

Such omission results from the general exclusion of incarcerated women's voices. As researchers Sharon McQuaide and John Ehrenreich wrote, "This lack of knowledge presents both a problem and an opportunity. There are few media images or academic studies of these women to guide or misguide researchers. The task of deconstructing popular or academic images is barely an issue."[1] Despite the growing body of literature about women in prison, McQuaide and Ehrenreich's observations are particularly relevant regarding the lack of research and prevalence of stereotypical written and visual images of African American women who have experienced incarceration. In this regard, bell hooks has written:

> I found that when "women" were talked about, the experience of white women was universalized to stand for all female experience and that when "black people" were talked about, the experience of black men was the point of reference. . . . It was clear that these biases had created a circumstance where there was little or no information about the distinct experiences of black women.[2]

In response to the situation that hooks describes, this book focuses on the lives of African American women. Their views on important social issues are considered significant and authoritative, particularly as they are informed by the women's direct experiences within U.S. society and the U.S. criminal justice system. Black feminist analysis provides the appropriate methodology for examining the criminal justice system in light of the women's knowledge and experience. According to sociologist Patricia Hill Collins, "[B]lack feminist thought consists of specialized knowledge created by African-American women which clarifies a standpoint of and for Black women. In other words, Black feminist thought encompasses theoretical interpretations of Black women's reality by those who live it."[3] In addition, Collins states that among the core themes of Black women's outlook is recognition that "in spite of the differences created by historical era, age, social class, sexual orientation, or ethnicity, the legacy of struggle against racism and sexism is a common thread binding African-American women."[4]

Thus, relating to the circumstances of African American women generally, and incarcerated African American women specifically, the continuing struggle for personhood, freedom, and justice comprise core themes of Black feminist thought. As such, Black feminist analysis has examined African American women's resistance to prevailing stereotypical or negative images, disenfranchisement, and social restraints from Black women's perspectives. Beyond focusing on African American women, however, Black feminist theory offers a path toward a distinctly humanist vision of society.[5] In this vein, the theory offers insight into the particular situations of African American women's lives, but it also provides a critique of the social and legal systems that purport to advance legitimate and equitable treatment throughout American society. Therefore, this study of African American women's experiences in U.S. criminal justice and correctional systems fills a void in the critical analysis of legal and social policies as informed by African American women's insights.

This book is organized into three parts that include a legal and empirical analysis, narratives of incarcerated and formerly incarcerated African American women and others who have relevant perspectives, and conclusions and recommendations based on information and insights from parts 1 and 2. Part 1 examines historical and contemporary issues with regard to African American women in the U.S. criminal justice system. Consequently, this section addresses the race, gender, and class-based determinants of criminality and punishments during the early and recent periods of American history. In addition, in part 1 I analyze prevalent criminal law doctrine and sentencing reform in the face of the unprecedented rise in the U.S. prison population. Specifically, this examination focuses on drug laws, three-strikes laws, and mandatory minimum sentencing schemes for their influence on the increase in African American women's incarceration rates.

Part 2 presents the narrative voices of African American women concerning their life experiences, events leading to their involvement in the criminal justice system, their relationships with children, family members and friends during and subsequent to incarceration, and their perspectives about the criminal justice and correctional systems. This section also includes perspectives from family members, legal professionals, correctional administrators, community volunteers, and transitional program administrators in order to better understand the institutional dynamics and community connections that affect the women's lives. In addition, part 2 includes photographs of those who are featured.

Finally, in part 3 I examine the larger societal implications revealed by the narrative discussions and analyses of contemporary criminal justice policies. Here I also include recommendations for alternative approaches to address criminality and punishment in U.S. society.

WHERE WE ARE

The United States entered the twenty-first century with an incarceration rate of two million people, thereby garnering the dubious distinction of having the largest imprisonment rate in the world.[6] Moreover, in recent years the number of women in U.S. prisons and jails has grown more sharply and more quickly than the male prison population during similar time periods.[7] Noting the increase in women's supervision within the criminal justice system, the Bureau of Justice Statistics (BJS) reported that between 1990 and 1998, "the per capita number of women under probation supervision climbed 40%; the jail rate grew 60%; the imprisonment rate increased 88%; and the per capita number of offenders under parole supervision was up 80%."[8] In an earlier report, BJS found that the total state prison population had grown by 58 percent between 1986 and 1991.[9] During this period, the number of women in prison increased by 75 percent, while the number of men increased by 53 percent.[10] Similarly, BJS noted that between 1986 and 1991, the number of female arrests grew by 24 percent, while the number of male arrests increased by 13 percent.[11] In 1998, the Federal Bureau of Prisons reported that, "since 1988, the number of [federal] female inmates has increased by 182 percent, compared to a rate of growth of 158 percent for male inmates during the same period."[12]

Even more disturbing than the overall increase in the number of incarcerated women is the fact that over two-thirds of women who are confined in local, state, and federal institutions are women of color—mostly African American women.[13] BJS projections of future incarceration rates for African American and Caucasian American women reveal expectations of even greater disproportionate representation of African American women in these ranks. Thus, while BJS projected a 15 percent increase in Caucasian women's incarceration rate, it projected a *95 percent* increase in the incarceration rate for African American women during the same period.[14] Moreover, the Government Accounting Office (GAO) reported that across all age groups, "[I]n 1997, black non-Hispanic females (with an incarceration rate of 200 per 100,000) were more than twice as likely as Hispanic females (87 per 100,000), and eight times more likely than white non-Hispanic females (25 per 100,000) to be in prison."[15] Updating their seminal 1990 report, *Young Black Americans and the Criminal Justice System*, Mark Mauer and Tracy Huling, of the Sentencing Project, noted that "African-American women have experienced the greatest increase in criminal justice supervision of all demographic groups."[16] Finally, BJS concluded, as it must, that "[w]omen in State prisons . . . were most likely to be black."[17]

As we will see in part 1, the overwhelming majority of incarcerated persons are committed for nonviolent offenses. Moreover, the growth in the U.S. prison population is related to changes in criminal justice and sentencing policies rather than to differential rates of offending; indeed, crime has decreased in virtually all categories.[18] Notably, during an era of declining crime rates, increased criminal penalties for drug-related offenses and lengthier sentences for a broader array of crimes has resulted in unprecedented levels of incarceration, including stark rises in the incarceration of African American women.

I NEEDED A MIRROR (I)

Charlotte Pierce-Baker's book, *Surviving the Silence: Black Women's Stories of Rape*, chronicles the seldom-heard voices of African American women and their experiences of rape. Her book recounts how the rapes she endured instantly shattered her and her family's well-being. She tells her own story and includes those of eleven other Black women. On the need to write her book, Pierce-Baker states:

> I entered therapy for the first time immediately after my rape. Somehow I did not believe that I could go through such a trauma and come out unharmed. I was assigned a counselor by a Philadelphia organization. It was not a satisfactory arrangement, so I kept trying until I found the right match. But it was not just a therapist I needed and was searching for; I was looking for another black woman—another rape survivor—who could understand the intricacies of my life and trauma, to whom I wouldn't have to explain my dilemma of being black and a woman. *I needed a mirror. The ones available were all distorted. I now know that I was not as alone as I thought. There were, in fact, other black women looking for themselves in mirrors—equally without success. All of us were looking in the glass silently.*[19]

Charlotte Pierce-Baker's discussion of African American women's experiences of rape and their need to connect with one another and see themselves in the others' reflections mirrors the experiences of many incarcerated African American women. In 1997, for example, the GAO reported that approximately 40 percent of female inmates in federal prisons and approximately 57 percent of female inmates in state institutions had histories of physical or sexual abuse prior to their incarceration.[20] Sixty-nine percent of women under correctional-system authority reported that physical or sexual abuse occurred before they reached eighteen years of age.[21]

A joint study by the National Institute of Justice and the Centers for Disease Control and Prevention on violence in the general population estimated that between 2.1 and 6.8 million women in the United States are raped and/or physically assaulted annually, mostly by intimate partners or others known to them.[22] The study found that over half of the women who reported being raped (54 percent) were raped before they were eighteen years of age.[23] Significantly, the researchers also found that victimization as a child doubled the risk of physical or sexual abuse as an adult woman.[24] These data indicate that the incidence of violence in women's lives is staggering. The data also reveal that while estimates of physical and sexual violence against women in the general population is high, even greater numbers of incarcerated women report experiences of such violence as children and adults. Thus, the need to address violence against women throughout the society, and with particular regard to women who become at risk for incarceration, appears patent and paramount.

Silence often enshrouds the pain of incarcerated women who must deal with traumatic abusive experiences. As is also applicable to the participants in *Inner Lives*, Pierce-Baker writes about the women in her book: "They represent the myriad voices that wait to be heard. In their chorus perhaps you will catch a hint of the pain but also the wonderment of their survivals and a glimpse of the diversity that constitutes our lives, our worlds, our traumas—our silences—as black women."[25]

Clearly, the absence of African American women's voices in much of popular and academic discourse transcends class and other characteristics and social distinctions in American society. Such exclusion highlights the importance of narrative to inform and critique existing social structures, legal doctrine, and imbedded biases in institutions such as the criminal justice system. For example, narrative has been effectively employed in legal scholarship, adding the distinct voices and experiences of women, people of color, gays and lesbians, and others who are frequently marginalized or objectified in the law. In 1990, for example, the *Berkeley Women's Law Journal* published a symposium issue that featured the narratives of African American women faculty members. As described by Emma Coleman Jordan:

> The story of black women law professors in the legal academy has yet to be told. This collection of essays begins the process of creating a record of our experiences as teachers, scholars, administrators and participants in the law school culture . . . the articles contained in this volume represent at once individual and collective efforts to undertake the difficult task of self-definition. For many of us, the process of self-disclosure represents a painful, but necessary, first step in achieving the larger task of identifying and sustaining a coherent research agenda that embraces the problems of black women. We offer a glimpse of our inner lives.[26]

The value of the women's narratives in this book, as Mary Frances Berry suggests, is that "they also show how stories change and how they remain the same. They should help us to understand how justice and injustice are dispensed."[27]

I NEEDED A MIRROR (II)

Inner Lives includes a visual component in addition to narratives and legal analysis—women who consented were photographed for the book. In this respect, the need for a mirror also speaks to the disturbing prevalence of stereotypical images of African Americans in U.S. media. Thus, visual images are integral to this book in order to include realistic and recognizable images of African American women who are or have been incarcerated.

Photography has contributed to the inculcation of negative imagery of African Americans in U.S. society. According to photographer Chester Higgins, who is African American, "Photographers and editors are socialized by our society, which sees nothing wrong with looking at people of African descent through the distorted lens of otherness."[28] Laura Wexler notes that "[p]hotography was part of the master narrative that created and cemented cultural and political inequalities of race and class."[29] Katheryn Russell provides an illustration of this point using an example from filmmaker Lewis Payton, Jr.:

> Lewis Payton, Jr.'s film, *The Slowest Car in Town*, centered on a young Black man's elevator ride. In the short film, a Black man dressed in a business suit and carrying a briefcase enters an elevator on the eighteenth floor of an office building. The elevator makes four stops before reaching the lobby. With each stop someone White enters the elevator. Each White passenger sees something different. At the first stop, a White woman gets on the elevator and upon discovering the race and sex of her fellow passenger, she makes a quick exit. Two White people get on at the next stop. They look at the Black man and "see" an African bushman holding a spear and "hear" roaring African drum beats. The next Whites who board the elevator envision the Black man as a shackled convict, wearing prison stripes. Other passengers visualize him as a drooling crack addict, who looks like a homeless beggar. By the time the elevator reaches the lobby, the Black businessman no longer exists—he has been reduced to the image projected onto

him by the White passengers. [P]ayton's short film captures much of what Black men and women face today—entrapment by media imagery.[30]

For Black women, "entrapment by media imagery," represented as authentic, generally results in typecasting of African American women as subservient, inept, oversexed, and undeserving. According to Laura Wexler:

> The valorization of the visual image of the middle-class white woman as the signifier of the category "woman" that makes other social relations invisible took shape in the early nineteenth century. . . . Photography, invented in 1839, was an even better technique than drawing or painting for making images of "nature," and photography was therefore conscripted for the sentimental cause. The idea was, if you could take a picture of something, it must exist. To the middle-class nineteenth-century viewer, a photograph was a "mirror" of nature, and not only that but unlike other mirrors it had a "memory" too. Photography inscribed, therefore, a very powerful image of the "real."[31]

Rarely do African American women see positive images of themselves as multidimensional beings in early or contemporary media. Controversy surrounded African American photographer Renée Cox's portrayal of the Last Supper, with a nude African American woman as the spiritual center, in her self-portrait, *Yo Mama's Last Supper*. Claiming religious offense, New York City mayor Rudolph Guiliani threatened to cut off funding to the Brooklyn Museum of Art, where the exhibit was shown in 2001.[32] It seems unlikely, however, that the mayor's response would have been as vehement had the artist presented yet another salacious image of an African American woman. In this regard, photographer Chester Higgins states, "People of African descent are most often portrayed, projected, stigmatized and demonized by our lowest common-denominators of behavior. Our humanity is often disfigured by people's victimization and the lamentable behavior of those on the fringe."[33] Thus it becomes offensive when African American women are portrayed as divine, rather than as derelict. Hence, historian Darlene Clark Hine expresses the particular importance of presenting realistic images of Black women:

Creating and disseminating a visual history is perhaps more important with Black women than with any other single segment of the American population. We know all too well what this society *believes* Black women look like. The stereotypes abound, from Mammy to the maid, from the tragic mulatto to the dark temptress. America's perceptions of Black women are framed by a host of derogatory images and assumptions that proliferated during and in the aftermath of slavery, and with some permutations, exist even today. We have seen Black women's faces and bodies shamed and exploited. What we have not seen nearly enough is the simple truth of our complex and multidimensional lives.[34]

In approaching the photographic component of this project, I was inspired by the work of African American photographers such as Gordon Parks, Carrie Mae Weems, Marvin and Morgan Williams, and Chester Higgins. I especially valued the work of Roy DeCarava, whose black and white photographs of Black Harlem residents confirm my belief in the power of black and white photography to convey the spectrum of African American life.[35] DeCarava's renderings of African Americans in everyday life appear deceptively unremarkable. However, his work is exquisite, as he deftly portrays his subjects in the available (often dark) light of their surroundings. Therefore, one must look closely and attentively at the faces and environments in his photographs in order to appreciate the details and nuances that one might otherwise overlook. Like Ralph Ellison's "invisible man," the subjects in DeCarava's photographs would ordinarily be relegated to invisibility but for the photographer's belief in the intrinsic importance of his subjects.

Of course, distorted images also abound in representations of those who are involved in the criminal justice system. As criminology professor and photographer Howard Zehr observes: "We tend not to see victims or offenders as real people. We seldom understand crime as it is actually experienced: as a violation of real people by real people. Rarely do we hear the experiences and perspectives of those most involved."[36] In the words of researchers McQuaide and Ehrenreich, "To see [incarcerated African American women] only as the prison creates her is to falsify her and to reduce her to her current social status."[37]

The women's willingness and courage to be photographed in *Inner Lives* provide additional opportunities for understanding beyond stereotypes and nondescript statistics. It demands more than a glance, however; one must actively look to see the human dimensions and complexity of their lives.

METHODOLOGY

This book is a multifaceted analysis of African American women's experiences in the U.S. criminal justice and correctional systems. It is informed by past and present criminal doctrine and practice, as well as by over one hundred interviews conducted over a three-year period with incarcerated and formerly incarcerated African American women, their families and friends, prison personnel, prison activists, and members of the bench and bar. The book features twenty-three extensive narratives of a broad range of individuals who participated in this project. Unfortunately, every participant's story could not be presented in the book; however, their experiences and perspectives are reflected in the data analysis of the *Inner Lives* participants, as well as in summarized accounts of the issues that many women raised.

I conducted extensive outreach in the latter part of 1998 to obtain participation of currently and formerly incarcerated African American women in this project. Potential participants were notified through mailings and e-mail postings to inmate organizations, prison newsletters, lawyers, law professors, grassroots and professional advocacy organizations, and individuals or organizations having related interests. The response was swift and encouraging, as incarcerated and formerly incarcerated African American women wrote to express their interest in *Inner Lives*. Most of them expressed surprise that their views were sought. Rarely, they said, had they been asked to discuss their own lives, the lives of loved ones, the offenses for which they were convicted, the experience of incarceration, and their visions and hopes for the future.

I endeavored to make this project as diverse as possible. In this regard, I sought to include African American women across geographic regions and ranges of personal and institutional experiences. Thus, I interviewed women in prisons, jails, transitional housing, and private residences in the East (New York, Connecticut, New Jersey, and Washington, D.C.), Midwest (Michigan, Ohio, and Illinois), South (Arkansas, Georgia, Louisiana, Florida, and Texas), and West (California and

Nevada). In addition to geographical diversity, the women represent a wide range of age groups, offense categories, and degree of correctional system oversight. I interviewed women currently incarcerated in maximum, medium, and minimum-security facilities; women participating in residential programs; and other women who resided in private homes while they completed parole/probation or after they completed it. In part 2 I provide more detailed descriptions and data analyses of the *Inner Lives* participants.

Despite my attempt to create a diverse and representative work, this book is not a scientifically devised statistical study. Rather, the women and other subjects in this study volunteered and thus represent a self-selected group, although they were initially targeted largely at random. Instead, the central technique with respect to the women's perspectives employs "life history" methodology.[38] As sociologist Beth Richie has described it, this method "offered a more intense opportunity to learn about subjects' backgrounds, opinions, feelings, and the meanings they give to the mundane events and the exceptional experiences in their lives."[39] Life history methodology complements the Black feminist analysis applied in this context. As such, Gwendolyn Etter-Lewis states:

> Oral narrative offers a unique and provocative means of gathering information central to understanding women's lives and viewpoints. When applied to women of color, it assumes significance as a powerful instrument for the rediscovery of womanhood so often overlooked and/or neglected in history and literature alike. Specifically, articulation of black women's experiences in America is a complex task characterized by the intersection of race, gender, and social class with language, history, and culture. It is oral narrative that is ideally suited to revealing the "multilayered texture of black women's lives."[40]

It is important to note that life history methodology, underscored by Black feminist analysis, need not entail direct comparison of African American women's experiences with those of, say, Caucasian American women. As the center of this analysis, the intrinsic value of African American women's experiences and perspectives are not predicated on comparisons or distinctions from others' life experiences. Instead, as Etter-Lewis articulates:

[B]lack women . . . are constantly expected to *prove* that their situations are radically different from those of white women. If not, then their lives are considered unremarkable. . . . In readers' minds, black women must earn credibility by claiming features unique to their own embedded subgroup. Otherwise, they are viewed merely as white women in blackface. Such attitudes are uninformed and counterproductive. Whether or not black women measure up to such superficial standards has little to do with the reality of their struggles and the quality of their lives.[41]

Thus, whether or not sharp distinctions can be drawn between the women whose life histories are presented here and others who may have had similar life experiences, the critical issues involve the authority accorded to African American women about their lives and the opportunity to express their self-knowledge in authentic voices.

In order to employ life history methodology effectively, I identified several major topics through a literature review of studies and interviews with women in prison, and through writings relating to African American women's life experiences. Many of these sources are listed in the bibliography.

Thus, the topics explored during our interviews included discussion of early years and adolescence, adulthood, onset of criminality, experiences during criminal adjudication, imprisonment experiences, resistance efforts, and release and transition back to the community. Within these basic areas, the women discuss their perceptions of the context and meaning of their life experiences and the crimes that led to their imprisonment. They also discuss the resistance strategies they employed to cope with seemingly impossible odds as youths and adults, including paying attention to their physical health, mental health, spiritual needs, and political awareness. In addition, the women discuss their preparation for release from prison and the challenges they face upon return to the community outside of prison.

While there is considerable diversity within their individual circumstances, the women often experienced similar traumas that began in childhood or developed later in adulthood. Invariably, their traumas resulted from family dysfunction; an inability or disinclination to make wise decisions about friends and intimate companions; the realities and perceptions of limited or nonexistent life choices; and a lack of alternatives for productive, fulfilling and economically viable lives. The persistent impact of structural gender, race, and class oppression that affected the women's ability to achieve or project an image of value as a productive member of society undergirds these difficulties. Thus many, although not all, of the women might identify with Beth Richie's definition of "gender entrapment": "African-American women from low-income communities who are physically battered, sexually assaulted, emotionally abused, and involved in illegal activity."[42]

While our interviews covered specific areas related to the women's incarceration and earlier stages of their lives, they also encompassed broader issues and concerns. The women expressed concern for their families, for the victims of their crimes, and for young people, especially young African American women, who need direction and support in order to avoid a similar fate. They expressed disappointment for unrealized dreams; remorse for self-inflicted harms and harms done to others; anger at real and perceived injustices in their lives; and determination and hope for self-improvement, betterment of their quality of life, and the betterment of society, despite the past. Strong yet vulnerable, the women revealed these innermost thoughts. In striving to express themselves, they risked further misunderstanding in the effort to contribute to greater understanding.

At the end of each interview, I asked each woman the same question: "Why have you participated in this project?" All gave thoughtful, personal responses as they seemingly rewound their histories in their minds and searched for the words to articulate the circumstances of their lives to themselves and others. When the women answered, however, invariably they spoke of meaning beyond their own lives and hope that others would benefit from their hard-won lessons.

Inner Lives participants had the option of using their real names or pseudonyms in this book. Almost all of the women who were interviewed chose to be identified by their actual names. I have honored this request with some modification. In the narratives in part 2, incarcerated women are identified only by their first names to provide a greater degree of privacy for them and their families. However, the formerly incarcerated women are identified by their full names, as each of these women has been active publicly on issues regarding women in prison. In some cases, the rules of the institution dictated the degree to which the women's identities could be revealed. Despite extensive discussions and assurances, for example, attempts to interview women in federal institutions and to allow use of their names were stymied by inordinate concerns of the Federal Bureau of Prisons.

Women also chose whether or not to be photographed for this book project. Ultimately, the choice of being photographed or not was also determined by institutional policy. Where the women agreed, and where the institution permitted, I took photographs during the course of the interviews. Individual interviews lasted from one and a half to three or more hours and were usually taped if the institution allowed it. My equipment choices were fairly spare. It was important to travel lightly into the facilities, particularly since I had to go through personal and equipment searches at several junctures. I entered the facilities with one or two bags at most, containing camera bodies, lenses and flash, notepads, a tape recorder, and cassettes.

Cynthia and the other women who were interviewed and photographed for this book entrusted me with sharing with readers the painful and embarrassing details of their lives. None of the women aspired to incarceration. The stories recounted here are the life histories of African American women whose dreams and promise were derailed at critical points in their lives. Without resources or recourse, however, prison became the inexorable endpoint for them when individuals and institutions ostensibly in place to prevent such outcomes failed. Thus, these stories consist of multiple levels of neglect and betrayal by family, friends, and social institutions. As the women are quick to point out, however, self-sabotage due to low self-esteem and poor decision making frequently contributed to their predicaments as well. Several women adamantly maintain their innocence of the charges that resulted in their incarceration; others acknowledge their criminal involvement and responsibility. In either case, as African American women, they are keenly aware of the disparities in their treatment and experiences within the criminal justice system and within American society.

Taken together, these stories attest to the entrenched devaluation of Black women's lives and to the corrosive forces of racism, sexism, classism, and multiple interlocking forms of oppression within African American women's lives. Invariably, the stories presented in this book are circular tales of the victimized becoming victimizers, who are in turn revictimized. It is important to note, however, these are also stories of triumph, resistance, self-awareness, and change. For some of the women, incarceration was an important step toward self-realization.

For these women, prison provided an opportunity for contemplation and commitment to more productive lives. For other women, the prison experience only compounded their difficulties in finding stability, good health, and new directions in life. As our prisons currently exceed two million people, disproportionately populated by African American women, it is imperative that we hear all of these stories.

If Cynthia's and the other women's trust in sharing their stories has been justified, this book will succeed in stimulating reconsideration of the near-exclusive reliance on incarceration for crimes in our society. To this end, the analyses of the women's experiences, empirical data, legal theories, and social policies will inspire greater commitment to alternatives to incarceration and the creation of safer spaces for African American girls and women in U.S. society. Our society must consider the particular circumstances of African American women in order to adopt effective approaches to crime prevention and public safety that are more rational and more fair. Whereas African American women's criminality very often is in response to harms or neglect committed against them, I argue that such alternative measures ultimately will better serve the public interest, enhance African American women's potential, and advance the democratic ideal for all citizens.

PART I

ANALYSIS OF AFRICAN AMERICAN WOMEN'S EXPERIENCES IN THE U.S. CRIMINAL JUSTICE SYSTEM

HISTORICAL BACKGROUND

In recent years, African American women have experienced the greatest increase in criminal justice supervision of all demographic groups in the United States. However, the disparity in African American women's representation in the U.S. criminal justice system is not without historical precedent. Indeed, throughout American history, Black women, like Black men, have always been disproportionately represented in the U.S. criminal justice system. It is also important to note that while incarceration has supplanted other forms of criminal punishment in recent years, this was not always the case. In fact, in the history of punitive apparatuses the prison is a fairly modern creation that was perfected and used in greater measure in America than in Europe, where it had its origin. The advent of the prison as the primary mechanism for criminal punishment became characterized by its racial disparity in these institutions. In this section I present an overview of these developments, followed by an analysis of data and legal trends in the current era.

RACIAL, GENDER, AND CLASS DISPARITIES IN EARLIER ERAS

In the colonial era, the criminal laws were especially harsh toward enslaved persons, servants, and women and were heavily influenced by existing religious ideals.[1] During this period, race gradually signified criminality among groups that previously had been considered relatively on par. For example, historian Winthrop Jordan noted that in the early seventeenth century, the terms "slave" and "servant" were used synonymously, suggesting only marginal distinctions between these two disfavored and disenfranchised groups.[2] This attitude changed, however, as Africans were deemed unfit to join the community of "civilized, Christian Europeans" because of their race.[3] As Judge Leon Higginbotham observed, "As it became increasingly evident that the supply of indentured servants and redemptioners was inadequate for the colonists' maximization of their profits, a far more cruel system of human bondage was chosen—slavery, where one's darker skin became a justification for Whites to subject Blacks to a depravity that had never been used against indentured servants.[4]

As greater distinctions were drawn between the servant-slave classes, criminal penalties became more disparate as well. Thus, while the typical punishments of shaming, whipping, and the death penalty were seemingly neutral potential criminal sanctions for all groups, they were meted out more frequently against enslaved persons.[5] This disparity in the implementation of harsh criminal punishments occurred in both southern and northern colonial America,[6] and increasingly race became the sine qua non for determining criminality and punishment. As such, early American legislatures designated behavior that may have been legal for Whites as criminal if committed by persons of African descent. As Paul Finkelman notes, "early America developed separate criminal procedures, protections, and punishments for blacks, whether slave or free. Race became the key to a fair trial and an impartial administration of the law."[7] As southern and northern colonies adopted comprehensive race-based criminal-law regimes, the notion of people of African descent as being naturally criminal was further inculcated into the evolving national consciousness. Such government-sanctioned racially discriminatory treatment also further legitimated the subordination of people of African descent in all areas of American society, not just within the criminal justice realm.

In addition to race-based punitive distinctions during the colonial era, gender also formed the basis for differential treatment. While Caucasian men and women generally received punishments such as public whippings or hangings for similar offenses, women were punished more harshly on gender bases. For instance, the punishment for adultery was more severe for White women than for White men.[8] Women of African descent were not thought to possess the virtues reserved for women of European descent. Therefore, Black women were not punished more severely than Black men on the basis of gender in this regard. While gender distinctions rarely applied in the punishments meted out to enslaved men and women, the offense of miscegenation was substantially defined by one's status as a woman of African descent.

In 1662 and 1692, for example, Virginia passed laws that outlawed interracial marriages between Whites and men and women of African descent. With respect to African American women, the 1662 act provided that "[c]hildren got by an Englishman upon a Negro woman shall be bond or free according to the condition of the mother, and if any Christian shall commit fornication with a Negro man or woman, he shall pay double the fines of the former act."[9] African women and their offspring suffered severe punishment under such statutes, as violations included physical punishment for the women and enslavement for the children determined by the mother's status. In most instances, White men were simply fined for violating miscegenation laws.

It was clear as early as 1643 that African women occupied the lowest social status in society, as exemplified by Virginia labor tax statutes. In 1629, Virginia had designated that "tithable persons" included all those who worked the land. In 1643, however, tithable persons were redefined to include all adult men and Black women. The distinction was significant because servant women of European origin were deemed appropriately employed in domestic settings, while Black women were accorded no such regard. Instead, as John Hammond of Virginia wrote in 1656 in reference to African American women, "Yet som wenches that are nasty and beastly and not fit to be so employed are put in the ground."[10] While this was not a criminal sanction, it clearly penalized Black women on the basis of their race and gender and consigned them to harsher working conditions in the fields. In 1662, Virginia enacted a statute extending the tax on women to all "persons [who] purchase women servants to work in the ground." Again, the racial distinctions were such that White women were tithable only if they were servants and actually worked in the fields, while women of African descent were tithable whether or not they were free.[11]

Once the system of chattel slavery was firmly in place in colonial America, new dimensions of race-based differential criminality and punishment emerged. Sweeping slave codes were enacted to regulate every aspect of personal status and social interaction involving enslaved persons. Black women were treated just as harshly as Black men under these provisions. In an oral history account, for example, a formerly enslaved woman named Elizabeth Sparks recalled: "Beat women! Why sure he beat women. Beat women jes' lak men. Beat women an' wash 'em down in brine."[12] Under the elaborate slave code system, the racial, gender, and class status of offenders and victims determined whether cases would be heard in designated White or slave forums.[13]

Further, under the perverse reasoning of slave codes, enslaved persons were considered property for some purposes and persons for others. This paradox is exemplified in *United States v. Amy*,[14] in which an enslaved woman, Amy, was accused of stealing a letter from the U.S. mail. Her attorney objected to her prosecution by arguing that she had to be considered a "person" subject to the penalties of law. Upon conviction, Amy's appeal was heard by Chief Justice Roger Taney, who explained the enslaved person's dual status: "He is a person, and also property. As property, the rights of [the] owner are entitled to the protections of the law. As a person, he is bound to obey the law, and may, like any other person, be punished if he offends it."[15]

Significantly, persons of African descent were targeted for inhumane public and private punishment by governments and slaveholders, and official law or law enforcement rarely protected them. Thus, most slave codes permitted Whites to "beat, slap, and whip slaves with impunity."[16] If Whites faced punishment for harms to enslaved persons, it was based on the excessive cruelty of the act. Under such circumstances, however, the violation was not against the enslaved person but against the White slave owner's property interest. Thus, fines, if assessed, were paid to the slave-owning family, not the family of the injured or murdered slave.[17]

Sex offenses provide the starkest example of double standards in the penalty and protection provisions of the slave codes. Under such schemes, Black men having sex with White women faced the severest penalty (hanging or castration), while White men having sex with Black women faced the lightest penalty (fines, public penance).[18] Black women were completely unprotected under these legal schemes. Rape of Black women was not recognized under most slave codes and consequently could be done with impunity, whether the perpetrator was enslaved, free, or White. In *George v. State*,[19] the court unequivocally ruled "the crime of rape does not exist in this State between Africans." To the extent that such offenses were recognized at all, it was due to alleged property damage to slaveholders, not injury to enslaved women.

Following the end of the Civil War, African Americans fared scarcely better under new racially discriminatory criminal law provisions, as "Black Codes" replaced "slave codes." Although the Recon-struction era reforms promised independence and self-determination for freed slaves, southern states responded by enacting laws that rein-scribed the perceived racial inferiority and inherently criminal status of people of African descent.[20] Mississippi led the way by passing its laws in 1865. It became a crime there for free Blacks to commit "mischief" and make "insulting gestures," and its Vagrancy Act defined "all free Negroes and mulattos over the age of eighteen" as criminals unless they could furnish proof of employment upon demand.[21] Other states fol-lowed suit and created a variety of vaguely defined offenses directed at freed Blacks. Like the slave codes of the previous era, Black Codes were replete in their regulation of Black activity.[22] As W. E. B. Du Bois stated:

> All things considered, it seems probable that if the South had been per-mitted to have its way in 1865 the harshness of negro slavery would have been mitigated so as to make slave-trading difficult, and to make it possible for a negro to hold property and appear in some cases in court; but that in most other respects the blacks would have remained in slavery.[23]

In the wake of Reconstruction era failures, Jim Crow legal schemes ushered in a new era of racially biased criminal laws and other regula-tions restricting Black life. Characterized by apartheid-like segregation, Jim Crow laws restricted Blacks' movement throughout the society and limited their social mobility and political exercise.[24] The prospect of Black liberation and full participation in American society unleashed an especially ominous threat by the Ku Klux Klan and other White ex-tremists, as lynching became prevalent in American society. The lives of thousands of African American men, women, and children were extin-guished by lynch mobs. Officially, over three thousand lynchings were recorded between 1882 and 1964, while unofficially the figure is esti-mated at above ten thousand.[25]

While lynching was an extrajudicial punishment for supposed criminal offenses or social transgressions by African Americans, it was often carried out with tacit or express official approval. One writer notes: "Whatever the cause of lynching's demise, the law had little or nothing to do with it. Throughout the Progressive Era, lynching re-mained a brutal crime that went largely uninvestigated, unprosecuted, unpunished, and undeterred by the agents of law at every level of government."[26] Offenses for which lynching was the prescribed punishment included perceived insults to White persons, to the more common allegation of rape by Black men against White women.[27] Although African American men were the most frequent targets of lynchers, African American women were also targeted for mob cruelty.[28] The *New York Tribune* reported one such incident involving the lynching of a woman:

> Mississippi 1904: Luther Holbert, a Doddsville Negro, and his wife were burned at the stake for the murder of James Eastland, a white planter, and John Carr, a Negro. The planter was killed in a quarrel which arose when he came to Carr's cabin, where he found Holbert, and ordered him to leave the plantation. Carr and a Negro, named Winters, were also killed.
>
> Holbert and his wife fled the plantation but were brought back and burned at the stake in the presence of a thousand people. Two innocent Negroes had been shot previous to this by a posse looking for Holbert, because one of them, who resembled Holbert, refused to surrender when ordered to do so. There is nothing in the story to indicate that Holbert's wife had any part in the crime.[29]

In another instance, *The Crisis* reported:

> At Okemah, Oklahoma, Laura Nelson, a colored woman, accused of murdering a deputy sheriff who had discovered stolen goods in her house, was lynched together with her son, a boy about fifteen. The woman and her son were taken from the jail, dragged about six miles to the Canadian River, and hanged from a bridge. The woman was raped by members of the mob before she was hanged.[30]

Regarding these vile events, which were committed in celebratory and carnival-like atmospheres, Randall Kennedy correctly notes, "Along with the unpunished raping of black women, lynching stands out in the minds of many black Americans as the most vicious and destructive consequence of racially selective underprotection. . . . Nothing has more embittered discussions of the criminal justice system than the recognition that among those who have insistently demanded 'law and order' are those who have been unwilling to take effective action to deter antiblack racially motivated crimes."[31]

Thus, enactment of racially specific criminal laws, discriminatory application of purportedly neutral criminal laws, and official failure to enforce legal protections on behalf of African Americans have created an enduring ethos of distrust of the U.S. criminal justice system within many Black communities across America. This distrust is reinforced by present circumstances in which African American men and women are disproportionately incarcerated under harsh criminal law penalties in the United States. Many share the disillusionment expressed by civil rights and antilynching advocate Ida B. Wells in 1887, which prompted her to ask, "O God, is there no redress, no peace, no justice in this land for us?"[32]

RESISTANCE

Discussion of the historical uses and abuses of criminal law to unfairly punish and disenfranchise Africans and Americans of African descent would be incomplete without recognition of their determined efforts at resistance throughout these periods. Throughout the assaults and indignities of the slavery era, for example, Black men and women resisted their capture in Africa and challenged the conditions of bondage once transported to the Americas.[33] Both Black men and women worked primarily in the fields during slavery, although it is often perceived that Black women worked under less arduous conditions. As scholar-activist Angela Davis writes, "Where work was concerned, strength and productivity under the threat of the whip outweighed consideration of sex. In this sense, the oppression of women was identical to the oppression of men."[34] Yet, women also experienced slavery in uniquely inhumane ways that were gender specific. Indeed, once Congress prohibited further importation of Africans into the United States for enslavement, Black women's reproductive capabilities became especially important to the slaveholders' economic interests.

Like Black men, Black women protested their enslavement and sought freedom through various means, including "stealing, burn[ing] gin houses, barns, corncribs, and smokehouses."[35] Resistance efforts also included poisoning, arson, escape, mass revolts, and the use of physical force to kill masters.[36] Historian Deborah Gray White notes that women generally had a more difficult time escaping than men.[37] Nevertheless, women often employed gender-specific means to undermine their enslavement, such as avoiding or terminating pregnancy, or took other opportunities to obtain freedom.[38]

After emancipation, African American women remained largely in domestic service, as racism excluded them from more skilled employment opportunities. In 1881, the Atlanta washerwomen's strike demonstrated Black women's collective strength in demanding better pay for their work.[39] In addition, African American women were prominent in the fight against lynching. Ida B. Wells, Frances Ellen Watkins Harper, and Anna Julia Cooper, for example, were ardent advocates for African American women and men; they demanded better living and working conditions and government action to eradicate lynching.[40] Black women also sought vindication of their rights through the court system, such as Ida B. Wells's 1884 lawsuit against the Chesapeake, Ohio and Southwestern Railroad, which denied her the purchase of a first-class seat. Earlier, Eliza Gallie, a free woman in Virginia, fought her accusation of petty theft in court. Historian Suzanne Lebsock writes:

> In November 1853, Eliza Gallie . . . was arrested and charged with stealing cabbages from the patch of Alexander Stevens, a white man. She was tried in mayor's court and sentenced to thirty-nine lashes. There was nothing unusual about this; free black women were frequently accused of petty crimes, and for free blacks as for slaves, whipping was the punishment prescribed for by law. What made the case a minor spectacle was that Eliza Gallie had resources, *and she fought back.*[41]

The racial hierarchies established during the slave era still persist in the contemporary social policies and institutions of American society, including the law. Negative stereotypes of African American women emanating from this era have also persisted.[42] These images provided justifications for Black women's continued subordination and have reduced their chances to lead healthy and successful lives. This even when in all periods in American history, African Americans have resisted negative imagery[43] and demanded recognition of their political, civil, and economic rights.[44] Black women led many of these early struggles and continue to assert their rights to human dignity and fair treatment within the legal and social systems in U.S. society.[45]

A BRIEF HISTORY OF THE U.S. PRISON SYSTEM

The ubiquity of prisons in American society belies the relatively recent ascendancy of this institution.[46] Before the eighteenth century, prisons were only one part of the punishment system in the United States.[47] Before the increased use of prisons, punishments consisted of mostly physical acts inflicted in public in order to instill humiliation and restore morality through penitence. Prison use increased in the late eighteenth and early nineteenth centuries after reductions in the use of corporal punishment and the death penalty, and as shaming became less effective.[48] After reducing the types of offenses that were punishable by death, the states determined that offenders should instead serve long prison terms.[49]

In the 1820s, New York and Pennsylvania developed competing models of the penitentiary, which continue to form the core philosophy and architectural structure of prisons in the United States. The New York model (Auburn Plan) was centered on the congregate system of imprisonment. Under this plan, inmates were isolated in cells, coming together for meals and work details; even then, they were forbidden to look at each other or converse.[50] In contrast, the Pennsylvania model (Cherry Hill Plan) was known for its near total separation of inmates. In this regard, inmates were housed singly in cells throughout their entire confinement; they ate and worked apart from others and were allowed only selected visitors during imprisonment.[51] Despite the contrasts in physical structure of the respective models, the New York and Pennsylvania models emphasized rehabilitation of the inmate by dint of a strict prison life routine. While both systems had staunch proponents, the New York model ultimately prevailed nationally as the less expensive and more profitable model.

By the post–Civil War era, overcrowding, brutality, and disorder characterized the growing prison system throughout the United States. Even in New York, inventor of the Auburn Plan with its emphasis on reflection and rehabilitation, an 1852 report to the New York legislature noted the problems associated with imprisonment. The report recognized that while prisons successfully removed the offender from society, thereby preventing further crimes during incarceration, "[i]f the object is to make him a better member of society so that he may safely mingle with it . . . that purpose cannot be answered by matters as they now stand."[52] Further, just after the Civil War, African Americans comprised

75 percent of prison inmates in southern states, a clear effort to replicate the conditions of slavery from the previous era. Indeed, as Edgardo Rotman notes: "The result was a ruthless exploitation with a total disregard for prisoners' dignity and lives. The states leased prisoners to entrepreneurs who, having no ownership interest in them, exploited them even worse than slaves."[53]

African Americans bore the brunt of the convict lease system, based on their massive rate of imprisonment under the Black Codes. In some states, African Americans comprised 80 to 90 percent of inmates and were the majority of inmates leased to plantations, coal mines, canal companies, brickyards, railroad companies, sawmills, turpentine farms, and phosphate mines in Tennessee, Alabama, Mississippi, Georgia, Florida, and the Carolinas.[54] Leased convicts worked under deplorable conditions that drastically shortened their life expectancy. Financial incentives further spurred criminalization of former slaves, as the fee system enriched local deputy sheriffs, police, and judges who received per capita payments for arrests and convictions. Upon request, former slave owners, construction companies, labor contractors, or the state itself were supplied leased convicts' cheap labor. When such needs arose, African American men and women were summarily arrested, imprisoned, and convicted. When they were predictably unable to pay their fines, they became leased convicts. As historian Bruce Franklin notes, "The convict lease system had a big advantage for the enslavers: since they did not own the convicts, they lost nothing by working them to death."[55]

Key prison reforms occurred during the Progressive Era of the 1920s. In one instance, prison reform was informed by adherence to behavioral science theories, as prison reformers applied therapeutic models to inmate rehabilitation. The medical or therapeutic model was based on the belief that inmates suffered from physical, mental, and social pathology or illnesses. Despite its asserted advantages, any promise of a distinctly therapeutic approach to criminality was undermined by inadequate investment of professional resources and research on the uses of therapeutic regimens in this context. In this regard, Edgardo Rotman has noted that "the ratio of professionals to inmate (one psychiatrist or two psychologists per five hundred or one thousand cell institutions) was so small as to render the programs ineffective."[56] Additional prison reforms during the Progressive Era included increased use of indeterminate sentencing, probation, and parole. Despite these promising reforms, the therapeutic model failed due to inconsistent and ineffectual implementation.

After World War II, penology was inspired by rehabilitative optimism. Reflecting this sentiment, the American Prison Association changed its name to the American Correctional Association and advised its members to redesign their prisons as "correctional institutions" and to label the punishment blocks in them as "adjustment centers."[57] Further, this optimism was formalized in the 1955 United Nations Standard Minimum Rules for the Treatment of Prisoners, which provided in Article 58 that a sentence of imprisonment can be justified only when it is used "to ensure, so far as possible, that upon his return to society, the offender is not only willing but able to lead a law-abiding and self-supporting life."[58] Prison reformers, lawmakers, and prison officials shared these principles.

The continued influence of the therapeutic model led to abuses that generated general opposition to rehabilitative ideal in the 1970s. As discussed, however, the attempts at meaningful rehabilitation were superficial at best. In addition, the prevailing indeterminate sentencing statutes led to disparities, arbitrariness, and disproportionately high penalties. After 1960, various forms of behavioral modification programs were used in American prisons. Many of these putative therapeutic programs in reality were abusive and violated inmates' civil rights and civil liberties.

Dispelling popular perceptions, criminology professor Norval Morris states: "It would be an error to assume that most of these late-twentieth century mutations of the prison tend toward leniency and comfort. The most common prisons are the overcrowded prisons proximate to the big cities of America; they have become places of deadening routine punctuated by bursts of fear and violence."[59] Despite their proliferation from the 1800s to the present, the efficacy of the prison has been questioned during every historical period. Norval Morris and David Rothman assert that "most students of the prison have increasingly come to the conclusion that imprisonment should be used as the sanction of last resort, to be imposed only when other measures of controlling the criminal have been tried and have failed or in situations in which those other measures are clearly inadequate."[60]

AFRICAN AMERICAN WOMEN'S EXPERIENCES
WITHIN THE HISTORICAL DEVELOPMENT
OF WOMEN'S PRISONS IN THE UNITED STATES

Women as well as men were held in the nation's early prisons. By the mid-nineteenth century the female prisoner population had increased in several states such that women required accommodations of their own. However, while some of the stringent rules of men's institutions did not generally apply to women, "Lack of concern, or worse, systematic exploitation meant that women often endured much poorer conditions than men convicted of similar offenses."[61]

Women's prisons lagged behind the theoretical advances of men's prisons. For example, the Mount Pleasant Female Prison for female felons in New York was built in 1839 on the grounds of Sing Sing men's prison nearly two decades after New York constructed the innovative male prisons at Auburn and Sing Sing.[62] Mount Pleasant represented a major turning point in the development of women's prisons because it was the first prison where women were housed in a separate building apart from men and supervised by a staff of women.[63]

Completely independent women's prisons did not appear until 1870, however, when Michigan opened a "house of shelter" for women.[64] In 1874, the Indiana Reformatory Institution opened as the nation's first completely independent and physically separate prison for women. Eventually, two models of independent women's prisons developed: custodial institutions that replicated the male penitentiary structure, and unwalled reformatories that consisted of small residential buildings strewn throughout expansive rural tracts.

Until 1870, the custodial institution was the only type of penal unit for women. According to historian Nicole Rafter, "The custodial model was a masculine model: derived from men's prisons, it adopted their characteristics–retributive purpose, high-security architecture, a male-dominated authority structure, programs that stressed earnings, and harsh discipline."[65] By the late nineteenth century, nearly every state operated a custodial unit for women.

While the custodial female prison model continued to develop, reformatories for women also emerged. In the late 1860s, the reformatory movement grew out of the social reform activism of middle-class women who had been abolitionists and health-care workers during the

Civil War. They became interested in the concerns of incarcerated women. Their reformist philosophy was reflected in the architectural design of women's institutions, rejecting the foreboding congregate interior and walled exterior style of men's institutions. Instead, reformers believed that unwalled facilities were more suitable for women inmates, who required fewer restrictions. This resulted in the prevalence of "cottage" plans among women's institutions, in which groups of approximately twenty inmates resided in small buildings with a motherly matron in a familial setting.[66]

Women's reformatories initially housed misdemeanants and tailored the late nineteenth-century penology of rehabilitation to perceptions of women's unique nature. As originated by the Indiana prison, other women's reformatories adopted the premise that women criminals should be rehabilitated rather than punished. Accordingly, it was believed that obedience and systematic religious education would help the women form orderly habits and moral values.[67] In this regard, domestic training was emphasized rather than vocational skills. During their sentences the women were taught to cook, clean, and wait on table; upon parole they were sent to middle-class homes to work as servants. Hence, women's reformatories encouraged gender-stereotyped traits of female sexual restraint, gentility, and domesticity.[68]

The women's reformatory movement met its demise by 1935, after a great expansion in women's prison building during the Progressive Era. As the population of female inmates changed, there was less sympathy for them: they were perceived as hardened offenders, unlike their young, vulnerable predecessors. Overcrowding and worsening conditions resulted from financial cutbacks while the female inmate population increased significantly. In addition, increasing numbers of African American women garnered less compassion than the previous, largely White inmate populations. Further, concerns about interracial sexual relations between inmates prompted an investigation at the Bedford Hills Reformatory for Women, in New York, forcing the institution to recognize that it was no longer performing its original reformatory purpose.[69] By the 1930s, it became too expensive to operate reformatories and custodial prisons for women and most states discontinued constructing them by the time of the Great Depression. Therefore, existing reformatories assumed greater numbers of more serious offenders and adopted greater punitive aspects in their overall operation. Thus, former reformatories became conventional custodial institutions upon the demise of the reformatory ideal.[70]

Race and class were starkly implicated in the development of women's penal institutions. "Women's prisons required obedience not only to prison rules . . . but also to cultural standards for femininity that fluctuated by race and social class."[71] These different standards regarding gender meant that racial imbalance already existed at the beginning of the growth of women's prisons. In reality, there were two bifurcated prison systems in the United States. One system was divided along gender lines, creating different institutions for men and women; the other was subdivided along racial lines, such that men and women's institutions were populated predominantly by African American men and women.

After the Civil War, African American women filled prisons at numbers far exceeding their representation in the general population in all geographical regions, but particularly in the South.[72] White women were systematically channeled out of prisons, while African American women were systematically channeled into them. Negative racial stereotypes justified these disparities by advancing the view that White women were victims of circumstance, while African American women were captives of lesser morals and uncontrolled lust. The convict leasing system best illustrates the disparities in treatment of White and African American female offenders. For an offense such as prostitution, for example, a White prostitute normally did not receive jail time while her African American counterpart usually was sent away to hard labor.[73] One example is Jane Jackson, a "colored" woman who was sentenced to ninety days, a ten-dollar fine, and court costs of fourteen dollars. When her jail term expired, she still faced and additional 240 days on the road gang to work off her twenty-four dollar debt. Historian David Oshinsky notes, "After three more brutal months, a white patron helped win Jackson a pardon by claiming, among other things, that a Negro could not be expected to control her sexual drive."[74] "I submit," said her patron, "that she has suffered sufficiently in view of the tropical origin of her race."[75]

In his study of Mississippi's notorious Parchman Prison Farm,[76] David Oshinsky notes:

> Like everything else at Parchman, the women's camp was segregated by race. The blacks lived in a long shedlike structure, the whites in a

small brick building, with a high fence in between. The black population ranged from twenty-five to sixty-five women each year, the white population from zero to five. . . . So few white females reached Parchman that a clear profile of them is impossible. Their crimes ranged from murder and infanticide to grand larceny and aiding an escape.[77]

As Oshinsky further notes, "[M]ore remarkable were the white women who were spared a prison term after committing a heinous crime." The cases of Marion Drew and Sara Ruth Dean exemplify this point:

> In 1929, [Drew] confessed to killing her husband, Marlin, in Ashland, Mississippi, near the Tennessee line. . . . The judge had never sent a white woman to Parchman. After conferring with the district attorney, he accepted a guilty plea from Mrs. Drew and then released her without bond. She would remain free, he ordered, if she behaved herself in the future.[78]

A few years later, Sara Ruth Dean went on trial in 1934 for killing her married lover, J. Preston Kennedy:

> The trial received national attention because both parties belonged to Mississippi's social register, and both were physicians. Dr. Dean was accused of slipping poison into Kennedy's whiskey glass during a "farewell midnight tryst." . . . It took thirteen hours for the jury to find Mrs. Dean guilty of murder. "We hated to send a woman to prison," said the foreman, "but we had no choice. It was either death or life imprisonment." Another juror agreed. "We wanted to make the punishment less severe, but we could not under the verdict we had to decide on."
>
> Ruth Dean remained at home during her appeal. When that failed, Governor Mike Conner issued a full pardon on July 9, 1935, after being bombarded with mercy requests. Though Conner claimed to have new information "not available to the courts," he never said what it was. His decision rested on politics and chivalry, Conner told friends. He just could not send a woman like Ruth Dean to Parchman, no matter what she had done.[79]

Underlying the differential treatment of women on the basis of race in the convict leasing system was the fundamental belief that some members of U.S. society were more deserving of criminal labels and harsher punishments under criminal laws. As the Parchman examples illustrate, even the most heinous offenses were deemed unsuitable for correspondingly harsh punishment if they were committed by White women. By contrast, the most minor offense alleged against or committed by African American women garnered severe punishment. In the convict leasing context, this often amounted to the death penalty, as many leased convicts were literally worked to death. Reform finally came to Parchman Farm in 1972, after the federal court, in *Gates v. Collier*, found numerous violations under the Eighth and Fourteenth Amendments at the prison.[80] Despite important rulings such as *Collier*, which ordered improvements in prison conditions and outlawed racial segregation and discrimination in prison operations, racial disparities in the U.S. criminal justice and prison systems continue to flourish. Indeed, as discussed below, such disparities in women's incarceration rates and treatment have grown rather than diminished in modern times.

AFRICAN AMERICAN WOMEN AND CURRENT CRIMINAL LAW AND PUNISHMENT

Modern Demographic Trends

In general, women comprise a small proportion of the total U.S. prison population. As the following data reveal, however, women have been the fastest-growing segment of the prison population in contemporary times. African American women are the largest percentage of incarcerated women. As figure 1 shows, women's overall imprisonment in state and federal institutions is characterized by sharp increases over the last twenty years. Women's imprisonment rose from just over 13,000 in 1980 to nearly 92,000 in 2000.

Moreover, as figure 2 reveals, African American women currently comprise the majority of incarcerated women in the United States. Almost half (48 percent) of female inmates across the nation are African American, one-third (33 percent) are Caucasian, 15 percent are Hispanic, and 4 percent are women of other racial backgrounds. In the federal prison system alone, African American women comprise 35 percent of inmates, Caucasians 29 percent, Hispanic women 32 percent, and women of other racial backgrounds 4 percent.

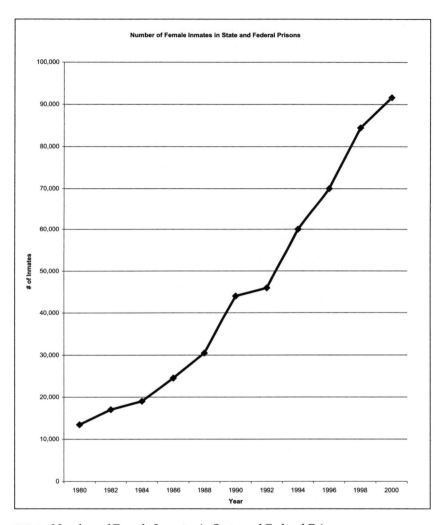

FIG. 1. Number of Female Inmates in State and Federal Prisons
Sources: GAO, Report to the Honorable Eleanor Holmes Norton, House of Representatives, Women in Prison: Issues and Challenges Confronting U.S. Correctional Systems, December 1999, at 3, 19; BJS Bulletin, Prison and Jail Inmates at Midyear 2000, March 2001, page 5; and BJS Bulletin, Prisoners in 2000, August 2001.

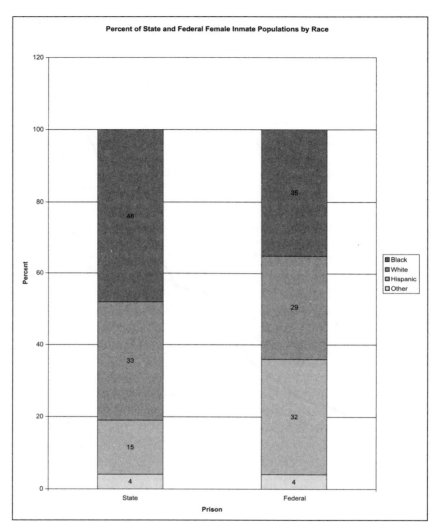

FIG. 2. Percentage of State and Federal Inmate Populations by Race
Sources: BJS Bulletin, Prisoners in 2000, August 2001.

Figure 3 further reveals African American women's disproportionate representation in U.S. correctional facilities.

Next, figure 4 shows clearly that women are incarcerated primarily for nonviolent offenses. Violent crimes by women were at their highest levels in 1980, decreasing markedly since then. Property crimes also were at their highest levels in 1980 and experienced substantial decreases between 1990 and 1999. Significantly, drug-related offenses were at their *lowest* level in 1980; however, incarceration for drug-related offenses reached their highest level between 1980 and 1990 and continued to climb between 1990 and 1999. Similarly, public-order offenses were lowest in 1980 and faced sharp increases between 1990 and 1999. These data correspond to changes in sentencing policy that instituted longer sentences for all offenses, particularly mandatory minimum sentences for all levels of drug-related crimes.

Finally, figure 5 shows extreme differences in regional incarceration rates for women. Although all regions experienced increases between 1990 and 2000, the Northeast consistently has had the lowest number of female inmates in state and federal prisons compared to other geographical regions. The Midwest has a female population slightly

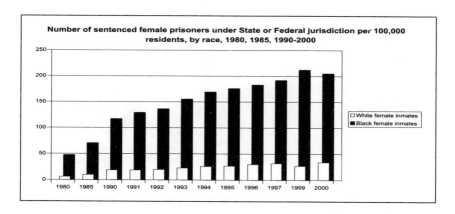

FIG. 3. Number of Sentenced Female Prisoners under State or Federal Jurisdiction per 100,000 Residents, by Race, 1980, 1985, 1990–2000

Sources: U.S. Department of Justice, Bureau of Justice Statistics, Bulletin: Prisoners in 2000; U.S. Department of Justice, Bureau of Justice Statistics, Bulletin: Prisoners in 1999; U.S. Department of Justice, Bureau of Justice Statistics, Correctional Populations in the United States, 1997; U.S. Department of Justice, Bureau of Justice Statistics, Bulletin: Prisoners in 1994.

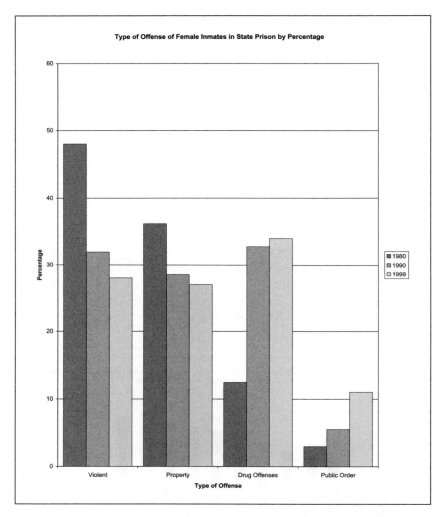

FIG. 4. Type of Offense of Female Inmates in State Prison, by Percentage
Sources: BJS Special Report, Women Offenders, December 1999, at 6, 14; BJS Bulletin,
Prisoners in 2000, August 2001.

greater than the Northeast, at approximately 7,000 inmates. The West had an increase of 10,000 female inmates between 1990 and 2000, placing it above both the Northeast and the Midwest. The most dramatic increase in the female prison population occurred in the South. Although there were more female inmates in 1990 in the South than in other regions, the increase climbed from just over 15,000 to nearly 37,000 incarcerated women in 2000.

Modern Legal Trends

Why has the imprisonment of women reached such unprecedented levels? Some researchers attributed the sharp increase in women's imprisonment to changing social mores regarding American women's roles.[81] However, the "women's liberation theory" of women's imprisonment ignores salient factors such as discrimination, race, poverty, and other social deprivations that account for African American women's incarceration.[82] By now, such theories are roundly discredited, as most experts acknowledge that the rise in women's incarceration is the result of changes in the criminal laws and sentencing practices over the last twenty years. As a recent *Harvard Law Review* symposium stated, "[T]he reasons for the dramatic rise in women's incarceration, both in absolute

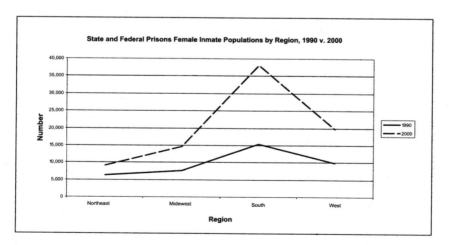

FIG. 5. State and Federal Prisons Female Inmate Population by Region, 1990 and 2000

Sources: BJS Bulletin, Prisoners in 2000, August 2001.

terms and relating to that of men lie not primarily in changes in the seriousness of female-committed crime, but rather in changes in criminal justice policy."[83] Thus, rather than representing liberation theory, increased willingness by law enforcement to arrest and imprison women for longer periods of time represents what sociologist Meda Chesney-Lind has called "equality with a vengeance."

These trends also reflect society's continued willingness to equate African American women with criminality, which in turn justifies disproportionately harsh treatment of them in the criminal justice system and throughout American society. Criminologist Norval Morris recognized that the gross demographic disparity throughout the criminal justice system "may reflect racial prejudice on the part of the police, the prosecutors, the judges, and juries, so that, crime for crime, black and Hispanic offenders are more likely to be arrested by the police and are more likely to be dealt with severely by the courts."[84] The legal response to drug-related offenses provides the most glaring example of racial-gender-class bias within the criminal justice system. These issues are examined with regard to their particular impact on African American women's lives.[85]

One of the hallmarks of the U.S. constitutional system is the right every American enjoys to be free from government intrusion without sufficient cause. In the area of Fourth Amendment rights, sufficient cause for government searches and seizures must be based on "individualized reasonable suspicion" of wrongdoing by law enforcement officers. These rights apparently do not extend to African American women, however, as racial-gender profiling has rendered them automatically suspect as drug couriers. While racial profiling is most often discussed in terms of affronts to African American and Latino men, experience suggests that African American and Latina American women are at greater risk for government abuse in this regard.[86] One particularly egregious example of such government excess involves the U.S. Customs Service.

In March 1998, Denise Pullian returned home from a business trip to Northern Ireland, where she helped establish a program for troubled youth. A U.S. Customs agent stopped Pullian upon her arrival at O'Hare International Airport, whereupon she was told to follow the agent. Pullian was told that she was targeted for a pat search because she was wearing "loose clothing." Upon being escorted to a small investigation room at O'Hare, Pullian's pat search transformed into a strip search. She finally cleared customs upon being forced to remove all clothing and a tampon to satisfy customs agents that she was not carrying illicit drugs.[87] When Pullian informed the Chicago NBC affiliate about her treatment, numerous African American women came forward to describe similar experiences:

> WOMAN #1: I had arrived at Chicago O'Hare.
>
> WOMAN #2: I was asked to step aside in another line.
>
> WOMAN #3: He went through all of my luggage.
>
> WOMAN #4: Then she told me to step this way.
>
> WOMAN #5: "We have to go to this room because we have to search you."
>
> WOMAN #6: She asked me to take my clothes off, take my hair down, spread my legs apart.
>
> WOMAN #7: And she had this great big gun strapped to her hip. So I did as she told me to do.
>
> WOMAN #8: I took down my shorts, took down my underwear, and I had to bend over.
>
> WOMAN #9: And then I was told to remove the pad, remove the tampon.
>
> WOMAN #10: And then she said, "Pull up your panties and get out." Those were her words.
>
> WOMAN #11: You just wanted it to be over as quickly as possible.
>
> WOMAN #12: And you feel stripped of your rights. And you get no explanation.
>
> WOMAN #13: I felt like I was being raped.[88]

The Chicago-area women's experiences were not unique. Particularly harrowing was the account by Janneral Denson, of Fort Lauderdale, Florida. Denson and her young son were stopped in February 1997 upon returning from Jamaica to Fort Lauderdale. Denson was nearly seven months pregnant at the time. She testified before the House Ways and Means Subcommittee on Oversight that she was stopped as she walked toward the exit with her luggage, then was searched. After being asked a series of questions about the purpose for her travel to Jamaica, she provided several pieces of documentation to verify her statements to the officers. Denson was left with another customs officer and waited, uninformed about the basis for her detention, for over an hour. Having not eaten all day, her request for food was ignored. After some time passed, she asked to go to the bathroom. She testified that she was escorted to the bathroom by two agents "where they had me lean against the wall, spread my legs, so that they could search me." The agent then read her some legal rights from a piece of paper, which she refused to sign. Her request to speak to a lawyer was denied. Instead, she was handcuffed and driven to Miami.

Upon arrival at a Miami hospital, Denson was told to change into a hospital gown. The planned vaginal examination was not conducted because a doctor decided she was too far along in her pregnancy. Instead, she was handcuffed again and taken to the Labor/Delivery ward. After long waits, she provided blood and urine samples. She then was put on a bed and handcuffed to a bed rail. The first customs agent and the doctor returned to the room. The doctor had a portable sonogram machine to conduct an internal check. This check revealed a difficulty with Denson's pregnancy, but it also revealed that Denson was not carrying contraband. Denson was then taken off the bed and handcuffed again. She reminded the agent that she didn't have anything in her luggage and had nothing inside her body cavities and asked if she could go home. Again, without explanation, her request was denied.

When Denson requested something to eat, she was told that she would not get anything until morning. The doctor then brought in a substance called "Go Lyte" and Denson was ordered to drink it. She was told that she had to pass three clear stools before she could leave. She testified, "I was scared to death for my child. I told the agent, that's a laxative and pregnant people should not take a laxative. I refused to drink it. They again handcuffed me to the bed; I laid there that night crying for a long time."

The next morning they gave Denson a cold breakfast that she was unable to eat. She testified further, "I had some orange juice and water. At that time, I heard the first agent outside my door call me a 'thing.' She said 'that thing's been here since Friday and she won't eat.'" That afternoon, Denson decided to drink the laxative to obtain her release. "There I was, one hand handcuffed to a bed, so scared that I drank a laxative that might hurt me and my child. I threw up. By the next morning, I passed two clear stools. About four hours later, the first agent returned to take me back to Fort Lauderdale." Denson was held incommunicado for two days: "They say they called my mother. The truth is that they never called my mother. My mother had been calling hospitals until she found me and then an agent told her I would be at the Fort Lauderdale airport in a couple of hours. I was taken to the Fort Lauderdale airport. Nobody was there. They just left me."[89]

Ms. Denson concluded her congressional testimony: "The very fact that I am here, speaking before you, points to the greatness of our country. But what I, and many other African Americans, have gone through, points to a great failure in our country. Conduct such as this is both illegal and Un-American, and, in the long run, can only serve to drive a wedge between you, the government, and the citizens of the country."[90]

Aside from sharing racial heritage as African Americans, the women subjected to such searches came from wide-ranging backgrounds, including age and occupations. In defense of the agency's actions, Customs Commissioner Ray Kelly advanced the "source country" explanation for the number of stops of African American women.[91] Accordingly, travelers, presumably of all races, from countries known to produce illegal drugs are theoretically targeted in greater numbers. A number of the women had traveled from Jamaica, which is on the source country list, so this explanation may be true. However, many of the women had traveled from cities such as Barcelona, Beijing, Frankfurt, and London and were still strip searched. Therefore, it seems more plausible that the Black women were searched by U.S. law enforcement agents based on their racial and gender identities as African American women. A Harvard University statistical report determined that African American women were stopped by customs at a rate eight times greater than that for White males, even though White males far outnumber any demographic group of travelers.[92] Customs' own study revealed that in 1997, an incredible 46 percent of African American women were strip-searched at O'Hare Airport.[93] Even so, Black women were found to be the least likely to be carrying drugs: at 80 percent, the percentage of *negative* searches was greatest for African American women.[94]

To add insult to injury, the Customs agency's form letter explaining its policy to those who had been searched stated: "To be frank, we are not at all sorry. As a matter of fact, we are pleased that you have complied with our laws."[95] Not surprisingly, over ninety African American women in Chicago joined a class-action lawsuit against the U.S. Customs Service, alleging constitutional violations. According to the plaintiffs, damage awards were not their primary motivation for bringing the lawsuit; rather, they sought government accountability for their loss of dignity and fundamental civil rights in the unbridled war on drugs.[96]

Another aspect of the war on drugs has adversely impacted African American women as their bodies became battlegrounds for ideological wars regarding reproductive rights and drug law enforcement. Dorothy Roberts addressed this systemic bias in her groundbreaking piece, *Punishing Drug Addicts Who Have Babies: Women of Color, Equality, and the Right of Privacy.*[97] Roberts argued that prosecution of drug-addicted mothers violated constitutional privacy and equal protection rights. Noting the government's extensive involvement in poor African American women's lives, as well as the women's limited options for birth control, safe abortions, prenatal health, and drug-abuse treatment, Roberts found that "[p]oor Black women have been selected for punishment as a result of an inseparable combination of their gender, race, and economic status," based on the "historic devaluation of African-American women's lives and roles as mothers."[98]

The problems Roberts had previously identified reappeared recently in the Medical University of South Carolina's (MUSC) agreement to work with police and prosecutors in an effort described by Vivian Berger as "[a]n unsavory amalgam of bad law, unethical medicine, and unsound policy."[99] In 1989, MUSC devised a "test-and-arrest" scheme, according to which patients whose urine tested positive for cocaine were referred for substance-abuse treatment, and those who failed to comply or tested positive a second time were immediately taken into police custody.[100] In *Ferguson v. City of Charleston, S.C.,*[101] the U.S. Supreme Court found that the hospital's coercive procedure to test women without a warrant, individualized suspicion, or special circumstances constituted a violation of the women's Fourth Amendment rights. While the hospital claimed that the policy was necessary to assist doctors in treating potentially difficult or dangerous pregnancies, the same ends could have been accomplished more effectively without the specter of criminalization and unnecessary governmental intrusion. Such was the disregard for the African American women's lives that "[s]ome were removed in hand-cuffs and shackles, still garbed in hospital gowns, bleeding and in pain from childbirth."[102] At least one woman was held three weeks in an unsanitary prison cell to await delivery of her baby.[103] As Berger states, "It is hard to believe that the authorities would behave so callously if the vast majority of affected patients were not impoverished women of color."[104]

While dire predictions about the harms to fetuses occasioned by maternal drug use have been overstated,[105] concerns about the health of unborn and newborn babies should not be minimized. Effective responses to such concerns need not entail further criminalization of African American women's lives, however. Notably, in *Ferguson*, the professed concern about African American women's infants, if not the women themselves, occurred when "[t]here was not a single residential drug-abuse-treatment program for women in the entire state [and] MUSC itself would not admit pregnant women to its treatment center. And no outpatient program in Charleston provided childcare so that pregnant women with young children could keep their counseling appointments."[106] In emphasizing arrest and imprisonment, the MUSC policy's absence of resources to facilitate African American women's access to prenatal care and drug treatment exposed its punitive and racially discriminatory design.[107]

The Customs Service has significantly changed its search procedures according to the recommendations of an independent investigation of its practices. The new procedures emphasize behavioral indices rather than racial or ethnic factors.[108] Similarly, the Medical University of South Carolina ended its racially discriminatory drug test-and-arrest policy.[109] While these are welcome developments, it remains doubtful that such embedded racial biases against African American women will cease rather than resurface in new guises. Indeed, racial profiling has assumed expanded proportions in the aftermath of the terrorist attacks of September 11, 2001. As such, U.S. citizens, immigrants, and travelers of Middle Eastern descent have come under increased scrutiny within heightened concerns for national security.[110] In this context as well, civil liberties cannot be jettisoned in finding the balance between security and liberty.[111]

Another area of drug-war enforcement that directly impacts on African American women's incarceration exists in the drug sentencing disparities. As previously noted, the U.S. incarceration rate has risen faster than the crime rate; more aggressive law enforcement efforts and longer punishment for drug-related offenses help to explain this anomaly. Mandatory drug laws and minimum sentencing, three-strikes laws, and sentencing guideline schemes have resulted in a greatly increased female prison population. In New York, for example, the Rockefeller Drug Laws require mandatory prison sentences of fifteen and twenty-five years to life.[112] The federal government's adoption of mandatory sentencing for drug offenses provides the clearest example of the racial disparities that lead to African American women's disproportionate incarceration.

Under drug laws enacted in the late 1980s, sentencing for minor roles and low-level participation in drug activities resulted in severe sentences and long incarceration for many African American and Hispanic offenders.[113] On the federal level, the disparity is built into the sentencing scheme. As such, possession of five grams of crack cocaine results in a mandatory five-year sentence. In contrast, the mandatory minimum sentence for possession of *500 grams* of powdered cocaine results in a five-year sentence.[114] This represents a 100-fold differential in sentencing disparity between pharmacologically identical substances. The critical difference is that crack cocaine is predominant in Black and Hispanic communities and powdered cocaine in White.[115] Beyond this, nothing rationally justifies the great disparity in sentencing for the two variations of this substance. Indeed, the *irrational* basis for the crack-powder cocaine sentencing scheme is evident in the absence of a legislative history on this crucial matter. As one commentator concluded, "Read as a whole, the abbreviated legislative history of the 1986 [Anti-Drug Abuse] Act does not provide a single, consistently cited rationale for the crack-powder penalty structure. In fact, there is evidence that Congress was simply pandering to the anti-crime attitude of the nation."[116]

The life-altering consequence of Congress's thoughtless action in consigning so many young men and women of color to prison under these laws is unconscionable, especially as the commission that recommended the scheme to Congress in the first place acknowledged the inherent unfairness of the sentencing disparities. In May 1995, the U.S. Sentencing Commission submitted a report to Congress strongly recommending abandonment of the one-hundred-to-one quantity ratio.[117] The commission unanimously agreed that the ratio should be abolished but disagreed as to the appropriate ratio. A four-member majority of the commission believed that the base sentence for crack and powder cocaine should be the same.[118] However, a three-member minority of the commission rejected the majority's one-to-one recommendation, finding that substantially different "market, dosages, prices, and means of distribution" enhanced the harmfulness of crack and warranted a greater sentencing differential.[119]

While the three-member minority did not view the issue as having racial implications,[120] others provided strong arguments to the contrary.

In *U.S. v. Clary*,[121] Judge Clyde Cahill found that the sentencing disparities for cocaine offenses evinced unconscious racism against African
Americans in violation of the Equal Protection Clause. Judge Cahill
thoroughly reviewed the racialized history of U.S. drug policies and the
pharmacological similarities between powder and crack cocaine, and
concluded that Congress's "[f]ailure to account for a foreseeable disparate impact which would effect black Americans in grossly disproportionate numbers would . . . violate the spirit and letter of equal protection."[122]

Despite the strength of the analysis in *Clary* and the obvious disproportionate impact of the cocaine sentencing laws on African Americans, neither Congress, the executive, nor the courts have deigned to redress their fundamental unfairness. In *U.S. v. Armstrong*,[123] the Supreme
Court rejected petitioners' request for evidentiary discovery to establish
their asserted equal-protection violation resulting from prosecutors' selective drug law enforcement. The federal public defender's office argued that African American men were selectively prosecuted under the
harsher federal crack-cocaine statute. Evidence revealed that in 1991, all
twenty-four federal crack-cocaine cases involved African American defendants. The public defender sought to establish that White crack-cocaine offenders were deliberately prosecuted in California state courts,
where the penalties were comparatively lighter. The Court ruled that
petitioners must offer minimal proof of racial discrimination prior to requiring the prosecution to disclose case records. The petitioners' burden
required "clear evidence" that the prosecutor's selective enforcement
policy "had a discriminatory effect and was motivated by discriminatory purpose."[124] As Katheryn Russell observes, "The *Armstrong* decision does not mean that the U.S. Attorney's office is not selectively pros-
ecuting Blacks in federal court. Rather, it means that the prosecutor can
withhold evidence of it."[125]

In addition to the basic unfairness of mandatory drug sentences,
they fail to consider extenuating circumstances pertinent to women's
lives. For example, even though women generally play subordinate
roles in drug operations, they often are sentenced more harshly than
their more culpable male counterparts. A 1994 Department of Justice
study on low-level drug offenders in federal prisons found that women
were overrepresented among "low-level" drug offenders who were
nonviolent, had minimal or no prior criminal history, and were not
principal figures in criminal organizations or activities; nevertheless,

they received sentences similar to "high-level" drug offenders under the mandatory sentencing policies.[126] Further, the majority of incarcerated African American women are single parents of one or more minor children. Thus, the impact of their incarceration inures beyond the individual inmate to her children and other family members (usually maternal grandmothers), who must care for young children during the mother's incarceration.[127] African American women rarely receive lighter sentencing based on their familial relationships.[128] They are also at greater risk than White women for loss of custody under the Federal Adoption and Safe Families Act of 1997 (ASFA), due to the length of the drug-related sentences.[129]

CASUALTIES OF WAR

Casualties of the war on drugs extend throughout American society, not just for African American women and members of other marginalized communities. In this regard, the erosion of basic constitutional rights through the enforcement of harsher criminal laws and penalties compromises the democratic system itself. As David Rudovsky argues, the very use of the "war" metaphor indicates tacit approval of the fact that such processes sacrifice rights.[130]

In addition to racially disparate legislative policies that erode our Fourteenth Amendment rights to equality and due process,[131] other freedoms guaranteed by the Bill of Rights are also implicated. For example, the First Amendment's respect for religious liberty is subordinated where religious practices conflict with the objectives of the drug war.[132] The Fourth Amendment, which generally prohibits warrantless and unreasonable searches and seizures by the government, has been severely undermined, permitting law enforcement practices that regularly exceed "reasonableness" in terms of citizens' privacy rights. In this context, in addition to the widespread use of drug-courier profiles that associate African Americans and Hispanics with drug use and trafficking, there are excessive and widespread drug-testing policies in schools and workplaces.[133]

Basic due process rights and the right to counsel are implicated in this war, as guaranteed by the Sixth and Seventh Amendments. As the courts are inundated with drug-related cases, the speedy trial guarantee of the Sixth Amendment and the right to a jury trial for civil matters in federal court under the Seventh Amendment are both seriously compromised.[134] These developments jeopardize every citizen's right to a fair trial.

Finally, laws that permit preventive detention and draconian punishment for drug possession denigrate the Eighth Amendment rights to bail and to sentences that are not cruel and unusual. The Bail Reform Act of 1984 similarly erodes key protections under the Eighth and Fourteenth Amendments, as the act fundamentally changed the bail system by authorizing the pretrial imprisonment of a person innocent of any crime on the theory that he or she would likely commit other crimes while awaiting trial,[135] presuming that a drug offense charge carrying a ten-year sentence makes one automatically dangerous. Accordingly, the act authorizes pretrial imprisonment based simply on a finding of probable cause for certain drug offenses. These provisions have resulted in the incarceration of thousands of drug defendants.

Predictably, the ill-advised war metaphor and its real-life consequences indeed generate casualties of war—predominantly among poor African American women who have been imprisoned in unprecedented proportions. Law and legal institutions have also suffered, however. And, while compromises to constitutional liberties may affect communities differently, the abandonment of constitutional rights has broader implications for the entire society. According to one expert, "We may soon discover that rather than freeing ourselves from drugs, we have simply given up our freedoms . . . our Bill of Rights and our political freedom will be the ultimate casualties of our war on drugs."[136]

PART II

PROFILES AND NARRATIVES OF AFRICAN AMERICAN WOMEN IN THE U.S. CRIMINAL JUSTICE SYSTEM

PROFILES OF *INNER LIVES* PARTICIPANTS

Eighty-four current and former women inmates participated in *Inner Lives*. Table 1 provides comparisons between *Inner Lives* participants and incarcerated women in the state prison system nationwide. The data for *Inner Lives* participants include currently and formerly incarcerated women. The comparisons are apt, however, as the data in the chart categories relate to the participants' experiences during their present or last incarceration. Therefore, the relevant information remains unchanged for both groups of *Inner Lives* participants.

The average age of *Inner Lives* participants at the time of interview was forty years. For *Inner Lives* participants, the average term for non-violent offenses is eight years and for violent offenders it is twenty-five years. Fifty percent of violent offenses carried the maximum possible sentence of life imprisonment. Not shown in the table is the statistic that drug use is implicated in 84 percent of the nonviolent offenses committed by *Inner Lives* participants. Of the violent offenses, homicide comprises 60 percent, with the other 40 percent being crimes such as simple assault, aggravated bank robbery, and child endangerment. Within the 60 percent homicide offenses, domestic violence was involved 40 percent of the time. Seventy percent of *Inner Lives* participants reported physical and sexual abuse during their childhood or adulthood, and 56 percent reported dropping out of school before the twelfth grade, prior to incarceration. The majority of *Inner Lives* participants are parents (88 percent), with an average of three children.

Table I.

Comparison between *Inner Lives* Participants and Female State Inmates Overall on Several Variants

	Inner Lives Participants	Female Inmates Overall
Average age	40	33
Charge	55%–NV	72%–NV
	45%–V	28%–V
Sentence[a]	13 years	18.5 years
Criminal justice history[b]	75%	65%
Substance abuse[c]	70%	74%
Abuse history[d]	70%	57%
Minor children[e]	88%	66%
Education[f]	43%	22%
Employment[g]	63%	51%
Economic status[h]	51%–poor	37%–poor
	49%–middle class	30%–welfare

Notes: V= violent; NV=nonviolent
[a]For *Inner Lives* participants, figure based on the averages for the maximum possible sentence. The computation excludes sentences for which the maximum possible sentence was life imprisonment.
[b]Prior incarceration in jail or prison.
[c]History of drug and/or alcohol abuse.
[d]Physical and/or sexual abuse during childhood and/or adulthood.
[e]Minor children during incarceration.
[f]Completion of high school prior to incarceration.
[g]Some work experience prior to incarceration.
[h]Economic status prior to incarceration.

Sources: BJS Special Report, Women Offenders, December 1999, at 6–9. GAO, Women in Prison, Issues and Challenges Confronting U.S. Correction Systems, December 1999.

NARRATIVES OF *INNER LIVES* PARTICIPANTS

This is not a small voice
you hear.

—Sonia Sanchez, "This is Not a Small Voice"

In Prison I came to know both extremes together. . . . In prison,
I remembered the way I had burst out laughing when a child,
while the taste of tears from the harshest and hardest days
of my life returned to my mouth.

—Nawal El Sadawi, *Memoirs from the Women's Prison*

This section includes twenty-three narratives on issues pertaining to African American women in prison. Most of the narratives are by African American women who are or formerly were incarcerated in the

United States. The women's narratives reveal the paradoxical situation, as suggested by Nawal El Sadawi's quote on the previous page, that for some women imprisonment was an opportunity for self-discovery while it was also the nadir of their life experiences. Although they do not speak for all African American women who have been incarcerated, the similarities in their experiences reflect the realities in many African American women's lives. These women's narratives are followed by commentaries of those who are active and knowledgeable on issues related to criminal justice, corrections, and advocacy on behalf of African American women in prison.

Because of the nonlinear nature of the narratives, I have edited them to enhance the coherence of the text without diminishing the individual's unique voice. Participants who are featured in these life histories were provided edited drafts of their narratives for their review. They made any necessary corrections, clarifications, or elaborations prior to publication.

Thus, speaking for themselves and about themselves, the women were willing to share their life histories in order to inform the effort to enhance general public safety, to devote necessary resources for violence prevention, to dismantle societal barriers, and to instill greater self-worth in all African American women's lives. Collectively, all of the participants' perspectives can aid the goal of promoting legal and social justice and reduce imprisonment rates of African American women.

A

CURRENTLY INCARCERATED WOMEN

I

DonAlda

DonAlda is currently serving a fifteen-years-to-life sentence resulting from the death of her abusive boyfriend. Although it is difficult for her to be separated from her three children, she refuses to let incarceration get the best of her. She continues to paint and to write and was the first Black woman to complete a course of study at the Children's Institute of Literature while incarcerated. DonAlda regards education as the key to reducing the number of Black women in prison.

DonAlda

I AM THIRTY-NINE years old; I was born in 1959. I have three children who are now ages fifteen, eighteen, and twenty-one. That's my whole life, my children. Even incarcerated, they're still my life. I live for them. That's what keeps me motivated in prison. I think that's what keeps me strong, it keeps me going, and keeps my hope alive that one day I'll be back home being a mother to my children.

I come from a family that has no understanding of welfare, jail, or anything wrong or out of the ordinary. First of all, we're Catholic. My mom works hard. She's always been a sales clerk. My dad's a career officer in the Navy. They divorced when I was around eight years old. My mom has my children. She's raising my children, and my two grandchildren. I have a real supportive family, and that helps too, in prison, having a supportive family. It really does.

Being Black and Catholic was very hard. I grew up on the lower south side, which is predominantly Black, but I went to Catholic school in the suburbs. All my friends who were White were not the friends that I went home to. I'm an only child, so I looked good and I dressed nice because there was only one of me. I guess I mostly wanted to be accepted, somewhere. It was hard. I was incarcerated in 1987 due to domestic violence. It was my boyfriend. We had two children together. He was a career criminal who had been in and out of jails. I guess somewhere along the line in jail he learned to beat women.

Just the attention that I received from my boyfriend made me feel that there was a connection between the two of us. My dad was in the service and was always away. My mom was sickly. She was always in the hospital. I was usually with relatives, most of the time. All of my friends were the White kids who lived in the suburbs. I was mostly around grownups. What does a kid do around grownups? You have no one to talk to but the dog, or the cat or the fish. It was kind of hard, just missing out on having a friend.

I ended up suffering abuse for years. We had two children. We got together around 1977, my senior year in high school. We started hanging out and stuff. I didn't know his other side. He was about two years younger than I was. He had been in detention homes. He grew up without his parents. His grandmother raised him. Basically, he did whatever he wanted to do. He wasn't violent when I first knew him. Not at all. He just always was the type that made the promises. He always made promises, but never followed through with them. He would say, "We'll live happily ever after," and "You and me against the world. So what if we're opposites," and "We'll be all right."

I didn't know that he was an intravenous drug user. He hid it well. I guess with the drugs and stealing or robbing people, or whatever, to get the drugs, I guess he was mad at me because maybe I was something that he wanted to be and couldn't be, so he took it out on me. He seemed to resent my education, the fact that I didn't use drugs, or that I had a level head. I worked. I went to work and I worked every day. When he was high it was like a Dr. Jekyll and Mr. Hyde thing.

The violence started after I had my first child with him, about 1980. I graduated from a Catholic high school, near Youngstown, a very good high school. I even went to college, Youngstown State University. I didn't finish because of him. He didn't like me going to college. He said things like, "If I don't go, or we don't have the same friends, then you don't go."

I studied graphic arts at Youngstown State University. I'm an artist, and a writer. I do my art every day. I paint every day. I use acrylics, because oils aren't allowed in our rooms. We have to be supervised with the oils, because of the chemicals. You have to use turpentine to clean, and so we're basically limited to watercolors and acrylics. Right now, my project is pillowcases. I sell pillowcases, usually for children. I love children, and in fact, I took a course of study from the Children's Institute of Literature. I'd like to write children's stories. I was the first Black woman, while incarcerated, to finish their course of study in the Children's Institute of Literature. They said they had a lot of guys take that course, but I was the first incarcerated Black woman. I don't let my incarceration stop me.

In 1980 the abuse started; it was after I had the first child. He became really jealous, really obsessively jealous. Shortly thereafter, I moved out, after I was beaten really severely. I moved out, moved back home with my mother, and, as always, you get the roses, and the apologies, and the "I'm sorry. It'll never happen again." Of course, I believed it, and went back. The next time I pressed charges, though. That violated his parole and sent him back to jail.

They sent him back to jail in 1984. They gave him six months in the county jail on a misdemeanor. That's when he vowed that when he got out, he was going to kill me for sending him back to jail. They wouldn't even charge him. I was beaten with the door molding, like the piece off the door with the nails in it and everything, from nine o'clock in the evening till four o'clock in the morning, all because he went to jail for stealing tape recorders out of parked cars on a busy street, and I wouldn't go to jail and get him.

When he finally did get out he let me have it pretty good so I had to escape from the house. He held me in the house, but I escaped and ran about twelve blocks to my mom's house, where I called the police. I had to leave my children in the house, and, when the police arrived he wasn't there. I pressed charges, they gave him six months, and he went back, and that's when he said he was going to kill me for sending him back to jail.

He got out in 1986. I hadn't seen him, but he had been looking for me. He'd been to my mom's house, saying he wanted to see the kids and different things. This one particular night, I took a friend to the grocery store, because her child was sick and needed cough syrup. We went to a 24-hour grocery store. While she was going to run into the store, I got a hamburger and a shake at the nearby drive-through and I was sitting in the car at the supermarket. Who do I see but him? He was with a group of people, and he sent one of the guys to the car to ask if he could talk to me. Before I could even answer the guy, he was walking toward the car. I had bought a gun after being assaulted so much. It was a sense of security for me. I never thought I would have to use it. I was about twenty-one years old when I bought that gun. I always took it out when I went out at night, and I had it under the seat of the car.

When he walked up to the car, he had a grocery bag in his arm, and he shifted the bag. Then I saw the butt of the gun in there. So, I reached under my seat, and got the gun and shot out the window, and shot at him. By now, my friend was coming out of the store, she was getting in the car, I was shooting out the window, just scared. I took off from there and went home and found out later he was dead. I didn't even know that I shot him. I knew I grabbed the gun. I knew I fired that gun. I didn't think I hit him. I hit him several times, I found out. Three times, as a matter of fact. He didn't die instantly, but, from my understanding, either he died upon arrival at the hospital, or on the way to the hospital. I didn't intend to kill him.

I was charged with Murder One. I had a trial. I had a private attorney. I felt really good about the relationship with my attorney because I knew him. I had retained him several times before to get my boyfriend out of jail. He was the only attorney I knew, only to find out that there was a conflict of interest. I didn't know that then. I know it now, but I didn't know it then. The attorney never explained that to me. He took my money, and then got court-appointed to me, so he got paid twice for my trial.

I never did a day in jail till I went to prison. I was out on bond a year waiting for the trial. Having no knowledge of the law, I didn't know that I could go before a panel of judges, that I didn't have to go through a jury trial. I thought that's how it goes, you commit a crime, you go through a trial. I had an all-White jury. This was not a jury of my peers. It was mostly males. There was one woman who was questioned, one Black woman, but because she had someone who was incarcerated in her family, she did not want to be a juror. She asked to be removed.

Nothing went through my head during the trial. I was on Zanex and Tranzene. I was numb sitting through the trial. My doctor gave me that. Behind the abuse, I started taking nerve medication. They said I suffered from high anxiety and anorexia. I weighed maybe 110 pounds, at the height I am now, five feet, eight inches. I used to pull my hair out; I would sit and twiddle my hair till I pulled it out. I was just a basket case during the abuse. When I would go to the doctor and say, "My boyfriend beat me up," instead of talking about it, or saying "Maybe I could refer you to someone to help you," he would just up my medication and add another pill to it. I was on a tranquilizer and a nerve medication. During the trial, of course, I abused them. I felt, "Oh, my God, my nerves are bad, I'll take, well, I'm taking three a day, I'll take six a day, or six an hour." I was taking them like Tic-Tacs, just shaking them out and taking them. I was aware but I wasn't aware. I was there, but I really wasn't functioning like I should have been. I just felt a grave injustice had been done to me.

I feel that, under the law, I should be punished. But, fifteen-to-life is a lot, that's a lot of punishment for someone who was abused, and for defending myself. I had the battered woman's claim, but at that time, it was not really known. The only thing that was out on the battered woman was the movie *The Burning Bed* at that time. Even though my lawyer questioned the jury on the battered woman syndrome, he really did not submit a lot of evidence on my behalf as far as the years of abuse and the different circumstances that led to that. He also had me take the stand in my own defense to testify about my relationship and the abuse I suffered. My attorney was trying to get me involuntary manslaughter, or manslaughter. Never once have I ever said that I didn't do it, or I'm not guilty of something. I'm guilty. I did it. I hadn't even seen him. That was the first time I had seen him since he got out of jail. The verdict that they came back with was for murder. I got fifteen to life.

Starting to do that time was hard. It was really hard, because with my time it makes me one of the close status, close to max status. That puts a lot of limitations on what you're able to do. You're not able to go to college. You're not able to go places unescorted. You start at the bottom of the totem pole, and you have to work your way up to minimum status where you can get privileges. At that time, a lot of programs weren't offered to lifers, which is what I was. A lot of things really discouraged me and made me angry, and I didn't know how to deal with people younger than me telling me what to do. I was not a career criminal. I felt that I was just as smart or bright as some people, just as educated as some people, and it was difficult to be talked to, sometimes, like a dog. I would curse and go off, and I'd end up in the hole a lot of times, so it was rough on me. I did a lot of time in the hole for my mouth, at first. It was a hard readjustment.

I couldn't have the medicine that I had depended on for so many years. I was not weaned off of this medicine. Then [when] I was here, I didn't have the crutch to lean on. I had to deal and I just couldn't. Not only dealing with the time, but dealing with the fact that I killed somebody that I loved. First love, only love. Despite the abuse, I loved him. I never had time to deal with that. I just kept taking the medication and being numb. Now it was time to deal with a lot of things.

First of all I realized that I was not okay and that I had problems and issues that needed to be dealt with. I think it really took me until maybe three or four years ago to really realize that I'm not as okay as I think I am, and I need to get with self, and need to do things to help myself. I need to start dealing, instead of pushing things, or hiding things, or not talking about things. I need to deal with them. It started through my writing. When I started writing my children's books, I started writing about things that happened to me as a child, but I would put them in my children's characters.

People need to know that we are still human beings, even though we have numbers. That, sometimes, things are out of our control, and people make mistakes, and because you make one mistake, your whole life should not be judged or determined. Your destiny should not be determined by that one mistake. People should know that even though you're incarcerated, you can still be positive, you can still be productive. I'm very productive, every day I'm productive. Prison—now, you might think this is crazy—but prison has brought out the best in me. It has brought out the best in me, because it makes me resourceful.

Both of my daughters have been to jail. One daughter was there for disturbing the peace. She was in a fight somewhere and they arrested her. Just recently, my other daughter went to school with a utility knife in her purse. She says she carries it—we live in a bad neighborhood—she carries it in her purse at night, and she forgot to take it out at school and it beeped the metal detector. They took her to jail, so she's been to court. She came out of it fine. She's made the honor roll since. She didn't let it deter her, but she realized a lot of things by those six hours in jail. She realized, "Mom, I see what you go through now."

I really want people to be knowledgeable. It's for people to understand this system, and maybe they can help people not return. You have a lot of returnees. You have young girls that don't have any direction, and they don't understand. They think it's a game. These young girls in prison, they don't have any respect for anything. They don't have respect for life, other people, and authority. We need to educate them. Especially the Black community, as a whole, because there are lots of things they don't understand about the system. Education is a must. I try to tell my kids that education will keep you out of here. Not just school education like myself, but education about different things, like drugs, domestic violence, all kinds of education because I didn't know anything.

2

Cynthia

Cynthia had a tumultuous childhood. Although she did well in school, participated in extracurricular activities, and dreamed of becoming a doctor, she began drinking at sixteen, became pregnant very young, and left home to live on the streets. She witnessed domestic violence between her parents and was sexually abused by a family member. Cynthia is currently serving thirty years without the possibility of parole for murder. She is dealing with issues of race, sexuality, and medical care in the prison system.

Cynthia

I WAS BORN and raised in Newark. I am the middle child. My brother is younger and my sister is older than me. My mother and father were married and they separated when I was about seven years old. I lived with my grandmother for a while until my mother moved next door to my grandparents. Basically, aunts, uncles, grandma, and granddad raised me.

My mother is from Georgia. She comes from a big family of seven brothers and four sisters. She was just busy living her life when we were younger. We did things in the summer. We would take some trips to amusement parks and we would travel south to see relatives and different things like that. But my mother is an introverted person. She believes in the old-fashioned way of "do what I say, don't ask questions."

Church was mandatory in my house. My mother made sure that we got up every Sunday morning and went to church or vacation Bible school. She always cooked and made sure we had nice clothing and a roof over our head. I guess that was her way. She just never talked. Even now when she comes to see me she just sits there. She holds a lot inside.

My father comes from a family of eight girls and three boys. He was a truck driver and I didn't see him often. He would stop in and say hi, though. I didn't have a close relationship with my father until I was older. When I was about twenty-four years old, I wanted to know who he was so I found out where he lived. I started spending more time with him prior to my incarceration. We had a good relationship.

When your parents are separated sometimes kids hear different things about them. Some people might say that he is no good or whatever, but that is still your dad. When he would come home on weekends, we would go shopping. I would cook for him so that he could just heat up the food when he came home during the week, because he would be really tired a lot of times. My father was an alcoholic and I realized what he had gone through. I got to know him and understand what it was like for him as a boy coming up in the South in Alabama, his pain. He had only a fourth-grade education. I just think that he held a lot in and tried to cover it up with drinking. He died in 1995 of emphysema and lung cancer.

I went to high school in Newark and graduated in 1977. I was active in sports like basketball and softball. I always liked math and science. I was in the biology club and the African American history club. A couple of teachers made impacts on my life—a math teacher and my biology teacher. They encouraged me to do things right, to expand. It just wasn't easy. I was considered a problem child. I was suspended from school for getting into a fight. I fought because I felt that I was being picked on because I was real shy. Now that I am older, I realize that I thought fighting was the way because my mother and father used to argue and fight a lot. They didn't call it that at that time, but there was a lot of domestic violence going on. I guess I had anger and I guess I was a kid crying for help but didn't recognize it. I wanted to go to college to become a pediatrician after high school. I studied medical books so that the material would not be so hard for me when I did get into college. But I couldn't get anybody to take me for an interview for college, even though I had a lot of family around me. My family wasn't concerned with that and the question of my further education did not really come up. This was a disappointment for me. It was the turning point in my life.

After the disappointment with school and the violence, I started drinking beer when I was sixteen. I was depressed but I didn't understand that it was depression. Being here, I look back over my life and I realize the pattern. I started drinking and I was trying to go to school and I was trying to find a job. I looked for any type of job I could find, like clerk jobs or working at a store. I couldn't really get a job because I didn't have any skills. I planned to join the service but I got pregnant. Then I thought, "Oh God, what am I going to do?" I was still naïve. He was using condoms but I still ended up getting pregnant. I thought that as long as you use the condoms everything would be okay.

I thought about having an abortion because I knew that I couldn't bring a child in the world living the way I was, but I didn't have enough money. I had always dreamed that if I did have this child I wanted to be a good mother. I wanted to have a better relationship with my child than I did with my mother. I didn't even know anything about adoption. I didn't think I had any choices. I was scared to talk to any of the teachers that had helped me before.

I wasn't living at home. Before I graduated school, I was living on the streets because I ran away from home. I used to live in abandoned buildings, train stations, and go to the all-night movies and stay there. I left the house because of my relationship with my mother. I was beaten or belittled a lot, so I just left. One day, I came in from school and my mother hit me. It was time to leave because I wanted to strike back. It was just the last straw and I just left.

That is the way that I lived until I graduated high school. I confided in a couple of teachers about my situation because I was going to drop out of high school. I only had two or three weeks to go but I was becoming stressed and I was just going to quit. The teachers told me that I came all this way and that it was not in my best interest to quit with only three more weeks of finals and then the graduation. A couple of them helped me out and paid for my graduation dues and fees, asking me if I wanted to get my class ring. Another teacher let me stay at her house for a while. They helped me out. They made sure that I ate and bought me lunch. They did my hair for me for graduation. They just talked to me.

At that point, I was glad that I had graduated, but I didn't know what I was going to do with myself. I had a boyfriend in high school and he was working. So I lived in an abandoned building for a few weeks and we saved up some money and I stayed at a hotel so I could wash up. Basically, until I was seven months pregnant, that was the way that I lived. I have a daughter who is now in her twenties. She is working and she has a little girl herself now to raise.

I didn't really open up and tell my teachers the extent of what was going on as far as sexual abuse and different things. I still held that in and only gave them bits and pieces and not really the whole picture. When I was four years old, I was raped by one of my uncles. People that were supposed to help you were the ones that were taking advantage. It went on for a long time, until I was about sixteen. I did not discuss it with anybody until just recently when I was able to talk about it to a counselor in prison in a program about sexual abuse. The counselor was pretty good and I felt that she was sincere. I was able to open up and release it for the first time. I started to talk about the sexual abuse two years ago. I sat down and I wrote about it. I like to write, and I just wrote. She had a special session with me and I read it to her.

That counselor is no longer here but I feel more comfortable with myself. I realize that I didn't do anything wrong. I released a lot of anger. I am learning how to nurture myself for once in my life. I can't change the past, but I accept it and I am just trying to move on. I have been able to see how different situations have impacted my life as far as me being withdrawn, my shyness, my addiction and some of the choices that I have made. It's like trying to get to the root of the problem because if I ever get a chance to go out to society, I want to be strong. I want to be better than when I first walked in here.

After high school, I worked painting apartments. I also was trying to go back to school. I was studying to be a paramedic because that would still be in the medical field. I felt that I couldn't be a doctor because I just felt that it was too late for me. I was about twenty-four or twenty-five years old. I went for a while. I almost made it for a semester, then something would come up and I would end up withdrawing. I might take my finals, I might do the midterms, but something was always going on. I was young. I didn't really know that I should have stayed motivated or tried to find other things. I figured that once my daughter was in school all day then I could go back, but it just didn't work out that way.

I became addicted a couple of years before I became incarcerated. I began using cocaine by trying to be part of the group, trying to be accepted. It started as a weekend thing. I realized that I had a habit because I started selling things that I had, putting things in the pawnshop and borrowing. I tried to get into rehab. I went to a residential program for about a week and started to feel a little clean without really understanding what the situation was. I thought I had everything under control, but little did I know that when I went back home and started being in the same environment, around the same people, that I would fall back into it. For a few days, I said "no thank you. I am not doing that." When they said, "Just take a little bit," that is all it took. I was back into the madness. I was also in a lesbian relationship and I realize that I was basically going that way, which had nothing to do with some of the things that had happened to me. My addiction problems started while I was in that relationship. Basically, that is why I am here. We were involved together for about eleven years. One particular night, I came home from work and another girl was at the house. I asked the girl to leave and told my wife that I wanted to talk to her. The other girl said that she wasn't going anywhere. I guess my wife was scared and thought that I was going to beat her up or something because I was upset. My wife was leaving to get her sister and brother. I got into an argument with the girl she was involved with. The girl swung at me and I told her to just leave me alone, that I had no problems with her. I just wanted to talk to my wife. I knew that my wife had to let her in, so I didn't blame her. I had blamed the person who I had made my commitment with. Anyway, my wife left and we argued in the hallway.

About two days after the argument, I left. I went to stay with my mother. I asked my sisters to mind my daughter while I worked. One night I realized that I hadn't eaten although I had been drinking, so I went to get some fries to put in my stomach. I just started walking around because I was depressed. I went back to the old abandoned buildings where I once used to stay and called home. I came upon the other girl by chance walking on the highway and I asked if we could talk. I told her that I didn't want to have any problems. We were on foot. I told her that whatever she and my wife did was on their part, but I loved my wife's children like they were my own and I wanted to see them. An argument broke out and she said, "I don't give a fuck what you want." And that is when the situation happened.

We started arguing. It was late at night, and I did have a weapon on me; I had a knife. She did not have a weapon and I didn't think that she did. It was just the argument. One thing led to another. I remember flashes of her coming toward me and thinking she was going to throw me in front of the trucks on the highway. I recall during the struggle that she may have grasped for something and that she stumbled. I just went into panic and I just ran. Some days later, I found out that she had died. I knew we had fought, but I didn't think that I had caused her death. Then everything happened so fast, like flashes. I didn't really understand the extent of what I had done.

When I left after the argument, I went to my mother's house. I didn't say anything. It was late. I guess I was in total shock. I just kept everything inside of me. I had called my wife a couple of days after the incident and I told her that I wanted to get things that I had in the apartment. At that time she informed me that the woman had passed away. Then everything just clicked.

I was scared. I called a therapist that I was seeing and I told her that I think I might have hurt this person. That is when the reality of everything settled in. The therapist told me to come in and she talked to me. I was put in a psychiatric ward at the hospital. The detectives came up. I recall him yelling and telling me that I killed this girl and he told the nurse to put a hold on me. I wasn't exactly sure because they gave me a needle or something and I was asleep. After I had taken the therapy, they had to release me. Two police officers came and picked me up from the hospital and they took me down to a holding cell in Newark. I stayed there for about a week or so. Then they called me upstairs to the courtroom and they gave me a green paper. I guess it was an indictment form and they told me I was being charged with first-degree murder. There was a public defender there and he said just don't say anything. Then the judge set bail. I went back downstairs until they sent me to trial. I didn't make bail. They wanted $50,000 in cash only, according to what the public defender told me. I guess nobody wanted to put it up. My mother told me that she didn't have that type of money, so that was it.

Basically, I only saw my public defender about four times prior to trial. He came up and told me the nature of the charge and what it carried. He told me that he really had no defense for me and that he would try to get me a plea bargain. He said that because everything happened really fast that night and I really only had bits and pieces in my mind of what happened. He mentioned murder, aggravated manslaughter, reckless manslaughter, and that's all that I can remember. He told me the sentence required by law for each charge. For example, if I got an aggravated manslaughter deal then I would have to do maybe twenty years; if I got a reckless manslaughter that carried ten years. He requested that I have a psychological evaluation. I saw a psychologist who showed me some pictures and asked me some questions. The next time the attorney came back he seemed sort of angry. I don't know why he was angry. He said that they were going to try to use the insanity defense, but he couldn't do that because the guy said that I had borderline personality disorder and that I was not insane. He told me that I had to tell this guy something to put the pieces together the best that I could. So when I saw the psychologist, even though I could only remember bits and pieces, I tried to fill in the gaps so that it made sense, because I really couldn't remember. I remember talking and starting the conversation. She struck me and we had an argument. It's like flashes like you would see in a movie, like scenes just flashing. I don't even know how to describe it.

We went for a jury trial. My attorney told me that they were not going to offer me a plea and that I had to go to trial. I don't know why the state didn't offer a plea. I think maybe it's because I am a lesbian. They were trying to say it was a lover's triangle type of thing. I believe that they were trying to say that society doesn't want people that are not in the masses, like a deviant or something. That may have had something to do with it. I really don't know.

When they got the jury, the judge told them that it was going to be a lesbian trial and started asking them if anybody had problems with it. The judge asked some questions and then my attorney asked some questions to see who could stay and who had to go. Some people were dismissed. I don't know what my attorney thought about the fact that the case involved lesbians. He never said. I just told him what happened that night and a couple things that happened prior to the incident and that was about it. I never really thought anything about that until recently. Now I realize that there were a lot of things that he should have asked me that he didn't ask.

For example, I think that when I was injected at the hospital with the medication and I was asleep when the detectives woke me up the way that they did. One guy said I was incoherent. The other detective said that I was not incoherent. I think my attorney should have asked about the effect that the drugs had on me. I think that he should have asked them if I was really read my rights when the guy said that I made the confession to him. I had never been involved with the law before. I didn't know what to expect or what was required as far as what attorneys could do. I thought that they had your best interest at heart. You tell them what happened and they take the facts and do the best they can to defend you. I didn't know that they were supposed to be aware of different strategies.

There were men and women on the jury. There were Blacks and Whites; some were older. I just prayed that the jury would be fair because I didn't really understand what to expect. While going through the process, I saw how the prosecutor could take one statement and turn it into something else and the people would think it was a fact. For example, he tried to make it look like she lived only four blocks away from me and that I had to know this girl—like I stalked her—which wasn't true. Different things as far as the medical examiner's testimony were twisted around. I guess they did what they thought was right to do. I knew that I deserved to pay for what I did because it was wrong. I always try to accept the consequences for my actions, but I didn't think I deserved to do thirty years in prison without parole. It wasn't like I was trying to say I am totally innocent, but looking back now, I don't believe that I had a fair trial. The trial lasted about a week. Only my mom came to the trial; I saw her there. When the final verdict came it was for murder one. I was sentenced to prison after the trial. I was at the county jail for a while and came to prison in August 1987.

Hell. It's been real hard. Basically I thank God for His grace because I think I probably would have lost it. This is a whole different world. When I came here it was scary because I really didn't know what to expect. I've spent time in lock for all sorts of crazy things. I feel that now I have been stripped of everything. I used to be shy and withdrawn but now I speak up. A couple of years ago, I was depressed because my father and grandfather died, and I was close to them. It was a rough period and I was trying to see if there was somebody to talk to. I couldn't see anybody, so I was sort of depressed. I also was trying to work on my legal papers. During this time, I just stayed in my room and went to work, so they wanted me to see the psychiatrist.

I went to the psychiatrist and I was telling her that I couldn't even grieve for my father. When I went to see his body, the officers were telling me in the van that when you get there and you show out you are coming back. If you see any of your family there you are coming back. I was trying to brace myself because I hadn't seen my dad in ten years. When I got there I couldn't show any emotion. I looked at him but my tears, my pain, everything . . . I swallowed it down inside of me because I didn't want them to say that I had done anything wrong. I didn't want to cry because if you cry you don't know how hard you are going to cry when you start. I held that inside of me and it really made me depressed.

I talked about those issues to the psychiatrist. She wanted me to take medication and I told her that I didn't need any medication and that I was okay. That is why I first started doing drugs, trying to cover up things and not deal with whatever I was going through. I wanted to deal with it face on. I was in my bed asleep and I was called and told that they wanted to come see me and that I was going to be committed. I thought, "Excuse me, committed?" They said that I told them that I was going to commit suicide. I went over the conversation and didn't know where they came up with this. I started getting nervous. There was nothing I could do. I went back to my cell. By the time I got there to light a cigarette, there were sergeants and lieutenants at my door. They took me to the hospital, started telling me to take off all of my clothes, put me in a gown and sent me to the mental institution for the criminally insane. I stayed there for two weeks because when I went there, I was angry and scared.

It was the hardest thing that I had to go through because I couldn't show any emotion. I am a murderer. They are going to think I am violent. If I cry, they say that I am depressed. So for those two weeks, I held everything inside of me. I just read my Bible. Then I started counting my blessings because I saw people there who were really way out. I had a meeting at a big long table with all types of social workers, psychologists, whatever. They talked to me and asked me questions about my background. They put me in a therapy class. I just did what I had to do. When I was there, another patient started groping me and I was scared to really hit him or anything because I felt they would use that against me. I told the staff about it and they said, "He always does that." So on top of everything that I had been through, like dealing with the other sexual issues, I felt violated all over again.

When I came back to the prison, I started having nightmares and night sweats. I was really traumatized but I couldn't let anybody know because I felt they would use that against me. I just think God's strength got me through it. Now I refuse to ever speak to a psychiatrist because that is too much power. I am dealing with some of the things like the past abuse by practicing yoga and meditating. I am being honest with myself. I realize that the only thing that I have control over is myself.

At the prison, I have tried to bring things to different people's attention, but that is about as far as it goes. Some things are worked out as far as the handicapped people that come in here, like making arrangements for them so they wouldn't have to step up. For example, when my grandfather wanted to come and see me, he couldn't step up in the van because of his legs. Now they drive people up here and they can get in. I just keep loose. I believe that one day I will have my opportunity to try to make a difference. It's not like the 1960s with prison reform and different things, but I believe that society needs a wake-up call. I lost friends in here because of the medical system. The medical system is privatized. To me it is basically about making money. For example, I have certain health issues like high blood pressure. Once, I was supposed to go to the clinic in April. I sent them a notice. I received no response. I didn't hear anything until October. They gave me medication and it was making me sick. I asked them about the side effects of the medication and they told me that they couldn't provide me with that information so I just stopped taking it.

A friend died here several years ago. She was having pains in her chest. She was complaining a lot that she didn't feel well. I remember a couple of times she came in from work and she was real weak, about to pass out. One time she did fall out and they said nothing was wrong with her. Eventually when they did get her to the hospital, they found that she had cancer and it was too far gone. A lot of times people that I live with in here are discouraged because they always say that it's in their mind. They say I'm not going to pay five dollars just for him to tell me that nothing is wrong with me.

What concerns me is that I still have seventeen years ahead of me and there is nothing for me to do here. Nothing constructive. If you already have a GED or diploma, you don't have any other educational resources. They don't really give you any training or marketable skills. They have NA and AA. I have participated in the drug program, but basically I just do the domestic violence group. I speak to the women about it. I wrote articles for them. I help organize different things. I also went to a group for long termers. They teach you how to cope with this time. To me it's like parenthood, you learn as you go along because things are always changing. When there is a rule today, there may not be a rule tomorrow.

Everybody has to have a job unless you are medically excused. The most that you can make is fifty-eight cents per hour. Some people get paid thirty-five dollars per month. Some people make two dollars per day. It varies depending on the type of work you are doing. They also have a sewing room so you can make things. I think that they should have more programs to give marketable skills, like repairing computers. There is the GED program but college courses are no longer offered. I was able to take some sociology classes and an Afro-American history class.

Some people in here get along and some people don't. There are some people that are prejudiced. Black people prejudiced against Whites; Whites prejudiced against Blacks. It works both ways. Sometimes they fight and they argue. Basically, if they argue or they fight they will end up going to lock. If there was some kind of racial problem, both women might go to lock but the woman of color might get more time. For example, I had an incident a while ago with my job on max detail. I completed my assignment but the officer was in a bad mood so she said I didn't work as much as the other girl. I ended up losing my job. It was like she was saying things to provoke me so I just laughed at her. If I cursed her out they would write me up to try to justify it so I just laughed at her and it really made her mad. The assistant warden came to see me. She reprimanded her, the White person, and she fired me. We had the same charges, even though they never explained why I got a harsher punishment.

For instance, there also is no loitering in the hallway and no room visiting. There have been women of color that have been caught in someone's room and maybe the charge is fifteen days LOP (loss of privileges). Whereas, they tell the other person just to get out of there. I just try to keep a low profile and do the best I can.

Sexuality is scary in here because the population has a high HIV percentage. I am open about my sexuality but I have been celibate. I talk to people but it is not in an intimate relationship. I try to get people to think and expand, try to help people, encourage people. I think there is a lot of pain in here. A lot of people have been through the things that I have been through as far as sexual abuse and the drugs. Sometimes they need somebody to look up to or to listen to them. They really never had any guidance. Like me, they had nobody just to say, "Hey I care." I try to encourage them to get their GEDs. I try to get them to believe in themselves. I tell them that there are different opportunities out there and that it is important to stay motivated. They should spend time with their children. I left my daughter when she was six, so I missed out on school plays and different things.

I think people should understand that everybody makes a mistake. I think that the judge should have more discretion when it comes to sentencing people because a lot of the get-tough-on-crime policies are not really beneficial because they don't address the total circumstances. The judge can't look at the whole situation and make a determination based on the evidence and the situation. I think that they need to realize that the same people that they have in jail today, that they are housing for five, ten, fifteen or some many years, are going to return to society. If they are not treated with compassion, then when they get out there they are not going to have compassion. Everything is closed in. A lot of times, the way things are designed, it makes you feel that everybody is against you. They have to address those issues to get them skills, get them tools, and show them that they have options. Give them programs, psychological counseling, whatever they can that will help them make a transition back into society. Everybody deserves at least one chance in life. I know that we have to have laws to keep things balanced or have some type of rule that is reasonable, but I think they should look at the whole person and not just the nature of their offense.

I really don't know what my future holds because right now I am still facing seventeen more years in here without parole. But if I could be free, I want to get out and work with young people in my community. I want to go back to school and get an education. I want to spend time with my family. I want to try to make a difference in the prison system. I really want people to understand a lot of things that go on behind these walls that they are not going to read about on the news.

Right now, I am thirty-nine years old. I will be fifty-seven when I'm released. I try to take care of my health because I think that the older people don't get the type of care they need. I try not to go too far because if I go too far, I might stress out and worry about things that you can't change. I try to live in the moment. I just try to say God is in control and whatever happens it is because God allows it. Whether it is pleasant or unpleasant, I try to deal with it with the best of my abilities. People do change, regardless of the circumstance and the crime they were convicted of. I don't think that locking people up for a long time is the solution. I've had the direct experience of being here and because I was outside prior to coming here, I can say that it is not going to work. The system as it is today is not going to work as far as the long-term effect of bettering society and stopping crime. Sometimes the person can come in here one way and when they go out they are in a worse state. There is a lot of bitterness in here. It doesn't make you better, it makes you bitter. Sure people have to take responsibility for what they did, but if you are going to incarcerate them, give them the mental help that they need. Teach them social skills because a lot of times people don't have basic skills to do basic things such as parenting or coping with abuse and other issues. I think yoga would be a good program to have in prison because it helps expand a person's perspective. It helps them look at themselves and stop blaming people and take responsibility for the things that they do.

Today, I can say that there was just the rage, the anger, everything and I lost my temper. I regret what happened. I have risked my life a lot of times trying to save people. I felt that what happened was totally ironic to what I believe my nature was. I really thought that if anything, I would die to save somebody else.

I do think about the victim. It took me a long time to forgive myself because even though I did this, I really love people. I never thought that I would be in this type of situation. I don't really like violence because I grew up in it and around it. It makes no sense as far as what my belief system is and how people like Martin Luther King, Jr., meant something to me as I was coming up. It hurts, the pain that I caused her family. Regardless of what happened, I never had a right to take anybody's life. I always pray for her family. I pray for them that they have peace and that maybe one day they will forgive me. Everyday that I live with myself it is there. It was a tragic mistake. I can say that because I was high, that had an impact on it, but it was wrong.

A person can snap. It is true that a person can only take so much. You just snap. Back then I was trying to get a job so I took the civil service test and passed. I had decided that I wanted to be on the police force. I had two weeks before I started the training and I got in this trouble. It was heartbreaking for me because I knew that I had a lot to offer society, but that night I made a bad decision.

3

Mamie

Mamie currently is serving consecutive sentences of ten to twenty-five years for involuntary manslaughter, based on the death of her daughter, and five to fifteen years for endangering children, plus a concurrent life sentence for felonious sexual penetration. She continues to grapple with many questions regarding her daughter's death, which she believes was never properly investigated. She also continues to struggle with the issues surrounding her conviction and sentence and believes that she is the victim of injustice in the legal system. She appealed her conviction, unsuccessfully. She maintains her innocence and relies on her faith to help her through her sentence.

Mamie

MY NAME IS MAMIE. I've been here ten years. I'm forty-three years old. We are originally from North Carolina. My mom was from South Carolina, my father was from North Carolina, and I'm from Winston. My mom was a midwife in North Carolina; she helped to deliver babies. My father worked at a major tobacco company for thirty years. I think he was a packer. My mom didn't get a job when we came up to Ohio. My dad didn't come up with us. My dad and mom had separated and had gotten divorced when I was three. I have four sisters and two brothers. I fit between the baby boy and the baby girl. My mom raised me until I was fourteen. In the household, it felt like my mom had more love towards my sisters and brothers, and later for my children, than for me. When my mother separated from my father, she would always tell me that I was just like my daddy. I never really knew how my daddy was, but the only part that I remember was that he wasn't abusive and my mother was.

Jail really didn't faze me because I had lived at home and I took the abuse. My mother made a closet and put a hole in it, and had a padlock. If we didn't do what she said, we would go into the closet. We would stay in there for three or four hours. If I wasn't sent into the closet, she would make us strip all our clothes off and she would use an extension cord or switch. I would go to my sisters and they would say just go back, it's going to be okay. I went to my dad and asked him why she treated me like she didn't want me and he said he didn't know. He just said bear with her because she's still your mother. You're under her roof and you have to do what she says. My father tried to get us, and the court system wouldn't allow us to go with him. They told him he had to remarry, but he didn't want to remarry for a long time after leaving my mom. I was in my twenties when my dad remarried. By then, I was grown and on my own.

I had left home at fourteen and I stayed with this guy. I ended up marrying him because in the early days, you had to marry the man if you had a child. That was my situation, even though this man was twenty-seven and I was still a baby. My mother said I still had to marry him. I met him downtown in Akron. He told me that he worked for the city. I remember that wasn't really where I wanted to be, but I had no choice.

Being married to him was just like being at home again because he was abusive. Every time he got drunk, he either wanted to beat me or I couldn't go nowhere. The abuse started two days after we got married. He had gotten drunk and when we got home he wanted me to do something. I got up and fixed the food, I did everything he asked me to do, but that wasn't good enough. Then he began to call me by his first wife's name, and I wasn't going for that. I told him, you're not going to disrespect me by doing that, and he turned around and busted me in the face. That was it. I was not standing for an abusive relationship for the simple fact that I had enough abuse at home. I didn't need anymore. I was married for six months and then I was gone.

First I went back home to North Carolina and lived with my cousin. I stayed there only two weeks because I missed my daughter. My daughter was born in December 1972. She was born at eight months, one month premature. She was real sickly. She had to stay in the hospital about five weeks because her heart kept giving out on her. She had tubes in her. The doctor kept telling me that he didn't know if she was going to make it. That's when I began to pray, asking the Lord to take me instead of letting her suffer.

When I left to go to North Carolina, my mother had my daughter because my mother thought that I was too young to care for her. I knew nothing about raising a child. Not only that, but my mother needed the money from welfare. She had me in and out of the Children's Service Board. My mother told them that I was an alcoholic. I never did drugs in my life. I may have taken one or two drinks in my life. The Children's Services took that and ran with it. They felt that the kids should stay in my mother's care. At that time, I was fifteen or sixteen years old. My mother wouldn't give up the baby, and my husband felt that I didn't need a baby anyway, so I should give her to my mother. My husband signed the papers giving temporary custody of my daughter to my mother. I didn't know that until a year later, when my mother told me that he signed the papers.

I stayed away for a while, but I went to see my child. I wanted my child to know that I was really out there struggling for her, that I wasn't neglecting her in any way. I walked in the snow, knee deep; I just had to be near her. My mother would always tell my daughter that I didn't love her. She would not give my daughter the things I had bought for her. It didn't make sense to me. But I was determined, and I was not giving up. My daughter is twenty-seven now; my mother turned her against me and she doesn't like me. I explained to my daughter that it was not my fault.

My mother kept me in the court system. She said that she didn't think that I was fit to keep my children. My attorney felt that I should have visitation rights with my daughters, but he said he had to go by what my mother said. I thought it was very unfair. The more I told them what was going on, it was like I was a liar. The attorney just said, "Well, I'll look into this and I'll look into that," but nothing got done. So they kept it the same, and the kids remained in her house.

When I came back to Akron, I got an apartment. They knew I had a one-bedroom apartment. I already had my baby with me, and my mother had the other two. I had to look for a bigger place for them, but in the process of looking for a bigger place for them, I had filed for section eight (housing subsidy). While waiting for section eight to come through, I was in and out of the hospital with my nine-year-old so that she could see a psychiatrist. They couldn't deal with her in school. The lady that checked her said that she had a problem and they were going to put her on Ritalin. At first, they put her on 10 mg of Ritalin. She was getting out of control, I took her back, and they gave her 20 mg of Ritalin. My daughter had gotten to the point where she started banging her head on the floor, and she would get a fork after my baby daughter. Then she would just calm down and go into stages like, "Mommy I love you," and "Mommy don't ever leave me." She went through four or five stages with me.

She had a problem. I tried to get help for her. The psychiatrist said, well, let's try her out on this, and if she needs any more help, we'll go further. Well, further was to put her in a place. I decided that I would not have my daughter placed in an institution. I didn't put her in a place; I worked with her. That was a hard decision because I never had a chance to raise my daughter when she was younger, and I wanted to be there for her. I wanted to do things that other mothers did for their children. I really didn't know what her diagnosis was. All I know is that they were saying she was hyper, and that's why she was on Ritalin. They didn't even tell me that she had seizures. I felt that if I was with her, she would change, but she didn't. I did the best that I could as a mother. I did what I thought was best, but that wasn't good enough.

I did everything those people asked me to do. I got the house. I tried for a job. I did all of this. When they gave me my kids, they didn't have clothes, anything. I had to scrape up some clothes for them, scrape up some food for them, because they left me emptyhanded. It was like you just go for yourself. They had given me the runaround for a long time, and I kept running for help, running for help. They never explained about their medical history or anything. They never told me what I had to face, so I had to face it alone and I had to deal with it day by day.

I have three kids of my own, one passed. That's what I'm in prison for. I got the kids in 1988, after my mother went to jail. My mother was charged with involuntary manslaughter. That's the only reason why I got the children. All I know is that they gave her twelve to twenty years. The prosecutor said that she was going to die in prison. My mother died in Columbus, in a hospital on the dialysis machine. She didn't die in prison, so he didn't get his wish. My mother gave them eleven years on her sentence. Before she died, my mother explained to my daughter that it was not my fault, and that she didn't allow her to be around me and didn't allow us to do things together. Once I got them back it was going smoothly, until that day, the day that caused me to be here.

I only had the kids permanently for three weeks. It was going well. The children were in school. I was on welfare because I had my baby. On this particular day, I had been home all day because I had a slight headache. I went to sleep and I woke up because the kids were at school and I heard somebody at my door. It was my husband, who had come home early. Around 4:00 P.M., I asked him if the kids had come in, and he said they were out in the yard playing. I went outside looking for my kids and they weren't out there. I came back up and told him that they weren't out there. My husband then said that they had to be in the bathroom. My husband was standing by the stove.

I went to the bathroom and the door was locked. I told them to open the door. When they opened the door, they had a douche bag. It was just the baby and the nine year old, and she had my douche bag in her hand and the nozzle towards her mouth. I was asking her, "What are you all doing in here? The clothes are all over the floor." They said "Nothing, Momma." "So why is the door locked?" Again, they said, "Nothing, Momma." The baby said, "Yes, you was trying to use this." I said, "No, you're not. I'm going to spank you." So I spanked them. They were fine. They returned to the room. Later, they came back and they said, "Momma, I'm getting my bath water ready for school in the morning." I said okay. This was about 8:00 or 9:00 that night.

My nine-year-old went in and ran her bath water, and the water was as cold as ice, so I got up to check the water. I added some hot water to warm it up. As I got ready to turn, she kept saying, "Momma, I could swim." Well, I never saw my children swim because I never had them.

I said to stop playing in the water. I turned around again to try to get all this clothes up off of the floor, and I heard this bump. I turned back around and she was going under the water and water was coming out of her mouth. I panicked because I don't know if she was hurt or not. I took her out of the water and laid her on the bed and put a cover over her. I returned to my room to get some clothes to put on. Then I laid on the bed with her in my arms. My husband was still standing at the stove; it was an hour later. But I wasn't thinking about that, I was thinking about my baby.

I ran into my bedroom and called my girlfriend. Then I called 911. When the paramedics came, they checked my daughter and they said, "Didn't you know she was in a coma." I said, "What are you talking about?" He said, "She's in a coma." I said, "What are you talking about? How am I supposed to know these things?" All I saw was her foaming at the mouth. That's why I ran to the phone and called somebody. I asked if I could ride with them in the ambulance and he said no, I had to get a ride. Somehow, my husband beat them there, and he called and said they wouldn't tell him anything. I told him I was on my way. By the time I got my baby and myself together, the police was at my door. They said they were taking me to the hospital.

When I got there, they questioned me. I was at the hospital, in the emergency room. I didn't see my husband or where they had arrested him. He was arrested at the hospital before I got there. The cop said, "What did you spank her for?" I said, "I spanked her because she had my douche bag in her hand going towards her mouth." He said I spanked her because of perfume. I explained to them why I spanked her and that I spanked both of them. The cop said it was like I had beat her with a board. I said I never beat my kids with a board, never in my life. He came up with every excuse he could come up with. When it hit the paper, it was a mother beating up her daughter about perfume, which was not true.

From then on, I didn't know what to do. I couldn't see my daughter, nothing. They kept questioning me, asking, "What did you beat her with?" I said I spanked her, but I didn't beat her with no board. I never spanked my child with a board. Before I had gotten her, she already had bruises on her. He told me, I'm not worried about the old bruises, I'm worried about what's happening now. She could have been hurt before I got her, because she had marks on her when I got her. I kept telling them that I didn't know what they were talking about, that I didn't beat my child with a board. I asked them if I could make a phone call, and I called my sister. I told her to get to the hospital because they said I hit my daughter with a board and that I knew better than that.

When my sister got there, she asked what they were doing. She said, "That is not like my sister. How are you going to say that she whipped her with a board, were you there?" The cop said, "No, and are you getting smart with me, because I could take you down." So my sister said, "No, I'm just telling you about my sister. I know how she is and how she's not." He was not trying to hear her.

They took my daughter, my baby, they checked her out and she was fine. And they took me to jail. The attorney came down to see me. I don't know who contacted him, all I know is that he was there. He said that something was shoved up my daughter. He was saying that I had shoved the board up my daughter, and that's sick. I found out later, reading the paper, that they found semen in my daughter. Semen comes from a man and not a woman. I'm not that stupid not to know that. I got convicted on sexual penetration. How, when it comes from a man? I have no understanding about that.

I also don't understand how it is that my daughter lived eight days, and they pulled the plug without asking me. She was in a coma for eight days, and they pulled the plug on her that night, and they called me that morning and told me they had pulled the plug on her. I was in the county jail. My bond was $50,000. I would call my sisters and brothers from jail. They said the doctor said it didn't look good, that her brain was swelling and they didn't know how long they wanted to keep her on the life support system. My brother told them that they weren't going to pull the plug, if that was what they were asking. Well, the eighth night they pulled the plug on my daughter.

The attorney told me on the phone that they had pulled the plug on my daughter. He said the judge ordered it. He said that I was going to be charged with involuntary manslaughter. When he came to see me, he said he was going to make me say who had sex with my daughter. I told him, "If I did know, do you think he'd be walking around. I don't think so, I don't think so at all." I would really be down here doing time if I thought for one minute that my husband or anyone else had anything to do with my daughter before I got her or after I got her, or whatever. They would not be walking around. I would always tell my kids if any man came near them or touched them in any way, let me know. My kids never came to me and told me about anything. All I know is that the child hit her head on the tub. The sex part really got me.

I was charged with involuntary manslaughter, sex penetration, and felonious assault. Then, the attorney and prosecutor took a plea bargain behind my back, while I'm sitting in the county jail. The ten to twenty-five; I guess there's a tail on it. The attorney told me that I had a choice to go to trial or take a plea bargain, but not to worry about it then because he was looking into something. My friend in the county jail told me to pick up the paper. I picked up the paper and saw that he had taken a plea bargain. When I found out about the plea, I was on my way here to prison. Before I got here, I called him and asked why he took the plea bargain, and he told me that he didn't want to talk about it right then. Then he said, when we get into court, do not say anything.

The attorney didn't want to go to trial. I knew that I had a right to a trial, everybody has a right to a trial. That's not what I got. What I got was, "You could be facing thirty years or death row," or "I didn't want to take it to trial," and "I don't want to talk about the plea bargain right now." That's what I got. When the attorney first raised the issue of a plea bargain, I asked what chances I had. He said it didn't look good, that it looked like I was going to do some time. But he said that we didn't want to talk about a plea bargain right now. If my girlfriend in the county jail hadn't been reading the paper, I wouldn't have known that he took the plea bargain.

We didn't go in front of a judge to accept the plea. I was in the county jail. Still, when they got ready to send me out, the attorney never mentioned the plea until I called him back. I asked him how he could take a plea if I wasn't there. He said don't worry about it. Okay, well, don't worry about it. When we went to court, they sentenced me to prison. I was just supposed to keep my mouth closed, and that is what I did. I did everything these people told me to do, and look where I am. I kept my mouth shut like he said—"Don't say nothing when you go to court." I did all this. I'm angry because I know that they railroaded me.

When I got to prison, I was a little lost and didn't know what was going on, didn't know how to go about it, didn't know who I could talk to, because you can't trust anyone in here. My theory is, the Man up above has brought me this far, because in here you have to be strong to deal with what's surrounding you. Other than that, I think I'm handling it pretty good. I'm not going to stop until justice is done, as far as my case. There are a lot of women in here that I really feel sorry for because they don't know how to get help. It's real, real deep. After these ten years, I can honestly say that I learned a lot of things that I did not know, and if God ever lets me out of this gate, I could tell it to my children. It ain't easy in here. Trust me.

It seems like prison turned my life all the way around because I'm not used to dealing with people like this. But I've helped a lot, too. It's like being a role model for someone, because there are babies in here. It's just like being a mother figure to them.

I've experienced hostility from other inmates. When I first got here, they said things like "you baby killer." But when I got out into general population, I said, "Anything you got to say to me, say it to my face. We're face to face now . . . yeah, I kind of thought so." I let them know that you're not going to keep badgering me about what I'm here for, because first of all, you don't know what I'm here for. Second of all, I don't owe you nothing and I'm doing my time all by myself, and you're not helping me. But I don't have a problem with them no more.

I dealt with a lot of them that have done something to their children, but I can't judge them. I can't say, "Well, she did it." How can I say you did it? I wasn't there. You may say whatever you want about me and it's okay, as long as in my heart, I know that it never happened, I did not take my daughter's life. I can't worry about it. I can still walk with that smile whether justice be done or not, as long as I know that Man up there knows it, and if He forgives me for anything that I've done, who are you to judge me. I went through that ordeal when I first got here, but it don't bother me now.

What makes it difficult are the different attitudes here. Some of the staff are really nasty to you. Then we have some real good ones who will hear your problem, will take a little bit of time out to hear you. Some of them snap at you like you're a kid, because they've had a bad day and they think they can take it out on us. We have bad days, too, because we have families out there, and that's what we have to think about, but they don't look at it like that.

Plus, it's sad when you can't get medical help around here. I experienced that. I almost died in here several years ago. It happened because they pulled the wrong tooth. They left in the tooth they were supposed to pull and the metal was hitting against the nerve and it turned into an abscess. It turned real black, then it busted and the poison went through my system. I couldn't move, couldn't walk, couldn't eat, couldn't do none of that. Twenty-two days I asked for help and didn't get it. There was one White girl that had the same problem, and they took apart the pharmacy that night, and they stole the medication and brought it back to me. I thanked her for it, because she didn't have to do that, because she could have gotten locked up.

I draw to occupy my time. Sometimes I go to the ball field. Sometimes I sit out in the yard. Sometimes I just sleep. As for programs, I did the domestic violence program, then I did Building Bridges, then I did 12-steps. I don't have a substance abuse problem, but I did it because I thought it would be interesting. I did it for myself so I could be prepared for anything when I do go home. I have a certificate in volleyball. I go to school now; I'm studying for my GED. I went to the 11th grade on the outside, but I was in the slow learning class. I was stuck on math then, and that's what I'm having problems with in here. I like math because it's a challenge. I like reading and language. So far, it's going good.

Ten years is a long time. Ten years from my children. They write to me, send me pictures. My oldest daughter understands more than my baby does. But she understands up to a point. They know in their hearts that I'm here for something that I really didn't do, and they're accepting it. It's hard to accept, but they're accepting it. When I first came here, I got letters from my husband, but I haven't heard from him no more. He did thirty days for child endangerment and he's back on the street. They told me nothing. My husband doesn't want to talk about it.

I was working with a guy who is a paralegal. He had gotten all my documents together and came up with twenty-one errors that they made in my case. I knew something was wrong. I tried everything. We went to the Ohio Supreme Court, the U.S. Supreme Court. I never got anywhere. I started writing the TV shows and everything. I wrote to Governor Taft. I wrote all of them and I never got any response from any of them.

All I am really asking for is justice, that's all. I want justice done and to get my children back. That's not much. Right now I feel empty because my children have been taken away from me. None of us is here forever and I wanted to enjoy and be a mother to my children, and that has been taken away from me. I want to find out who had sex with my daughter. I want it analyzed. I want to know who had the right to pull the plug on my daughter. I want to know how they could take a plea bargain behind my back. I want to know who did this to my daughter.

I won't be all right till I find out. I'm not going to be all right because I don't know; but when I find out, I will be all right with it because I'll give it to God and I'll let Him work it out for me. Until then, I'm not going to stop. I want this pain to go away.

The hardest part of being in here is your family. You wonder from day to day whether they are laying in the gutter, are they laying in the hospital, is there something wrong with them. That's the hardest part. Other than that, you can get through the whole day. I talk to my brothers and sisters on the phone. They have me laughing when they come to visit. My baby came down a couple of months ago. I didn't know who she was, because she was 5'7" and she was real slim and skinny. I was like, "Who are you?" And she said, "Mom, this is your daughter." We sat there the whole time and we just bawled our eyes out. It was a nice visit; I was glad to see her after ten years. Now she's getting ready to go to college. I'm happy for that. I can't say nothing but I've been blessed, because she could have been with the wrong crowd, with drugs and all that. But she didn't, and she said, "Momma, I want to make you proud of me." I told her, "I am proud of you, but don't do it for me, do it for yourself." That's the way she looks at it now. I hear from her all the time. My family tries to stay in touch.

I think it's important for all the women to know that they should let go of things in their life that they've been keeping in. They should talk to somebody about it, reach out for help, because it's out there. They should get with themselves and get with somebody to help them know right from wrong and to know that justice can be done. Nobody out there hears me and don't care to hear me. To me, I was just a nobody. Today, I can't say that, because today I can say I am somebody. Where women over there might shut the door, there's a door over here that can be opened. I want women to think that there is hope somewhere down the line.

4

Elizabeth

Elizabeth is serving a fifty-year sentence for drug-related offenses. She has been active in political movements throughout her life and continues her activism in prison. In addition to fighting her own legal battles, she assists other inmates with their legal problems. She is an outspoken critic of the prison system and the institution in which she is incarcerated. Among her complaints is the small number of persons of color working in choice positions within the institution. Elizabeth believes that her conviction will be overturned and plans to open her own legal research firm when she is released.

Elizabeth

I WAS BORN in Chicago, Illinois, in 1945. My father's people are from a little town in Crittenden County, Arkansas, Gammonsville. My mother's people are from a little town in Mississippi County, Arkansas, Osceola. My parents brought me back to live with my mother's parents when I was about two weeks old. My mother was young, about nineteen or twenty. My parents moved to Florida in 1950. They became labor contractors; they hauled migrant workers up and down the eastern coast of the United States, from Florida to Maine. I spent the school year with my grandparents and the balance of the year with my parents. Arkansas was the only stable place that I lived. I still consider Arkansas my home. I have four children, four daughters.

Most of my mother's people are gone from Arkansas. My mother and grandfather died and are buried in Florida. My father and brother live in Florida, and have done so for years. My father's remarriage resulted in six children other than my brother and me. I am the only pea remaining here in Arkansas, just my kids, my grandkids, my great-grandkids, and me.

I attended a country school about five miles from Osceola. During my elementary school years, often I was the only kid in school. All the Blacks and poor Whites lived out in the country. They had to go to the cotton fields instead of school, weather permitting. Many days, I was the only kid in school. I have always made good grades. My teacher was working on her master's degree. I had an extremely legible handwriting, so to keep me busy, she put me to hand copying her submissions. I picked up lots of knowledge from those writings. I love reading and read anything from garbage to the classics. When I finally made it to high school, I had such a background that I was far ahead of the other kids. I easily graduated valedictorian of my class. Not much of a class; there were only twenty-two of us. I graduated in 1961. I was fifteen. I went to college shortly after my sixteenth birthday. At that time, the college was known as Arkansas A.M. and N. College. Now it is known as the University of Arkansas at Pine Bluff. I was a liberal arts major. My career choices were limited. More than likely, I would have ended up teaching.

I started working with SNCC (Student Non-Violent Coordinating Committee) while in college. Many of the SNCC members lived at the Freedom House on King Street. We were kicked out of school because we staged a sit-in at a store in downtown Pine Bluff, Woolworth's. They were kicked out of school for about three to six weeks. The sit-in was in 1963. It was just before the March on Washington. Orval Faubus was governor. This same Faubus physically barred Black students from entering Central High School in Little Rock. I still fantasize over those days.

Until then, I had never experienced racial prejudice, per se. My father's people had a whole town in Arkansas named after them, and the inhabitants were directly or indirectly related to him. My grandfather on my mother's side owned one of the few Black businesses in Mississippi County. As a sideline, he was a realtor, for Blacks only. The Whites owned the shacks but they wanted them rented to Blacks. My grandfather was paid to collect the rents. This gave him a lot of undeserved, and often misused power. He also had some weird beliefs that he unsuccessfully tried to impose upon me. To his dying day, he never understood why I could not accept the principle that I'm inferior to Whites. He lived for over a hundred years.

Other than this, growing up, I experienced very little discrimination or was mostly unaware of it until I sat-in at the Woolworth's. People were spitting on us just because we were Black and dared to sit at the "Whites only" lunch counter. I had never really confronted hate until then. Nor did I know the danger of my actions until much, much later. I never really thought about danger. Even when I did, I did not seriously do so. It still amazes me that people can hate you for things you have no control over. We protesters starved together and suffered together. It was just like the big close-knitted family I always wanted. Growing up, there was just my little brother and me.

I also moved into the Freedom House after I got kicked out of school. In 1963, a group of us opted to go to Lake Providence, Louisiana to register voters. Truly, ignorance is bliss. Danger did not cross my mind until years later. I moved to Florida in November 1963. I worked with my parents as a subcontractor. We hauled migrant workers up and down the East Coast. Out of gratitude, I married in 1964. I had my first child in 1965. By 1968, I was again in the struggle. I was at Grant Park when the hippies were beaten by the Chicago Police. I worked with Operation Breadbasket/PUSH and the Black Panthers.

In 1970, I moved back to Florida. By October 1970, I was in prison for attempted armed robbery. Two girls and I attempted to rob an Armour meat truck at gunpoint. We pulled this gun on the driver of the truck. The gun had no firing pin. The driver jumped out of the truck at a traffic light. Neither of us could drive a stick shift. We were arrested right there in the middle of Miami. The crime was so stupid and ill-conceived that I only received two years. I served fifteen months.

It was 1988 before I got in trouble again—possession of a controlled substance. I was guilty as hell. I owned and operated a game room and recreation center in a little town called Turrell, Arkansas. The arrest occurred at my place of business. I had almost three keys (kilograms), plus a gun that had been stolen from the police station and pawned to me. My being female worked for me. The police thought that I was just running the place for someone else—some male someone else. Females in most parts of the country do not really handle large quantities of drugs, so the police did not think of me as anything but a minor nuisance. The police never found the gun and the three keys. They only found some small amount planted on me by one of my workers or the police. I had a good lawyer. I was sentenced to eight years in prison. I served two years.

I was paroled in 1992 and rearrested in 1994. I have never been tried for the crime that I was rearrested on in 1994. I have never been arrested for the crime I am now locked up for. I am innocent and I am not. I did not commit the crime I was tried for. The details of the crime I was arrested on remain so ambiguous and contradictory that I do not know whether I committed it or not. However, since I was never tried for it, it is a bit late to wonder now. I did not deal any street drugs while on parole. I supplied two people. I would go to Florida, pick up a couple of keys, and bring them back to Arkansas. These sales were my main source of income while on parole. I doubled and tripled my money. I would pay around $11,000 for a key, transport it to Arkansas, and then sell it for $35,000. If the quality was real good, I would add cut to the product and then sell the keys for $20,000 to $25,000 each. The police figured that I had to be doing something illegal because of the amounts of money I spent. I spent lots of money because I was super lucky on the crap tables and at the casinos. I also had a place of business in Turrell and a barbeque stand in Blytheville.

I was arrested and charged with selling a lousy $60 worth of crack cocaine. The judge set my bond at $250,000—cash. For a number of reasons, I was unable to make bond. At first, the amount of cocaine was $50 worth, two loose rocks, the sale occurred in Blytheville, the confidential informant was male, and there was a buy tape. By the time I made it to trial, the amount of cocaine was $60 worth, several rocks in a plastic bag, the sale occurred in Osceola, the confidential informant was female, and there was no buy tape. The undercover agent testified that he was able to identify me because I "stood in a well-lit area" while making this sale. The undercover agent wore glasses to correct a bad case of night blindness. It was the middle of February—at nighttime. The address finally decided on by the state as being the crime scene had no electricity at this house but I was convicted anyway.

It was not my house; I did not even live in that town. The woman that lived in the house testified on my behalf. She admitted to knowing me, but not well enough to give me free run of her home when she was not there. She was not accused of selling drugs. Her house was not a drug house. It was never shown how I may have gained entry to her home. My luck just ran out. I was tried as a habitual offender and sentenced to fifty years in prison. But I was not a habitual offender. I continue to fight my sentence because I was never arrested for the offense that I was tried for. Much of my paperwork shows this; however, I am unable to have my claims heard on their merits because of one procedural default after another.

After I got to prison, I tried to fight my conviction. At that time I knew very little about the law. The prison officials would not let me do peril-free work on my case. They would store my paper work in inaccessible places. When this did not deter me, I was unable to get my prescribed medical care. Therefore, I started filing civil cases. I alleged that my diseases were not being treated properly. The U.S. District Court agreed, and we settled out of court.

I have lupus, sarcoidosis, and osteoporosis. I have been on steroids for over twenty-two years. I had medical slips saying that I must have access to water. I did not have access to water. I went to the hole. While in the hole, if I asked for water and did not ask politely enough, or if I disobeyed my keeper's orders and asked too often, then I received another disciplinary, and more hole time. I ended up doing about forty-five extra days in the hole, losing about 200 days of good time and other privileges—this because I needed and asked for water. I sued again.

I also stayed in trouble for helping other inmates by doing free legal work for them. After a while, I just did not care anymore. I was frustrated and showed it. When I get frustrated I often say things I have no business saying, so back to the hole I would go. I filed over three hundred grievances. At the bench trial, the district court dismissed my case because it found that even though I filed three hundred grievances, the administrators lacked the requisite degree of knowledge to be held liable for my wrongs. I appealed to no avail, even though the law states that if a convict files grievances or gives some other type of administrative notice, then prison officials cannot deny having knowledge of the complaints. I was in a private prison until July 2001. Profit was their bottom line. When my rights and their profits were in conflict, my rights suffered.

There are about six hundred people here, about three hundred are Black. When we first arrived here, it was real hard on us Blacks because of open discrimination and racial prejudice. They were not accustomed to Blacks. Hardly any Blacks live in this area. Out of about one hundred officers, only three or four officers were Black. Now there are a few more. Until recently, there were few Black inmates or staff in clerical positions.

I subscribe to darn near every type of magazine or prison advocacy group that I can relate to. I became a member of the Prison Advocacy Network, a South Carolina–based group several years ago. I coauthored an article for them entitled "Leveling the Playing Field." I believe that I am the only convict in Arkansas that is a member of the National Lawyers Guild. I have been a member since 1994. I am also a very good jailhouse lawyer.

I think that all women, no matter what color, should learn what the rules are and then have the courage to exercise whatever few rights those rules give them. Many people are afraid to even attempt to exercise their rights. They would rather leave it up to someone like me to fight for their rights for them. It's an uphill burden, but I am willing to help.

I want people to know what life in prison is like and some of the ways someone can end up here. For example, if someone pleads guilty to a charge, whether they are guilty or not, they are told that they won't do a day of time—maybe two or three years or probation or suspended sentence. Say they take the offer. Then, about a year or so later they commit some minor infraction. If that happens, they will have a revocation hearing and about 90 percent of people who are taken back for revocation are found guilty. Once they are found guilty, they could receive ten or more years of prison time, not the balance of time remaining on the suspended sentence.

Once people are in the system, many of them fall through the cracks and never see daylight again. Education is the key to stopping this. I want to educate as many inmates and convicts as possible regarding their rights. I advocate change through education, not violence.

5

Rae Ann

After pulling herself out of a life of prostitution, Rae Ann struggled to balance employment, school, and motherhood. In an attempt to earn money to feed, clothe, and house herself and her children, she began holding drugs for a boyfriend. Rae Ann is serving two life sentences in Louisiana for two counts of distribution of illegal narcotics. She hopes her story can help other women to stay away from the life that took her freedom from her.

Rae Ann

I'M FROM NEW ORLEANS. I was born and raised in the housing projects. I can't find any faults growing up there, except that my father and mother split when I was a baby. My father wanted to do some things that my mother didn't approve of, so they separated. My mother was the father and the mother. She was real firm. You did what was supposed to be done and that was it. My father was a barber by occupation. He did that until he died. I was able to be with my father as a small child. He lived with his mother and on weekends that's what I did. My father's mother was a nurse, so she worked. I was six or seven, around that age.

I was raised in a Christian environment, more or less. Religion was stressed on one side of the family, but it wasn't stressed on my mother's side. Whenever I went to my father's house (actually his mother's house), I had to bring some church clothes and that's where I learned about God. I didn't learn it with my mother. My mother didn't become a born-again Christian until many years later. I remember coming back from my father's house with the feeling of God but being young and not understanding. I was the only person in my household on my mother's side that went to church. It was okay for me to do this but it wasn't in the home. You wouldn't hear your mother saying "God this, and God that" and that was okay.

Living was not hard except that in my later years, I believed that a lot of things would have been different if I had two parents. I had friends that had two-parent households and they were happy. The mother and the father had a combination income. My mother had all the bills. She had to buy the clothes and the shoes and the necessities for bathing and washing. My mother was a floor worker for the federal building. She also was a nurse-midwife. She was actually delivering babies. She would come home and tell us stories. I was proud of her, that she was doing this on her own. My mother did what she could with what she had. She went from working to being on welfare, and welfare in Louisiana was not her thing. It was a handicap.

We were raised on the basics. I remember my mother only being able to afford certain things to eat. She lived by buying rice and beans and if she couldn't get meat, she didn't buy it. She made gravy from scratch, so we had gravy and rice. We had beans when we didn't have broccoli and cheese. Whenever she could afford to do something good for us she did, especially for Christmas and birthdays. I didn't remember having an ugly time. I remember getting games, and maybe an outfit or a pair of shoes. There just wasn't a lot. I guess then it wasn't hard as far as me not having expensive clothes. My mother taught me that whatever you don't have you do without. If it is something that you really need then you will really get it. That was my childhood, leading up to my life.

I have two brothers. One is less than a year younger than me. I was born in 1957 and he was born in 1958. I also have a baby brother. He has a different father. My mother didn't remarry, but her friend came to live with us. He was a chef and a dry cleaner. It wasn't an unhappy thing because he was a father figure of sorts and we loved our brother. Later my mother remarried when she was in her 50s. I wasn't incarcerated then, so I remembered that.

School was great. I was in public school and I went all the way to the twelfth grade. It could have been raining, storming, snowing whatever, and I would go to school. I graduated from high school. My high school days were good, with the exception of one incident where my mother beat me half to death. I don't mean that literally, I am exaggerating some, but she caught me shooting hooky one day and I got a beating for it. After that I did not miss a day. In fact, I had to check in with the principal to ensure their peace of mind that I was there. Other than that, I graduated fine. My aunt in Detroit bought my class ring. I had my gown. I have my high school pictures that you do for the yearbook. I have no complaints. My complaints come later.

I'm the oldest girl and I was first, so I had a lot of responsibility. My mother had a lot of pride about herself and I used to watch her and listen. She was my role model. She loved us. We had rules. We went to school. We came in. We played in the yard and by a certain time we bathed and we were to go to bed. That was it, that was the routine. Outside of that, I can only say that everything was okay during my childhood with my mother until after the graduation and I felt grown. That's when my mother had to take a stand. She was fine with my boyfriends, she was fine with my friends, but I had a curfew and I had to be inside at a certain time while other girls stayed out later. That was something I didn't like as a child or as a teenager.

I wasn't abused, but I got my share of whippings if I did something that I wasn't supposed to do. If she told me to be in at a certain hour I would get punished; I couldn't go outside the next day. She would tell me to go up to my room and find a book. She was firm about home-work. If I didn't bring a book home she felt that I was being lazy. I had to bring a book home even if I didn't have homework.

I was an avid reader and I was a curious child. I became a curious teenager. I liked boys at a young age. I was a pretty girl, pretty lady, so I had boyfriends. I had several at one time sometimes. I was pregnant from my childhood sweetheart, when we graduated from high school together. He was going into the military. It occurred to me, I'm gonna have all these boyfriends, you already have a baby and if you have any more boyfriends and are active sexually, you are going to have more ba-bies. How are you going to take care of them? Part of me didn't want to work after I graduated from high school.

I graduated in May 1975 with a nurse's certificate. I found out that I was pregnant, which I didn't know at graduation. My pregnancy was a surprise, but I had been sexually active. I was taking pills and I stopped. I had this illusion that I wanted to have a baby. All teenagers have that. When I stopped taking the pills, I wanted to get out of my mother's house. If I had a boyfriend and we were trying to plan things for ourselves, then I would leave. Then my boyfriend immediately drafted into the army. I was thinking of leaving, too, and was waiting for him to send me a ticket after basic training. I was willing to be a mil-itary mother and military wife. Things just didn't work out. He ac-knowledged the child and sent me some money through the mail, but he did his thing in the army while I was stuck here in the city waiting on him.

I started to have these ideas about prostitution. I thought that if a woman's body was going to be used in that way, she should be paid. I met a guy that was already in that life. Call him player, pimp, whatever. At first, I didn't know what he was but I was attracted to him as a man. I was eighteen years old. So my first act of crime was prostitution. I was pregnant at the time.

He explained that if I were his woman, I could make money, and I would have my share and he would have his. If I made $200, $100 would be for me and $100 would be for him. That made sense to me. I was young and was ready to get out there and do my thing. I guess I could have pounded the pavement for a job, but I saw all this nightlife and activity going on and I liked it. I was down in the French Quarter of New Orleans, and I met this guy. My boyfriend left me on the corner to go do something. I don't know what he did but he turned his back. I was fresh and they saw it. The guy said, "Hey, how are? Are you look-ing for a date?" I said, "Yes, let's go." That was my first experience and that was my first arrest. I went to court, and I got probation and I went home. I later had my baby in February 1976.

After I recovered from my pregnancy, I was adamant about going back on the street. It had nothing to do with how I was raised. My mother told me that it was not nice. My mother taught me that the body was not to be used and that I didn't need all these different men having me. She told me to find somebody who would be mine and mine alone. That is what I was raised to believe. But I went back to it and I learned a whole lot more. I was put with a girl who showed me some things. For a long time, I was even afraid and shy. After my experiences with men, though, I wasn't shy anymore. I made more money in prostitution than a person working five or seven days a week. The guy didn't railroad me or sugarcoat anything. He didn't put a gun to my head. He straight up told me what we could have with what I could do. Going in, I knew he didn't work; I knew that he wanted me to do the work. I was all right with that, and it didn't bother me.

That life ended in 1979, when I decided that I needed to make a change in my life. I went through a transition period after I had my daughter, and in 1979, I had my son. This was not something that I wanted to make a career out of and I stopped. I was tired and pregnant, having my son. I knew that this guy was not going to be the person that was going to marry me and come out of that life. I thought, "Okay, that's you. I'm not mad at you, not angry, but this is not what I want to do anymore." So I went to work.

I worked several jobs. The first job I had after that life was working with the mayor's clean city committee. I was a supervisor. I had many arrests prior to this, but luck would have it that nobody questioned me about that. From there I went to the New Orleans World's Fair. I worked with the housing authority where I was a community activity worker, and I went into the houses when the cable company ran cable through all of the apartments. Actually, I used to beg for jobs. When I got that job I was begging the manager, "I need a job. I want to work." I would go patiently down to the office. My mother worked there and literally begged, and eventually the housing authority hired me.

I also went back to school. I thought I would try something else and would refresh myself with nursing. I had lived in my own apartment after the life that I led, and then I came back in the environment of the projects when my whole objective was to leave the projects. It wasn't a good environment. It just brought you down, everything in it, everything about it. You see the same people everyday; you see them doing the same thing everyday, all day. I didn't want that. During my teenage years, I wanted my mother to move. I would say, "Why don't you move out of the projects." My mother would say, "I'm not going no where. People prosper and succeed. You can be what you want to be and still live in the projects." She didn't lie; it was the truth.

I was going to college for nursing and I had to do my on-the-job-training. For the training, you have to go to the hospital or the nursing home, wherever they assign you. Working nursing hours meant that I had to be on the wards until 6:45 P.M. My kids had been in preschool at the age of six months. It was something that I did, if I found a job. My discouragement came from not having anybody to watch my kids. That was really a sad thing. I had cousins that could have done it, even my mother could have done it, but she was working. In finding jobs, I would say to myself, "Well I can't work at night because I can't get nobody to watch my kids." I'm still on welfare now, trying to go to school. If I find a job far out, where am I going to find the money to bus myself from here to there.

The welfare money was $192 a month and I had two kids. You weren't actually allowed telephone, furniture bills, all of that, but I had a telephone and I paid for that. Now if I got a twenty or thirty dollar telephone bill and a twenty or thirty dollar rent bill, that is sixty dollars of the $190. If I have to buy soap powder, deodorant, cleanser for me and my kid, then that is some more of the $192. The children needed socks or shoes and that was some more; so how was I going to allow thirty or forty dollars out of the check to go back and forth to work. I had all this to deal with, so I just didn't get a job. I kept the welfare and I stopped going to school because I couldn't get anybody to watch my kids.

The choice that I made was to deal drugs. I was introduced to it socially at parties. When I was introduced to selling drugs, I saw money. I saw a means to get a whole lot of things that I couldn't have because I couldn't work. I was a working person. Honestly, I would have preferred to work. I just felt so discouraged. When I got introduced, they said, "Girl you can make a lot of money now." I knew that I saw that happening around me. I met this guy who was already dealing and I said, "I need money. If you're going to be something to me then you are going to have to help me, okay." He said, "Okay if you want me to help you then you are going to have to help me, all right." I first started holding drugs and that got me by. After that, in holding the drugs, I started to do the drugs.

At this time, I got into another relationship with the guy I caught the charge with. Now I had the money to do the things I needed to do. I didn't want to do this too long, but when you are young, every penny goes to something that you see that you want, if not for your house, for your kids, or for yourself. You never make enough money. You would have to be the supplier, not the pusher. This guy was just a small-time pusher. He would go on the corner every day, and would sell three hundred to four hundred dollars worth of drugs. Out of that my holdings might be sixty or seventy dollars depending on what the market was and depending on how much you sold. In the end, I learned that he was holding back on me.

I was holding a few dozen bags here or there. When he went out there and did his thing and came back with the money, he was short or didn't sell what he thought that he would sell. That means that I wouldn't get my cut. I got tired of that. We were in a relationship and we were getting high. We were constantly getting high, so we got habits. I believe that he furthered my habit to further my need for the money. At first, I was just a nose person and eventually I became an I.V. drug user. I used coke and then heroin. We were simply snorting drugs at liberty just because we had it. We thought we were straight and that the high wasn't going to lead to anything else, but it did lead to the addiction.

Heroin relaxed all of the body nerves. I wasn't dysfunctional, I wasn't obnoxious, I wasn't doing things that I didn't have any business doing. I wasn't jumping off buildings. I wasn't going to rob people. The I.V. drug use was a whim. I tried it for about six months. Later, I went to detox. My boyfriend insisted that I go into detox, so I don't fault him for that. Detox was for 72 hours in a New Orleans hospital. I didn't want to stay. At the time the hospital was not accredited. A lot of things were going on in that hospital that shouldn't have been happening and eventually somebody filed suit. I felt that I was supposed to be paid attention to. Maybe not round the clock, but maybe every so many hours. I was completely on my own in the hospital.

After detox, I got busted. Detox was January, February, and March. I didn't go back to I.V. drug use when I came out of detox. I was just trying to get myself back together, but I ended up going out there and helping this guy. I was watching his back while he sold drugs, literally. If the police came, I held it. He still had access to my apartment while I was in the 72-hour detox. It was a live-in thing and the drugs were still there. I would hold it for him when we would go out. We would go to a bar where users could buy drugs. I was not holding the drugs in my house, only on my person. In April I was busted. I was arrested for distribution. They said that I had sold some to an undercover agent. I wasn't the seller, I was the holder.

This is why I am here now. I was arrested in April 1988. They indicted me for the three counts from an operation that lasted a year and netted some ninety-seven people, and I was one of them. The charge was distribution of heroin for sale of narcotics. I have two life sentences for two counts. I was found not guilty on one count and guilty on two counts. I got a life sentence for each count, running concurrent. Distribution for the sale of narcotics is a mandatory life sentence. They said I sold to the undercover agent on three separate occasions.

I was reverted back to a first-time offender because I hadn't committed a crime from 1980 to 1988. The law states that if you don't commit a crime within five years of a prior record or criminal activity you revert back to a first-time offender. I allegedly sold three bags of heroin. But here is this other person who comes into court with me that was busted with one hundred bags. You give me a life sentence and you give him ten years. And I was due parole.

I was sentenced in July 1989 and started doing time here in September 1989. As a result of investigating things when you come into the institution, you learn that the law library is there. The guys that were on the charge with me taught me some things about the law. I learned that one of several officers that worked within the operation, not necessarily an officer who testified against me, had received a life sentence. He (the officer) made the remark that "he'd be prisoners' get out of jail free card; the investigating officers were all corrupted." It took me a long time to find that out.

I can't expound explicitly about racial issues because I don't want to say something that may make the prisoners think that I am racist or militant. I don't want to be labeled, but some things that happen with Blacks don't happen with Whites or some things for Whites don't happen for Blacks. I might get in trouble for something that a White girl might not get in trouble for, or I would be penalized harshly and she wouldn't. It is everywhere.

For example, the charge that I got wouldn't have happened to somebody else that was White. In one of the surrounding parishes, one of the White girls I know had two or three hundred bags of heroin. She got ten years. If the charge wasn't for distribution for the sale of narcotics, what was she going to do with it? If you ask a lot of other Blacks about their charge, you find that distribution could be just standing on the corner selling or the attempted distribution is just to be in possession of it. I just can't believe that a society would want to keep a person locked up for so long as to take away their whole life.

As far as rehabilitation, I think that if you sit yourself down, or if you had been made to sit down a certain amount of time and really look at what is going on with you, then you could minimize the risk of coming back. The majority of the people that come back are the people that go right back out and do drugs and abuse drugs. They may have two years left on parole. The parole people go after them again and when they come back they're doing a year and a half left of that. When they leave, they walk around with this air that, "Oh, I don't have a life sentence so I can live and do what I want." That makes me feel disgusted because you give me a life sentence, but I have all these people around me that are constantly leaving saying if I come back I'll do just six months, whatever is left of my parole time. In essence, the probation and parole system is not doing an accurate job. Whites get more favor with pardon and parole than do Blacks for the same charge. I watched it every time they have a board. It starts with the legislatures who enact the law. It is not working to hold a person like this.

In the late 1990s, United Way petitioned us for some money and the women's facility raised $50,000. In society, they have the notion or stereotype that we should remain locked up and have the key thrown away. I just want it noted that we as convicts and prisoners raised that fifty grand, we sold everything. We had dances and all sorts of food sales. We even sold off days when you could buy a friend's days off. They say a lot about us, but when a specific organization needs something, they come here.

Volunteers come in to help us. They come in to sit with us and discuss what we go through. You could be going through some really mental things in here about your crime. There is a group for battered women, women that have charges that they killed their spouses. You have all this documentation in the state of Louisiana that this person battered you mentally, physically, emotionally, and nothing was done for the women. The only thing that they could do for them is give them a life sentence for a crime that they committed. So you can kill me, and the man might get no time; but if I kill you, I am going to get a life sentence. These groups come in to help us and they do help.

We also have Alcoholics Anonymous and Narcotics Anonymous and the drama club. Drama helps you feel comfortable with your inner self. I'm a tour guide, a volunteer within the institution. I do tours and I go on speaking trips. I have been to LSU (Louisiana State University) speaking to the criminology department. It's good. I like to be able to give something back.

I disappointed my mother. I disappointed my family, my kids. Me being in prison caused a lot of hardships for my mother. My son was nine and my daughter was twelve, so my mother's life essentially stopped because she had to take care of them. My daughter is now twenty-five and my son is twenty-one. Children in turn have a different attitude about life because of the way their parents were treated. My son is rebellious. He feels that if I was just trying to pay some bills and take care of them, he and his sister at the time, then I shouldn't have my whole life taken away.

I think about a lot of things that I did in my life and it's nobody's fault. I'm not blaming anybody; it's just that you make mistakes and a lot of things happen that cause you to veer off. I just wanted help. My family now supports me wholeheartedly. I might get a visit three times a year.

My co-defendant is more or less where all my anger is. He forced me to testify. He was brutal and he was threatening. They severed us on the morning of trial for him because of a conflict of interest. I wonder what was the conflict of interest. I said a lot of things at my trial to help him. Initially, I thought he was going to help me when he got out. I wouldn't have left him high and dry because we were in it together. I wasn't trying to put all the fault on him. I was trying to pay some bills. Maybe I was trying to buy furniture, maybe I was trying to buy my children some tennis shoes or whatever. I wouldn't have left him like that, but he didn't do anything. He came up here one time to see me.

Prison has made me a better woman. I could have been this bigoted person. I was bigoted when I first came. I didn't want them telling me nothing. If they said something to me, I had something to say back. I wanted to have the last word. What I learned is that this is not what this is about here. They didn't put me here. They are only here for care, custody, and control. I was always saying, "Why, why I can't do this? Why do you ask me this?" The place doesn't make you or break you. You make or break yourself, depending on how you live with yourself. If you walk around with a frown on your face every day, then that is how you are going to live, and that's negative. If you live and think positive, no matter where you are, you are going to be okay. I am not a negative-thinking person. I've always been positive through all of this.

I just had to adjust to prison life—getting up when they told me to, going to bed when they told me to, going to work when they told me to, or going to the kitchen. It was difficult because you can't just say I'm going to the kitchen because I am hungry right now. Adjusting means to just keep in mind that this is not your home. It is a place where I am sentenced to do time. That's it. You can be free with that.

The absence of God is very important. I was recently baptized. Getting to know Jesus is the best thing that has happened to me aside from giving birth to my darling son. I want young people who think of doing what I did to think long and hard about the consequences. It wasn't worth it, period! So think before you act. You control your own fate. If my story helps somebody or reaches out to some young person and prevents her from doing the wrong things, I think it will be positive.

6

Donna

Donna has been in and out of the Texas prison system for over twenty years. She graduated from high school as a young mother and went on to college, but her involvement with an older man when she was younger had negative consequences for her. Prostitution and drug use became patterns in her life. A cycle of incarceration soon followed. She was on a ten-year probation term during the initial Inner Lives *interview; she later returned to prison on a probation violation after resuming drug use. She is trying to remain strong, plans to continue her education, and ultimately hopes to be an example for young Black women so that they will stay out of the system.*

Donna

I'VE BEEN THROUGH the Texas prison system since 1981. I'm forty-five years old. I grew up in Overton, Texas. It's a small country town in the eastern part of Texas. It was a close-knit community. Everybody there was like family. I went to an all-Black school back then. We weren't integrated. The schools were integrated after I got to the seventh grade. It was kind of lonely because I was an only child. I was real tall and skinny, and I was kind of smart. I used to win spelling bees when I was in sixth grade. I was always winning something. I won a presidential fitness award during the time that Lyndon Johnson was president. Basically, I had a pretty well-rounded education coming up.

I came up through the period where racial discrimination was legal. I remember when I was a child, my mother took me to the Dairy Queen and I had to get ice cream from the Black side. I remember that water fountains said "White" and "Colored." Blacks lived on one side of the tracks and Whites lived on the other side. My grandmother used to iron clothes for White people to make money to send me to school. My grandmother used to be on her knees cleaning in the hospital to send my mother to college and to send me to school.

My grandmother raised me. She raised every grandchild; she even raised my daughter. When I was a child, my mother lived in Dallas, while I lived with my grandmother in Overton. My mother left home to find work. She would come home to see me once a month. We were close. I didn't question it. My grandmother would tell me, "You live here. Your mother lives there. I'm taking care of you. Your mother loves you."

My mother was killed when I was in junior high school. A squabble broke out between her boyfriend and his uncle, and she got caught in the crossfire. That threw me back a ways. At first, I didn't accept it and I almost had a nervous breakdown. My grandmother was very close to me and we were devastated. I went to see our family doctor; we didn't have money for counseling back then.

I continued with school because they pushed me. I finished junior high school, and went to high school. I focused on the right track; it took a while, but I got back. I enjoyed school until there was integration and we had to go to the White school. The White kids thought they were better than us. One called me a nigger when I was in gym class. She said that the Black students were supposed to change in a separate area. Although the school was integrated there still was segregation. It was just the practice; it was unwritten. Things changed and I became more radical. I had teachers who were working with me and I started to like school better. There were teachers who didn't see a person's color. They saw that we were children trying to get an education. They knew that I was from a good background. My grandmother was good people and everybody knew her.

I got pregnant during high school, but I was determined to finish and to be something, to be somebody. I kept my pregnancy hidden because they would have kicked me out of school. I graduated from high school in 1972. I also decided that I wanted to go to college. I asked my grandmother if she would keep my baby for me and she said yes. So I moved from Overton to Tyler, Texas, to go to college. I majored in elementary education and minored in law. During these times, there was Martin Luther King, John Kennedy, and there were other issues. There was also Angela Davis. I knew that things were wrong and I thought that I would be a lawyer.

I thought I was going to get a job or that Prince Charming was going to come and take me away. He did come, but it wasn't the Prince Charming that I wanted. I met a guy from Dallas. He was in the hustling life. I met him at an after-hours club in Dallas. I just looked at him and it was like, "God, he's so handsome. He's pretty snappy and cute." He was much older. He had all this jewelry on and he had a pretty car, and he had all this money. I knew what kind of life he lived because I wasn't crazy. My girlfriend told him that I was looking at him and he came over and asked me if I wanted to have breakfast with him. I said yes and we went to breakfast and we talked.

I was still in college, in Tyler. He came down and asked if I wanted to go back to Dallas with him. I told him that I did, and that's how I got started in that life. But in the meantime, I went to college and I dropped out in my junior year when I was about nineteen or twenty. I didn't know this was a kind of game with these guys. For months, I didn't know that he had women that worked on the street. He would take me through this block where all these ladies were, and I knew they were prostitutes, but he didn't tell me that two of them worked for him. He would park in the back and the women would hand him some money, and then I understood.

When he brought me to Dallas, he put me in a motel and paid for my room. He gave me money and bought me nice clothes and jewelry.

I never did anything. He had a three-bedroom home, and he said, "Look, I'm going to stop paying all this rent for this motel. You can come live with me." So I went back to Tyler, and I told my grandmother that I was with this guy and that he had a square job. I came back and moved in with him. One night, he asked me if I knew what he was doing. I told him that I did, so he brought his ladies home one night to meet me. I told him that I wanted to go with them the next time they went out. He said, "No, you don't." I said, "Yes, I want to see what you are doing on that street." So I went.

I never was just a square person, but I wanted to know what that fast life was like. I wanted to know what they did. I just wanted to know and experience it for myself. People told me that drugs were bad for me, but I didn't listen to them. People told me that being a prostitute was not good, but I wanted to experience it myself. I liked the money, and I liked the high. I was real dumb, and I didn't know what I was doing. He tried to discourage me, but I thought I was in love with him and I felt obligated after being with him for so long. I thought that was what he wanted. I wanted to show him that I could do what they were doing. I wasn't ugly at the time; I felt kind of attractive.

After I went out, he saw that I had a weakness, and that weakness was him. I worked in the Black neighborhood. Back then, guys only gave you ten or fifteen dollars for dates. So, he started to emphasize that I go and that I learn what to do. He put one of my favorite sisters with me and told her to show me what to do and how to make a lot of money.

This went on for about ten years; I stayed with this man for that long. In those ten years, I ran into lots of problems. One time, a guy drove me to a lake, and nobody else was there. He was choking me, trying to rape me in his car. It was around two or three o'clock in the morning, and from nowhere, these White people showed up. I know that God sent those people there. They heard me scream and they came to the car and they said, "Get away from her. What's wrong with her? We're going to call the police." I got out of the car and I ran down to the beach. The man kept pulling me back, trying to drag me back toward the lake. This White guy ran up behind me to get him and I got away and ran. The people asked if I wanted them to call the police, but I just asked them to take me to a phone so that I could call a cab. When I got to the phone, I looked back and they were gone. When I got back, I told him, "I don't want to do this anymore. Somebody tried to rape me and take me off." He said that I should have known better than to get in somebody's car. He got mad at my favorite sister and slapped her, because she wasn't supposed to let me leave.

During those years, it turned out that he had a temper. I had a lot of physical abuse. One night, I went off with my favorite sister and we didn't come in when we were supposed to check in. Instead, we stayed out all night. Back then, the police were real bad and he didn't always want to get us out of jail. When we didn't come home, he beat us up. Another night, when I didn't come home with a certain amount of money, he beat me up real bad. The way I saw it, I was his woman and I couldn't leave. That's your man, your pimp and you stayed with him. That was the code, the ethic that you lived by. So, if you leave him and he finds you, he beats you up and brings you back home. The only way to leave him is to pay, to run away, or to get another pimp. That's the only way out of the game; you can't get out.

I thought that the violence was part of being a whore. I'd see my other sisters going to work with dark shades on. He beat me up so badly one day till you couldn't tell who I was. I used to cry. I was hurt, but I loved him so much. It had gotten so deep that I didn't really know how pain felt anymore, because I had lost it. I had medicated my pain. My drug use started when I was about twenty-one years old. I started smoking weed, and I would drink. When he would hurt me and do things to me, I would go and drink. I also started taking pills. Then, I would go to work. In a way, I lived two lives because I would go back home to see my grandmother and my baby. My family thought that my man was earning the money at a job. I always sent money home.

The first time I went to prison was in 1981 for aggravated robbery. I was working on the slab, as we called it, with another sister and we weren't in a mood for dating this particular night. So we got in this White guy's car and just took his money. We threatened him with our guns. We split the money in half, and she went her way and I went mine. Well, the guy came back in the neighborhood and told people that he was looking for us. Later, he picked my picture out of a lineup. I had already been to jail for prostitution, so my picture was there. The police came and arrested me. They knew that another girl was with me, but I never gave up my fall partner. I received two years probation for that charge.

I stayed in jail for a week or so, and when I got out, I got busted again. This time, I got the original five-year sentence, because they violated my probation. My man got angry because he thought I was using drugs at a time that I wasn't. He beat me up real bad, and he jumped on me to check my arms for tracks. I didn't have any tracks, but pretty soon, I started using heavy drugs. I started shooting speed, and from speed, I went to heroin. I went from heroin to cocaine. I started doing heroin because the people who turned me onto it showed me how to steal money without having to lie on my back for it. They were using heroin and they were sharp every day. They had money in their pockets and you could not tell that they shot dope because they were clean, they smelled good and they dressed nice. They had a code of ethics, even among the boosters. Even though you steal, you don't steal from your friends. So, I thought, "This is what I want." I was living in a fantasy world. I was in another world and I never thought that this would catch up with me. I never thought that one day, I would be old and gray.

When I went to prison in 1981, on the five-year sentence, I was kind of scared. I had a reputation for fighting and a reputation that I didn't play, so I didn't have a problem. Also, I knew people there from the street. I was in the maximum-security unit in Mountain View. I was placed in the dorms for the aggravated robbers and people who had murder cases. I didn't get any visitors, but my man wrote to me and sent me money and pictures. I did my stretch. Back then, you weren't considered a real street player if you didn't go to prison. My grandmother was upset with me. Thank God, she had my baby.

I became a Muslim in 1981. I was raised in the Baptist faith. When I changed to Islam, I became more disciplined about myself. I stayed clean for a long time and I got in touch with myself. It was a more disciplined religion. I used to watch how disciplined they were. When I saw Muslims come out of their service, they didn't go to a liquor store. You didn't see them get out and curse. They would go into the neighborhood trying to help the community. I liked the way the women carried themselves; they looked so stern and they didn't wear makeup. I loved the way they prayed. The Koran teaches us that our bodies are beautiful. We also understand that God is not responsible for what is wrong with us; we do this to ourselves.

When I went to prison the second time, in 1993, it was for forgery. We made company checks and we'd write them out, and go to the bank and cash them. I went back to Mountain View. I was there from 1993 to 1995. My friend Joyce Brown had gone, but Joyce Logan was still there.

Joyce was there for me as support. The second time in prison was different. I became radical.

I was involved in a protest at the prison; I think it happened in spring 1994. The prison didn't want to give us proper food. They were housing us in lock-downs for no reason. They were writing us up for everything and they spoke to us really badly. They would go into our lock boxes and destroy our property and do whatever they wanted. It was too overcrowded, and they were stacking us at fifty or sixty women in a dorm that was meant for thirty. The medical system wasn't good. We thought that women were being overmedicated. There were women walking around like zombies. And it took months to see the dentist. In the winter, the dorm was cold, and in the summer, it was hot. So, we protested. Nobody went to work. We asked for the director of corrections, Mr. Estelle.

They took us down to a lock-down, single cell. When the administration got there, he pulled us out one by one and asked us, "What do you want?" We told him and they called the warden down, and she talked to him and she talked to us. Some things changed. They eased the overcrowding by opening other units for women. The food got better. Some people never get visits, so the only thing they live for is maybe to use the telephone. The telephone policy got better, and there was help for indigents. The heating was fixed.

We felt that Mexican and Black girls were treated differently, especially in terms of jobs. While I was there, I worked on the yard squad cleaning up the grounds, and the hoe squad augering the dirt. That's real punishment, when you're out there augering and chopping all day like the men. It's usually in the summer, in the hot sun. I also did data entry and keypunch work, and I helped with orientation for new inmates.

I started to think about my life and the vicious cycle that kept me coming back to prison. When I'd get out, I said, "Well, I'm going to do this and I'm going to do that." Then, I'd get out and I didn't get a job or somebody would come over and I would get busted again. I've gotten tired, though. I've been in recovery before. I stayed in denial in recovery. When I went to Gainesville, I was in denial. I decided that I would humble myself before God and see what happened in my life.

While I was inside, I kept saying to myself, "Hey, nobody's writing, nobody's coming." When I was thinking about this, I also got a new counselor. This guy was really good. He talked to me and he told me that I had a lot of anger issues that I needed to set free. He told me that I didn't have to keep using drugs and killing myself. He said that I could be a gift to society, to my people, to myself, and to my daughter and my family. But, first, I had to learn to love myself. My grandmother loved me, but I was looking for something different. I just wanted someone who would say, "Donna, I love you as you are, for what you are, and I want to help you." My pain was covered up with drugs, so I started thinking about the things that I wanted to do.

Even after I converted to Islam in 1981, my real power was not strong enough when it came to drugs. When I have a crisis now, these sisters—the Joyces—tell me when I'm doing wrong. I have this guilt, this shame about me. In Islam, if you do wrong, you walk in shame for four months. I've done this a couple of times. But each time I go, I get back into this drug thing, or the money situation. I was too proud to ask my friends or family to help me with rent, or a car note, so I went to where I knew the fast money was. I will have to use the tools that they taught me in counseling to cope with these things or I will keep doing the same things and keep getting the same results.

I'm getting a little stronger; I'm getting a little better. I have times when I want to give up, but I just try to pick myself up and try not to use drugs. I want to do things differently. I've gotten into African American history, and I think about those people that did things to help us, and it hurts. I think about slaves, and how they were beaten and whipped. Sometimes, I come down to earth and get real with myself, and I think about my grandmother and the things she had to endure. I think about the people that I have helped, and none of those people that were in that fast life were there for me when I was really down and out.

Since I've gone through it, I think that the best way to help people on drugs is to send them to more treatment places. Teach them more about the legal system. I have seen that Black women are not very knowledgeable about how much time we can get in prison. Some of them have no money to fight their cases, so they take state-appointed attorneys, and they come to them with whatever agreement they can make. The women accept it because they have been trained about what to accept since the very first time they go to prison or get locked up. Most of them are addicts and they want to take whatever time they can and get out as fast as they can. We're not legally educated and we'll take anything.

Also, as far as my Black sisters are concerned, we need to go out in our neighborhoods to speak to each other. We need the younger generation working with the older people. We need to show that we care about each other and that we care what we think. They need to see me not selling drugs and see me not using drugs again in our community.

7

Martha

Martha was convicted of three drug-related charges in 1989. She is currently serving a twenty-years-to-life sentence. She was sixty years old at the time of sentencing. Prior to the drug sale that led to her conviction, Martha had ended her foray into selling cocaine because of the harm it caused to others, including her daughter. After getting out of the business, a former friend and buyer asked Martha to help him purchase cocaine. After refusing several times, Martha contacted a seller for the friend, who was an informant. After a joint trial, Martha's co-defendant, the alleged supplier, was acquitted. Despite persistent health problems, Martha has participated in numerous educational and self-improvement programs in prison. Her clemency appeals have been denied twice. She perseveres and looks forward to being released and spending her remaining days with her children and grandchildren.

Martha

I WAS BORN in a little town called Lumpkin, Georgia; it's near Savannah. I grew up with my mother, father, and two older sisters. My sisters and I were born a year apart. My older sisters were born in 1927 and 1928, and I was born in 1929. My parents and sisters are deceased now. One of my sisters died in 1993, while I've been incarcerated. She was sixty-eight years old when she died.

We left Georgia and moved across the river to Eufaula, Alabama, when I was a baby. That's where I grew up. We used to walk the truss to cross the bridge between Georgia and Alabama. Our town in Alabama was in a dry county. People had to go to Georgia to get alcoholic beverages.

My father tried sharecropping. It was kind of hard. If you wanted to sharecrop, you would make an agreement with one of the White fellas who had a lot of land. They would furnish you with everything for the year, such as your food, money, seeds, and fertilizer. At the end of the year, the owner got half of whatever you grew and you would pay back the money they loaned to you. But we never cleared anything. The White folks took it all.

I also worked hard in the field. I started in the field when I was eight years old. When we finished working our crops, I would do day work for about twenty-five cents a day. I have always given a person an honest day's work; I don't care how hard the work was.

All we got were hand-me-down clothes from White people. I used to go to school with bare feet in the wintertime. I got tired of that situation and ran away when I was fourteen years old. A traveling show came to town in 1943 and my father gave us a little change to see it. They were looking for a dishwasher, so I decided this was my chance. I worked with them for a while. At the time, shoes were rationed, and sugar also was rationed. Since I was a minor, the boss got my sugar stamps; I didn't need sugar because they were taking care of me. They bought me clothes and shoes and things, so I was in pretty good shape.

At fourteen, I was a pretty developed young lady. There were two White guys in the show who did an act in blackface. They started to fondle me and I ran away from the show. We traveled all over the South. When we got to Selma, Alabama, I wandered home with them and I never went back to the show. Another show came to town, a Black show, and I joined them. I was a dancer in that show and I stayed with them until I was about sixteen.

On one of my nights off, I met a guy when I decided to go to the movies. He was sitting behind me. We got into a conversation and he asked me to go home with him. At first I said "no" many times before he persuaded me to go. He didn't have any bus fare, so we walked about ten miles from town to his house. There was one bus the next day and I missed it. We did not get married, but we stayed together for eight years. Our relationship was good for two years, and then he really dogged me for the other six years. He used to beat me and finally I got tired of it and I left him. When I would leave, he would find me and beat me until I went back. When my oldest daughter was two years old, he beat her with a wire coat hanger. She was hollering and crying. I just couldn't take that and I knew that if I stayed with him, I would kill him. I packed my stuff while he was at work and just walked away. He visited but I never went back to him. We were living in the country at the time, and I left to go to the city, to Birmingham.

He found out where I was living in Birmingham. At one point, I had gotten hurt and was in the hospital, and he begged me to go back with him. His mother had my baby. When I got out of the hospital and went to see the baby, he tried to beat me to make me stay with him. They finally arrested him. After they arrested him, I got my baby and went to live in the city. I had a good little job there.

I met another guy in Birmingham. Since I was working, the mother of my baby's father—I called her Momma—took care of the baby. My new friend and I went to visit the baby one day. He wasn't working at the time, so my baby's grandfather asked him if he wanted a job. My friend said yes and he went to work in the coal mines. We got married and moved about 200 miles away to live in his family's house.

My husband's family also were sharecroppers, but we lived pretty well out there. Then I started having babies. We stayed together for five years. He had become very jealous and he didn't want me out of his sight. We had left his mother's house and returned to my hometown of Eufaula. He was working and then he started messing around with other women. That's when I decided to come North. We were living in the projects and the lady in the rental office asked if I knew any girls who wanted to work in New York City. Her brother worked in an employment office in New York. I told her I was interested and she bought a ticket for me. I told my husband that I was going for two years to give him time to make up his mind whether he wanted me or that other girl.

I came to New York and got a job. It was a good job, too. I worked for a family on the West Side; he was a Broadway producer. They had two girls and a boy, and they were wonderful children. My boss sent for my husband to come up from Alabama. We were going to live in the apartment upstairs and we were going to send for our other two children, who were still with his mother. My husband messed up, though. He kept calling his girlfriend in Alabama. When my boss and his family returned after being away for the weekend, they got the phone bill and fired me on Monday.

When they fired me, I didn't have anything. I told a policeman that I didn't have any money or a place to go. They sent me to the Bowery. I was pregnant. When I got to the Bowery, the man there was so nice. He told me that I shouldn't stay there in my condition. He gave me six dollars and told me where I could find a little cheap motel room that night. Later, the welfare office sent me to my oldest sister in Newark, New Jersey. I stayed with her until I had the baby. After the baby was born, my sister and I didn't get along too well.

I met a guy while I was living in New Jersey, and we hit it off really well. My mother was in the hospital in upstate New York and I wanted to see her. I stayed there for a couple of months and picked beans and other vegetables. I told my mother about my children and promised to bring them to see her. In 1963, I went to see my mother again and stayed for the season. In 1966, my boyfriend and I moved to King's Ferry, in upstate New York and did migrant work there.

My daughter got pregnant in 1969, and we moved to Syracuse so that we could get health care at the clinic, and we stayed. Around 1980, my daughter was going with a guy and they started taking cocaine. My two older daughters started taking it, too. I couldn't believe it. That hurt me so bad. They were really strung out and I didn't know what to do.

I got involved around the time that my son bought me a car when he was home on furlough from the Army. I gave the car to my grandson. Something happened to the car and my grandson needed money to fix it. I had a little money in the bank and loaned him the money to fix it. Then a guy came along the street selling a TV. My grandson wanted the TV, too, so I loaned him the money to get the television. Then there was no money to fix the car. My daughter told me that if she had twenty dollars, she could make enough money to get the car fixed.

I didn't know what she was talking about, but I had twenty dollars, so I gave it to her. We were riding in my station wagon and she bought this cocaine. In less than twenty minutes, she had about $200.

I didn't know that she had been selling cocaine before this. I thought, gee, if they make that kind of money, maybe I had better try this. I was broke, and it occurred to me to get some money out of the bank and get some cocaine. I took a few hundred dollars out of the bank and told my daughter to get some of the stuff she was selling. I told her to buy seventy-five dollars worth, and she doubled the money. That's why I'm in prison.

All my life, I had been using hand-me-down clothes. Even when I was raising my kids, we went to the rescue mission and bought hand-me-down clothes and used furniture. I really saw a chance to get something I never had. It was really fast money and my goal was to sell it and get what I wanted and then quit. That's what I thought.

I was fifty-eight years old when I started selling cocaine. I didn't even sell cocaine for a whole year; it was more like nine months. Within that time, I had everything that I needed or wanted in my house. I had nice clothes and a few dollars in a safe deposit box. In October 1988, one of my ex-customers came to my house and wanted cocaine. I told him that I was not in the business anymore. He said, "But you know people . . . I need some bad." He wanted an ounce. I called some guys to see if they were still in business. They were still selling and the customer came to my house and picked up the ounce of cocaine.

A week later, he called me and wanted eight ounces. I said that I would have to call to see if the guys dealt with that amount. My customer was a White boy and he called me "Momma." He said, "Momma, please try." Sure enough, the guys didn't have a problem with it. The customer was with a friend, who really was an undercover state police officer.

The customers came to my house. We were drinking beer, waiting for the guy to bring the stuff. When he came to the house, I took the stuff and told him to wait in my kitchen for his money. The rest of us went into the bedroom. The snitch said, "Hurry up, I'm getting nervous." I said, "Me, too." All of a sudden, I heard somebody say, "Freeze!" When they said freeze, the officer flipped me over on my back like I was a piece of paper, put an elbow or knee in my back and said, "Don't move." I was handcuffed behind my back, which hurt because I have arthritis in my joints.

A female officer asked for my ID and I told her it was in the pants on the chair. When she checked the pants pocket, she found my wallet, seven $100 bills, and half an ounce of cocaine that I was holding for my daughter. The police searched my house. My sister came up from New Jersey and cleaned my house before I got out of jail. She told me what they did to the house. They took all my clothes off the hangers and threw them on the floor. They took the garbage out of my garbage can. They poured flour and rice around. The one thing they didn't do was beat me up.

The police claimed they found a little packet of cocaine under my sofa, on my coffee table, the eight ounces that I sold to the undercover cop, and the stuff that was in my pocket. They got me for conspiracy. They gave me eight-and-a-half to twenty-five years for conspiracy, and twenty-to-life for possession in the first degree. I got twenty-to-life for sales in the first degree and one year for possession of drug paraphernalia. They also indicted me for one ounce from the first time they came to my house; I got three-years-to-life for that charge. The charges ran concurrently, so it was like having one twenty-to-life sentence.

They offered me a plea bargain. My lawyer wanted to meet with me on Saturday to discuss it. He told me that they offered me six-to-life. Then he told me that I didn't want the plea because he could beat that. He called me in jail to tell me that I didn't have to appear to accept the plea because he would appear to accept it for me. My attorney didn't tell me how much time I would get if I lost the trial. He just said, "I can beat that." I had $12,000 in a safe deposit box. The police knew I had it in the safe deposit box and I was scared they would take it. I asked my attorney to get it. My attorney's partner brought a note for me to sign to get the money from the safe deposit box, but I never got the money from them.

When I won the appeal for a new trial, I was offered another plea of ten-to-life. My attorney told me to take it. I wondered why he wanted me to take ten-to-life, but wouldn't let me take six-to-life. I thought that maybe I had a chance this time, so I refused the plea and went to trial again. I was convicted and got the same twenty years again.

It's difficult to explain how I reacted to the sentence. I'm a very tough person. The way I was raised, if something bad happens and you can't change it, put it in God's hands. So that's what I always do. When they told me "twenty-to-life," it didn't even hit me. After I got to prison, I thought about it a lot. I miss my kids. I miss my grandkids. I have five children, twenty-one grandchildren and twenty-two great-grandchildren. We've always been a close-knit family. We were happy. We played volleyball. We went swimming together. All of them like to fish and I would take them fishing. We liked cooking out. Now, a lot of the older ones come to visit. Some of the other ones don't come to visit, though. I don't know why they don't come. Sometimes, the older grandchildren will come by themselves for Christmas. But they really don't visit me like they should. I guess money is tight.

I was sentenced in 1989, so I've been here for over ten years. The thing that sticks out in my mind is that I can understand that I did wrong for selling the cocaine, but I think they gave me a harsh sentence. Since I've been in prison, I've met people who are here for murder and they got eight-and-a-half to twenty-five years. People would tell me that my case was like first-degree murder. But there are people serving time for first-degree murder down here who got seven-and-a-half to twenty years, or eight-and-a-third to twenty-five years, so why did I get twenty-to-life? I did not have any prior drug convictions before this.

It's really hard for me in the institution. You have to be a very strong person to be in here; you have to keep your sanity and stay out of trouble. Like I said, I am strong. When I first came here, my son and my youngest daughter sent me money. My husband would send me money, too, even though we were not together. I was in pretty good shape and I could go to the commissary regularly. Most people here can't do that. If others can get something from me, I'm the sweetest thing on earth, but if I say no, I'm this old bitch. This is how it works in here. That makes it hard. There's something going on every day. There's an argument about anything you can think to argue about.

In 1993, I fell in the shower and hurt my back. I wasn't going to do anything about it at first. Whenever I went to the hospital, they said nothing was wrong and it was just arthritis. I fell on the weekend, so I couldn't get it X-rayed because no one is here to X-ray on the weekend. On Monday, they X-rayed it. I was going to school at the time. I had stopped school in the third grade because we had to work on the farm. I was bent over in pain from my fall. They made me go to school. Another day after the fall, I fell and hurt my knee again while I was on my way to school. All of a sudden, about three inmates picked me up and brought me to the hospital. My knee was skinned up. The nurse cleaned me up and told me I could go on to school because nothing was wrong with me. There were no X-rays or anything. I went to school.

A couple of days later, it was pouring raining. I was sixty-seven years old and the teacher called me to come to school, and said if I didn't come to school they would write me up. I told her that I was not going because my side was killing me and I would be dripping wet by the time I got there. I would get to sit up in the classroom for two hours, dripping wet. It was October or November and I thought I could catch pneumonia like that. I didn't go, and that was my first misbehavior since I've been here.

I finally got to the place where I didn't want to go to school anymore. My sister had died while I was taking classes and I stayed out of school for a couple of days. I was told to go to class or get a misbehavior report. I'd just had a death in my family; why would they do that to me?

People out there should understand not to ever come in here. My goal was to buy things, but then I lost it all. I think about it quite often, all the stuff I had. I had nice clothes and now everything is gone. When I leave here, I will have only what I have on my back. In here, all we have is hope. I tell a lot of girls in here that if you lose hope, you don't have anything. I talk to Him—God—every day. He's making me strong enough to bear whatever happens.

8

Marilyn

Marilyn is serving twenty-two-years-to-life for participating in an armed robbery in which one of the victims was shot and killed. Marilyn was not present at the shooting, but she was charged with aggravated murder in addition to burglary and several counts of robbery. She initially faced the death penalty before pleading guilty to murder and robbery charges. Earlier in life, she had pursued a modeling career. After dropping out of school in the ninth grade, then marriage and pregnancy at a young age, Marilyn set aside her plans. After her husband's violent death, she became involved with an abusive boyfriend. Her boyfriend initiated the robbery and did the shooting that led to her incarceration. While in prison, Marilyn overcame serious mental illness, obtained her GED, completed numerous certificate programs, and obtained her cosmetology license. She also organized a charitable fund-raiser for breast cancer research. Marilyn has twice been denied parole. The dispute concerning Marilyn's parole status is featured in an exposé on the Ohio parole system in the **Cleveland Free Times.**[1]

Marilyn

I AM FORTY-FOUR years old. I was raised in Cleveland, but I was born in Newport News, Virginia. My mother had ten kids. There are five girls and five boys. My family struggled. We didn't have a lot of money. I never was mentally or physically abused by my family. They were always good to me. They gave me what they could give me, but it still was a struggle, considering that we were a big family.

I have three daughters and three granddaughters and one grandson. I stopped school after the ninth grade because I got pregnant and I just kind of quit. I wasn't really encouraged to continue school once I was pregnant and I didn't want to go anymore. I had my first child when I was fifteen. I had my second child when I was seventeen. Then I got married at seventeen. My husband was a year older than me. He worked for a bed manufacturer. My youngest daughter was born while I was in prison. I really feel like her surrogate mother because I wasn't there to raise her as I raised my other children.

I've been a widow since 1976, when my husband was killed. My husband was killed on the Fourth of July; actually it was around 2:00 A.M. on the fifth of July. We were riding down the street and this White guy that we didn't know shot him for no apparent reason. I was twenty and my husband was twenty-one when he was killed. My sister and I were also in the car, but we were very fortunate.

I never got any counseling when my husband was killed. I was very lonely and I was still mourning. I guess it was just a combination of things and I got involved with this guy who had just gotten out of prison after serving five years. I didn't know anything about him when I met him. When we first met, he was nice. When he moved into my house, he became very abusive. He didn't abuse me physically very much, but he abused me mentally. For example, he always had this gun and threatened to use it. He would find me if I would leave. He wanted me to prostitute for him. It sounds strange, but I was brainwashed by this man. I couldn't think. I got to the point where I went to my parents and wanted to move back home, but I wasn't woman enough to say, "Mom, I'm moving back home because this man is running me crazy." He didn't want people in my house; it was strange. I think my mother and everybody knew that he was abusing me. My kids were young, so they couldn't really understand what was going on. I always tried to make them go to their room so that they couldn't see what was going on. He and I were together for under a year before I came to prison with this life sentence.

Then one day he led me to believe that we were going to his mom's house. She lived above an after-hours place. But when we got there, his mom wasn't there. We had a few drinks at the after-hours place and he started robbing the place. He told me to put stuff in the bag and I did it. I was really afraid of the guy. I was scared if I didn't do it, he would smack me around. There were about two people in the place. I did not have a gun that night. When I left I got in the car that was parked two streets over and then I heard a gunshot. He never told me that somebody was killed that night; he told me that he got into a fight and the gun accidentally went off. I was two streets over when the guy was shot. When we were arrested, I admitted my crime. I knew it was wrong; I did take someone's stuff. They kept asking me where was the gun. Two witnesses said I had a gun and two witnesses said I didn't. I did not kill anyone. I did not have a gun.

This was in April 1982. They charged me with aggravated murder—with specification, burglary and robbery. I was facing the death penalty. They said I could be the first woman in Ohio to get the electric chair. When I first was arrested, I did not have a lawyer present. I made a statement to the police because they told me if I made a statement and told them what happened, they would just charge me with robbery. But they charged me with both crimes.

My bond was $200,000. I had never been in prison; this is my first incarceration. First, I had a public defender, then I had a private attorney. My parents hired a lawyer and paid him $4,000. At first, I didn't feel comfortable with the public defender, but looking back, they were doing more for me than the hired attorney. The private attorney told me that I might as well plead guilty because I had already made a statement to the police. I thought the lawyers would have reinvestigated on their own. They just wanted me to plead guilty. On the plea bargain, they gave me fifteen-to-life for the murder, and two terms of seven-to-twenty-five years. One term of seven-to-twenty-five years runs together with the fifteen-to-life sentence. That means you have to do your first sentence and then start all over again.

I took the plea. I was on suicide watch. I didn't know I was pregnant at the time. I was taking mind medication and they told me that if I pled guilty and testified against my co-defendant, I would get fifteen-years-to-life. I never loved this man; I was afraid of him, and I wasn't well. But I believed that people who actually killed someone got fifteen-to-life, so I did not testify against him and I wound up getting all of this time. I felt that I should have gone to a jury trial if I was going to get a twenty-to-life sentence. My co-defendant went to trial first and the jury found him guilty, so they really didn't need me then. My co-defendant got thirty-years-to-life.

I feel that I'm a role model prisoner. I don't get in trouble and I don't get tickets. When I went to the parole board in 1996, I had already done fourteen years and they required a psych evaluation. So I got the psych evaluation and I went back and they gave me five years. I told the parole board that I needed counseling. I knew I needed counseling with all that has happened to me. I didn't think I would get five more years because I asked for more counseling. When I finished the five years I went back to the board and got three more years. I go back to the board in 2003.

I was on all types of medications when I was first arrested. I was on a suicidal ward and taking mind medication—psychotropic drugs—to calm me down. I wasn't upset and I wasn't acting bizarre, but I was facing the death penalty and they felt they had to keep me settled. I was interviewed twice by a state doctor to see if I was mentally competent. I don't believe that I was, but they said I was. How could I be mentally competent when they put me on the suicide ward? I was on the medications for a long time. Then I went to the hospital and found I was pregnant; that's when they had to stop giving me the mind medications.

I wish that I had not been pregnant when I came to prison because I didn't know anyone when I came to prison and I was fighting two battles just to survive for me and my child. After I gave birth to my daughter in December 1982, they wanted to take my baby. I had a complete nervous breakdown in February 1983. They called it postpartum depression. After a while, I was sent to the mental hospital at the forensic center. I stayed there for about six months after I was sentenced. I had the breakdown because I was stressed. I had a twenty-two-years-to-life sentence, I could face the electric chair, they tried to take my baby, I wasn't going to be home with my family . . . it was a combination of things.

How could I fight if I wasn't mentally competent? When I came back from the mental hospital, they wanted to put me on more mind medication. Mind medication is not the answer. It doesn't make you think straight and you hallucinate. I stopped taking the medication because I wanted to get myself back together. After a while, I got myself together and I started going to school to get my GED.

All of my sisters graduated from high school. I was the only one who didn't graduate. Before prison, I went to modeling school and I got a certificate. I also enjoyed designing my own clothes. When I got to prison, I became determined. I said, "Well, I'm incarcerated; I have to do something." If you wanted to do anything like go to college, you had to have a GED So I decided to put my mind to it. I took my GED seven times; it was hard, but I did it. I was very proud of myself; I had had a complete nervous breakdown and got myself back together. After I got my GED, I went to school and got my cosmetology licenses for instruction, managing, and operating.

When my friend, Carmen, another inmate, was here, her mother had cancer and she wanted to do a cancer walk-a-thon. So we did a walk-a-thon. If you paid ten dollars, you got a dinner. We had a banquet and if the women wanted to walk, they walked. The women won prizes and things. We raised one thousand dollars in the cancer-walk-a-thon. I really liked doing the benefit. It was very exciting to get so many people involved in it, even if they didn't have cancer or know anyone with cancer. We could do benefits for so many other illnesses like AIDS and diabetes. I'd like to do more benefits like this if I ever go home.

Some days, it's very hard to be in prison, but I came to the conclusion that I just try to take one day as it comes. If I wake up happy, I roll with it. I have gotten much stronger since I've been incarcerated. I'm very independent now; I don't depend on anyone. Before, I was following people; I was weak and gullible. Now I make my own decisions. People come in and ask me how I did more than twenty years in prison. They may have a year or two years to do and they ask, "How did you do it?" I explain to them that it wasn't that easy. It's not like something I can take off the shelf and give you. I find that you have to take one day at a time, find something interesting to do that will benefit you and keep your mind occupied. Some days, I feel depressed and don't want to get out of bed, but I tell myself that I have to get out of bed and go to work. I work for the laundry here and I do the inmates' clothes. I like that job. It keeps me busy and it keeps my mind from just thinking about doing my time.

My family members were very close to me when I was first incarcerated. Now that I've been away so long, I'm afraid that they don't really know me. A lot of people come to prison, they could be any race, and their family members just don't understand the prison life and how lonely and depressing it can be at times. At first everyone is helping you out, then they forget about their loved ones. We're still women, we're still human beings; we just made a foolish mistake. It could be anybody, your priest, the cops, your best friend, rich or poor. Family members should be more supportive of some of the people that are incarcerated. Some inmates never receive any mail, no money orders, no food boxes, none of that. That makes a person get bitter. It's important for people to get mail, visits, and money orders. We have to survive in here, too. They're not giving away personal items, we have to buy that stuff. Everything is expensive for us, too, even if we are in prison.

A lot of women in here won't be woman enough to say that they were abused by a man. I want women to know that I was abused by a man and I'm doing time for a man, and that's something I'm never going to do again once I'm released. I'm not that proud; I was used by this man, I was abused by this man, and I went through enough. I don't think domestic violence is dealt with enough in the Black community. I think there should be more information and pamphlets that are directed to the Black community in order to recognize the abuse in the community. I never went to a domestic violence shelter because I didn't really know that it was abuse. In prison, they started domestic violence classes and I realized my experience was abusive. The community should not be so harsh on inmates. Because some women have low IQs, low self-esteem, or can't read or write, when they try to defend themselves they still get a life sentence.

When I came to prison, my oldest daughter was twelve and my youngest was ten. My parents raised them. They are doing fine; they're good girls. They didn't get into drugs or anything. They've been to college. My oldest daughter is a beautician and is renting a house. At one time she had custody of my youngest daughter, but the youngest is an adult now and takes care of herself. My second oldest works for a law firm. They went on with their lives. My youngest daughter had a difficult time during my incarceration. She was in a foster home and some treatment centers after suicide attempts. She's a good girl, she gets good grades in school; she just misses me. She knows why I'm in prison and she knows why her father is in prison. I didn't cut any corners with her. She asked me why I was in prison and I told her because I have no reason to lie about that. Each of my daughters is very open. They have tried to talk to lawyers and they have done everything possible that they could do to get me out of prison. They want me home. My grandkids are growing up and I haven't been there for any of them.

The staff gives me my respect and I give them theirs, too. I don't disrespect anyone. I think they give me a little more respect because of the cancer-walk-a-thon I did at the prison. I try to be cordial to other people because I know there are a lot of women in here who have mental problems, even though they might not recognize it. Some of the women come here with flat time and they go home. They ask me how did I do my time. I tell them I didn't take any pill to do this time. I got off the mind medication and I got my thoughts back. Whenever I get out of here, I want to be a clothes designer, a singer, and do lots of charity work. I want to go to college and finish my degree. When I start something, I like to complete it.

B

FORMERLY INCARCERATED WOMEN

9

Bettie Gibson

Bettie began her life in rural Mississippi. At a very young age, she was aware that belief in African Americans' racial inferiority was ingrained in the social structure. She also experienced sexual abuse by an overseer at her family's farm. She moved north to Chicago to live with her parents, who later divorced. After difficulties at home, she left and embarked on a self-destructive course that included prostitution, theft crimes, and drug addiction. She took the opportunity to complete her last sentence at Grace House, in Chicago. There, she received support to address her pain from sexual abuse and drug addiction, as well as support to complete her education. She is now well on her way to achieving the personal and educational goals she set for herself.

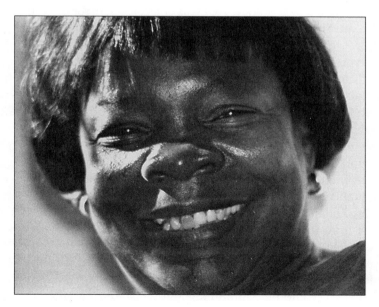

Bettie Gibson

MY NAME IS BETTIE. I'm forty-nine years old. I was born in Delta City, Mississippi, on a sharecropped farm. My parents were sharecroppers. My father's mother was a schoolteacher. She kept me when I was born. She was a very fair-skinned lady, with long hair; she was more Cherokee Indian than anything else. My mother's mother had my complexion; she had dark skin and woolly hair. I was the middle child, and I had three other sisters.

I think one reason why I fell into crime was that I wasn't educated. My father's mother had a lot of high ideas for me. Even though she was educated and taught the Black kids in the school down in Mississippi, I didn't have enough time to be around her. I didn't understand how important it was to be around someone with a stable foundation and an education. She lived well and got the things that she needed and wanted. With my skin color, though, I wouldn't have gotten too far. I would have to go through another door because of my skin color.

When I was young, there was a show in town. We had to sit in different places than the little White kids. Then, at the end of the show they would have a Black man wrestle a bear, and then a Black kid would wrestle a bear, to win money. That was entertainment for the White people. Because of my grandmother, I got to do things that other Black kids didn't get to do. There was Sears and Roebuck, for instance. It was a big deal if you shopped out of their catalog. My clothes and Christmas gifts came from Sears and Roebuck, but the other Black children didn't have that. You had to have money to order something from Sears. But even though I had all of that, the feeling of being inferior brought me away from that place.

Sharecropping was very similar to slavery. The overseer on the farm would try to have sex with us when we were children. He used to come over and try to put his penis into my cousin and me, and give us money and other things. We never were penetrated, but I felt that fondling and having to put our hands on his penis was just as bad. I was scarred from that. I never told anyone about it until I was grown. He would come inside my grandmother's house. She and the other Black people were so afraid of the overseers and the other Whites. They would find women chopped up on the river with axes, dead. It was just hush-hush. I would hear mumbling and whispers, but when the overseer came around, they would be quiet. So as early as the age of three, I knew that we were inferior to White people and I couldn't take it. I knew that something was not right in the house, that my grandparents were afraid of those people, and that we were beneath them. I said, "If my parents have a better place than this, I'm leaving."

When I was about four or five years old, my father decided to get out of the South and come north to get a job. We came to Chicago to try to better ourselves. I should have stayed in the South with my grandmother, but I wouldn't listen. I would have gone to college or the military. I just wanted to be a government person. But I always thought that everyone was equal and no one was superior. Everything was supposed to be uniform; what applied to you should apply to me. So when I was asked whether I wanted to remain in Mississippi or move to Chicago with my parents, I chose to go with my parents to get away from Mississippi. Since I had lived with my grandmother, I didn't know anything about my parents.

My dad got a job as a welder when they came to Chicago, and made pretty good money. He didn't really bother about education, though. My mother and father had only a third-grade education because they had to drop out to pick cotton in Mississippi. In this way, we were a dysfunctional family because two people didn't know anything except how to go to work and make some money. They didn't know how to tell us that an education was essential if we were going to lead productive lives. That wasn't instilled in us even after we came to Chicago.

I started school in Chicago, but I never liked school very much. I found math especially difficult. I couldn't come home and ask my parents, because they didn't know. Back then, they would pass you from grade to grade based on your height. They didn't have meetings with the parents to discuss what was going on with the children and their grades. Most of the teachers were White and didn't seem to care. They were getting a paycheck. If you weren't outstanding, they didn't put too much energy into you. It seemed as though the rest of the kids were on top of what they should know, and they caught on quickly. I was much slower. Maybe if someone had shown me a different way, I could have caught on. You have to use other approaches for people who are slower learners, especially when they come from family backgrounds that do not have much education. I am thankful to see that the education system has changed for the better.

My mother and father didn't have very good communication between them. When I was twelve years old, they talked about separating.

We had to decide who was going to live with whom. My baby sister and I picked my father, because it just seemed that my mother and I never had a good relationship. My other sisters went to live with my mother. After my sister and I stayed with my father for a while, we went back to our mother because my father lost his eye in an accident at his job. I was about fourteen years old then. When I went back to my mother's house, I kept running away from home. I started drinking alcohol, going out, and staying out. I would sneak out when everybody went to sleep. I just wasn't happy there because I was always being labeled. I got through school and I couldn't wait to get out of the house.

The first guy I met was what you'd call a pimp and he was from my neighborhood. I was eighteen years old, and I must have stood on the street as a prostitute for about two months. I don't know if it was because of what the overseer tried to do to us when we were kids, but I thought certain sex things weren't normal. So I started to go out on the street and pick men's pockets and take their money. I started to get good at it. I would go down on Rush Street, to the Gold Coast, where all the leisure trade people come from all over the world and I would get into the men's pockets. I would pick rich men's pockets of thousands and thousands of dollars, because I would dress up real nice, and they always wanted to get close to me. I had gotten so good that I could take their money out their wallet and put the wallet back in three seconds. Then I used to steal their credit cards and sell them.

Once I found out that I could pick pockets, I was able to leave home and have my own place. This is what drove me into the street, and I felt that was really the thing to do. I lived in nice apartments. I had jewelry, nice cars, and my kids were dressed nicely. I had gotten so good at picking pockets that I was really making money. The biggest one I ever took happened when I was nineteen. The guy had a hundred $100 dollar bills; he had ten thousand dollars in his pocket, probably from the race-track. I started buying a lot of nice things. The pimp started coming around, trying to get me to do this and that, and that's when I started using drugs. I was nineteen years old when I first sniffed heroin. One of my sisters did it, and my boyfriend did it. I started getting curious because it looked like they felt so good, and I just had so much pain. I didn't like myself. I thought that I never would reach my potential. At first the heroin seemed good, and then after I started taking it, I knew my life had become a whirlwind. It was going around and around, going nowhere, like a merry-go-round. I got strung out quickly because I made a lot of money; therefore, I had a lot of money to do drugs. A lot of people who didn't make a lot of money start shooting because it's direct contact through the veins and the high is supposed to last longer. But I didn't like needles.

Then one night I was on State Street and met this guy that owned a steel corporation. I picked his pocket. He had about sixteen hundred dollars in his pocket. I was caught because the doorman, a Black guy, told that I had the man's money. I gave the money back to him since we had gotten caught. The guy ran down the street after I gave the money back and slapped my boyfriend and me. My boyfriend was a big pimp from Chicago. He got out and beat the guy up with one of those clubs for the steering wheel. They put a warrant out for our arrest. This was the first time I ever encountered the penal system. This was in 1975.

My lawyer was well known in the county. He said, "Bettie, you know the judge is my father-in-law. If you plead guilty today, they're going to give you six months." I turned down the six months because my boyfriend told me, "Don't plead. Don't take six months for something you didn't commit." Therefore, we took it to trial. In the end, guess what we wound up with? It was five to fifteen years. They had charged us with armed robbery. The lawyer was so mad at me. He said, "Bettie, I'm not even coming back anymore. I'm going to send my protégé because I don't even want to see you."

When they slapped me in jail I was eight months pregnant with my youngest child. I have four sons. My oldest son was born in 1967, and my next son was born in 1968. My third son was born in 1972. When I got down to the penitentiary I was dilating. They got the car and the man driving was doing one hundred miles an hour to get me to the hospital. When we got there, they treated me so badly; they put me in a closet. They wouldn't even take me to the delivery room because I was Black. They let me have my baby by myself, almost in the closet. The corrections officer, a lady, was standing there. They were going to call my doctor at the prison. The CO said, "Well, she can't wait until the doctor gets here. The baby's coming." I started pushing and the baby came out right there.

I didn't get to keep three of my kids very much. My boyfriend's mother was given custody of them. When I got out of jail, I got a place in an affluent suburb and lived with my two youngest sons. I asked them if they were involved with any gangs and they said, "No, Mama, we're not in no gang." I said, "Look, I'm going to tell you something.

You don't be out here in these gangs. You going to school." They kept saying they were going to school. So one day, when I went in their room to make sure their beds were made, I found some gang literature. They were thirteen and fourteen years old. I got in the car, and I went and found them. No kid of mine was going be a gang banger. I told them to go back to their daddy and his sister's house, because I wasn't going to put up with it. I know where I went wrong. I know where my parents went wrong, and I was not going to be a part in destroying their lives.

Both of them were selling drugs. The older son got out of it, but the youngest one didn't. It's going to take more than talking to him to get him to stop because the money, big jewelry, and the cars got him caught up. He needs to go back to school. They need to send him to some type of program that says, "You either do this or you'll never get out. You either go through this program and wake up because if you don't wake up, you're going to get right back out here and do the same thing and get killed or end up back in here." Because the court system is waiting. Once you've been convicted of a crime in the state of Illinois, you can rest assured that you will be a repeat offender over and over again, because whatever they say you did, you did it. You cannot stand up in a court of law and take a trial on anything with your background and this is what they play on. Plea-bargaining is a very big thing in Illinois. Even people that shouldn't be in jail, that don't even commit crimes, plea-bargain to get a lesser sentence so they can hurry up and get in and get out. The jails are so overcrowded and filthy. The food is bad. The health care is lousy. And some of the guards are physically abusive.

Now the prison for Black women is what I call just a warehouse for people. They don't have programs to help you come back in society, to help you with your problems as to why you wound up there. It's just to get the money every time you come through the door. It's a lucrative business. So here you are going right back out there to do the same thing with fifty dollars. What is fifty dollars, with no skills and no training and no education, going to do for someone? Getting out of jail with fifty dollars would make me want to go use some drugs and forget what's going to happen two days down the line when I wake up with no money and no job. You would see women go out and come right back. There are three basic life-sustaining things that you have to have in life: food, clothing, and shelter. They don't come free, and you can't get them for fifty dollars. They know when they let you out that you'll be back, unless you get fortunate enough to have a program like this to help you. And you have to want it. People fail to realize that all the people out here on the street that they see walking down the street using crack cocaine and stealing don't do that because they want to do it. They have no other way.

My first incarceration was for armed robbery, the one in 1975. I received a sentence of five to fifteen years, and I served five years. On the second one, I received seven years, three times, but concurrent, which left me with seven years. That charge was robbery and I served three-and-a-half years. That was in 1984. In 1992, I got three years for petty theft, for pick pocketing; I served a year. Then in 1994, I served fifteen months of a three and one-half year sentence. Just as I was coming out, I got three-and-a-half more years. This happened at the end of 1997 or the beginning of 1998. I'm on parole for that one now. I went to school when I was in jail. Don't think I just sat there. It took me four times to pass the GED. It took me four times because you are a product of your environment and what your parents are. If my parents did not have an education, where did that leave me? Now, I also have credits from local universities and junior colleges.

I didn't understand that my life-style was an act. I was on stage until I was almost fifty years old. I was really on stage being an image that somebody else had built me up to be. It wasn't what I really wanted to be, and I learned to come offstage. I'm offstage now. I also learned that I suffer from bipolar mental condition. It was a long time before I knew why I suffered from this depression. I found out later that bipolar is a disease that you inherit, usually from a parent. Looking back on it, I think my mother suffered from bipolar because she suffered with a lot of depression.

I thought there would be some way to break that cycle, because I heard that people that did these programs were successful. This is why I asked for Grace House. I could have been with family members, but I didn't want to go back into the streets again, and there was no structure with my family members. I would not have found a job. Instead, I would have started stealing. The program was the best thing for me and I'm grateful to have been picked and to have this chance. I'm going to do this program successfully because I'm doing the things I'm supposed to do in order to stay here.

Now I take the bus where I'm going and I don't want diamonds. But don't get me wrong, it's okay to want these things, because this is what makes each of us individuals. That just isn't where my priorities are anymore. I want to reach my potential. I am someone that likes to explore in her mind, because I do have one. And if I had been able to cultivate what I know, and use what I got, I would have been sitting somewhere trying to help somebody. After all the money that I made, money is really nothing; it's just something to show, to glamorize. But can you live simply? When you can do that, then you know that you're somebody.

The Grace House is the best thing that could ever happen to a Black woman, or to any prisoner, because it will help you get back out in the community where you can be productive. You can get a job. My main thing is to get my degree. I have those academic credits, but I don't do math well. I need to pass math to get my degree. Grace House has a tutor who will help. I think that I could counsel someone and help them because how do you expect somebody that comes from one of the ritzy places in New York to come down and interact and try to tell somebody from the ghetto what to do and how to do it? They can't do it, because first of all they have to identify with them. You have to give inmates some type of encouragement to want this, and they have to see something on the outside. They have to see someone who's been there— someone who has been using drugs since 1972, and who has straightened up and is functioning. That would have a big impact on another drug addict. It would give them some incentive to want to stop from committing suicide, because in reality, using drugs is just like Russian roulette. Just because you didn't get it today, doesn't mean you won't get it tomorrow, because it slowly deteriorates the body and the mind.

I think that I need to take a look at the things that I'm doing and not look at what others may have or may be getting or what others, in my family maybe, can do for me. Instead of socializing with some of the people or going to places I've been around in the past, I need to try to omit that from my mind. That would bring nothing but trouble to me. And I need to be patient. That's first and foremost. I'm going to have to stay focused on the things that I might do that could lead me back to the penitentiary, and what it will take for me not to do those things. I want to stay focused on being an everyday person, without drugs and knowing within my heart that I don't need to have some type of mind-altering narcotic to make me normal and feel like I'm supposed to feel.

I see myself getting to the point to where I have a nice job and my degree someplace on the wall. And I see myself volunteering to help others, and putting back what I've gotten out of it. I am working on my

Bachelor's in social work. This is a good match for me because I can share what I learned in my text, and I can share what I learned from firsthand experiences in life. There won't be any dressing up or sugar-coating. I'll just put it out there like it is, hoping that they won't take the same path that some of us have taken.

I think that a lot of people should know some of the things that I've suppressed in me. I think maybe once they know that there are people that can bring out things that they kept inside so many years, they also can begin to open up and talk about their problems. I feel it is important that you don't have to be ashamed of what you've done, where you been, and the kind of family you may be from, because a lot of people come from dysfunctional families and they just try to cover it up and dress it up. But, I want to be open with it, so people will know that they are not alone and that there are places and programs that can help them work out their problems. I want to be part of that solution. Finally, I feel loved, cared for, and have a sense of self-worth. I would like to thank all the people who came into my life that believed in me until I believed in myself. I thank them profusely for the tools that got me where I am today and for lighting my way. I'm feeling very optimistic about my life.

10

Joyce Ann Brown

Joyce Ann Brown was accused of the heinous murder of a local Dallas, Texas, furrier, a crime that she did not commit. After serving nearly ten years in the Texas prison system, she finally was released when the Texas Appeals Court overturned her conviction based on the state's un-lawful withholding of evidence that pointed to her innocence. In prison and upon release, she became an ardent advocate for incarcerated women and men, and their families and supporters. Her story is told in her book, **Joyce Ann Brown: Justice Denied (1990).**

Joyce Ann Brown

I WAS BORN in Willis Point, Texas, a small town east of Dallas. I grew up in the Dallas area. My mother had ten children and she brought us to Dallas when I was in the third grade. My mother and her thirteen siblings had not been educated, except for one brother that ended up in the service. I'm talking about first, second grade, maybe, and that was it. My mother was married at thirteen; therefore, she did not get an education as far as school was concerned. But she was determined that her children would be educated before they left her house.

I graduated from Franklin D. Roosevelt High School in 1965. I had to take on a different role, because I had to be the second mother. Living in that environment made me want a better life for all of my siblings. I am the third child, but the oldest girl. I was a child, but I took on a grown person's role, by cooking, making sure the children ate, making sure they were able to get up, get off to school, and so forth. When my mom wasn't there, I was the one in charge. I took care of everybody. I also think that was a good thing, because it got me ready for womanhood. It made me a leader; let me put it that way. It made me always want to be in charge. If someone was weak and being abused, I always wanted to be the person that could tuck them under my wing.

When we grew up and went through elementary, junior high, and high school, there were a lot of things that we weren't able to participate in because we didn't have the finances. But because everybody around us was poor, we didn't realize how poor we were.

My brother, Robert, was the smartest person that I have ever seen in my life. He made A's and he went to college. He was the first of our family to go to college, and that made me proud. When I graduated from high school in 1965 and he was getting ready to enter college, I chose to get a job so that I could help him. I think that came from that upbringing provided by my mother. We didn't know anything about grants then. We didn't know if there was college money out there for African Americans. That hadn't been taught to us in our schools. Our parents weren't educated to know how to go out and get it, therefore college was just a no-no. We were taught to finish school, to get an education, to get a job. We were not taught to be entrepreneurs. I used to think, God, there's a better life than this. There are other things that you probably can do and I need to try to find out what those things are, because I want more for my sisters and my brothers.

I really didn't think about my own future because I had been taught that if you got a job, you were doing it. You were an A-OK Black person. When I was coming up in the '60s, young Black women didn't know about being a doctor or a lawyer, and those types of careers. All we thought about was being somebody's secretary and I fell into that mode. When I came out, there was Texas Instruments. All the Black folks were working for Texas Instruments. They were driving their own cars and living in their own homes, so, you thought Texas Instrument was it. Then I realized that when you paid your rent and bought a few other things, the money wasn't so great, even though I was staying at home with my parents. I had my siblings and they wanted to be in the pep squad, or the cheerleading squad, or other school activities.

Then I realized something else, because at that time, we kind of had integrated a little bit and we were able to go to the White clubs. Of course, I loved to dance and go out and have fun. It appeared that White men would always get attracted to me. At that time, I was a little afraid of them, because we had never been around them, especially in a loving way, or in any type of social way. After they bought you a drink, they would want to dance, and they would tell you how beautiful you were. Then I met a young lady that was a call girl. She looked like me and was built like me, so a lot of them had gotten me mixed up with her. We became friends and she eventually told me what she did. She used to say, "Girl, you could make a lot of money." I said, "Get out of here. I don't want to do that. My mom would kill me." But the White men kept coming, and we kept talking.

Eventually, I found a secretarial job for the school community guidance center in Dallas. I was the only lady. There were six men there, and I was the secretary to all of them. By that time, I realized that the money I was making was not going to allow me to help my siblings participate in the activities they were interested in. Some of those men that called themselves liking me, started leaving money on my dresser whenever they would leave my apartment. Then, my siblings could participate in all of the things that school had to offer and they didn't have to worry about how much it cost. My parents didn't have to worry about it, because I was going to take care of all of that. I wanted them to have an easy mind. All they had to do was get their homework, participate and be the best in what they were doing, and I was going to take care of it. That was it.

Mothers spoil their sons and discipline their daughters, especially the Black women. It wasn't instilled in my older brothers that they were responsible for their younger sisters and brothers. My brothers didn't have to get up and change diapers. They didn't have to cook with a baby on their hip. They didn't have to do any of those things. That was always the woman's job. Young Black men would get a job at somebody's golf course, caddying. When they came home they expected to eat and take a bath, rest, and go to bed. That's what our fathers, as far as we know, did. That's the way it was. I think it stopped with me, because I really didn't think it was right, and I didn't think that the other children should be in control of the other younger children.

So I lived a double life for a while. In 1970, I gave up the secretarial job and decided this was what I was going to do for a time. But I didn't want my mother to know, so I moved to California. I lived in San Diego and that's where I conducted my business. I came back to Dallas from California in 1975. I simply lived on one side of town, and my mom lived on the other side of town. I always had a front, always had a job, or they thought I always had a job. I've always said that if the state government could put a tax on prostitution it would be legal, but they could never put a tax on it, therefore it's illegal. Now, within my heart, I knew it was immoral, and I knew that it was a sin against my God. But other than damaging me, I wasn't damaging anybody else.

I wasn't the type to rob a person, or misuse a person. I did what I said I was going to do, and that was it. And I got paid good money for that. I was one of the top call girls in California, and in Dallas. I always had dignity, pride, and respect because I never brought it to my Momma's house. I knew that she would literally have a fit about that. Even though you think that you are pulling one over, actually, you're not. She probably had figured it out, but simply just did not want to accept it. So, she allowed me to front, and she accepted the front. Nobody can tell me that my mom didn't know, and nobody ever questioned where the money was coming from. They just accepted it. Later on, it would be said that even though we knew you couldn't afford some of the things we got, we never questioned where it came from. We're not going to question it now; we're just going to give back to you what you gave to us. They became my support when I was in prison, so it kind of worked out. To this day we've never really talked about it, never. It's as if it didn't happen, no matter how much they read about it in my book, no matter how much I talk about it.

I've never been ashamed of anything that I did and if those same little sisters and brothers were there, I would do it again without blinking an eye. It's just that, if I had the knowledge then that I have now, I would never have had to do it in the first place. If I had known about scholarship monies, about ways to get me and my sisters and brothers into a college without burdening my parents, there's no doubt in my mind that I would've found those monies.

After I came back from San Diego, I did the same things off and on. Then in 1979, I decided it was time to turn over a new leaf. My daughter was in school. My stepson also lived with us. During that time, I was at the PTA and every activity. My daughter was a cheerleader and Lee, Jr., played for the little league teams. When they were fighting for the championship, I would write all over the car, put the streamers all over the car and make sure that they got there. I was there to cheer them on. Then at night, I would go and do something different, but I was back at home before it was time for them to go to school the next day. Then I decided that this was not it. I've got children coming up now. I am going to do something different.

I've always been good with typing and shorthand, and paperwork and math. I carried the A's in Algebra when I was in school, but I did not know how to use it. I didn't realize there's nothing in the world that you can't do with math. A girlfriend called and said she heard that I was looking for a job. She knew that I was good with bookkeeping and all of that and she encouraged me to apply. I went over with my little resume. I had never really done bookkeeping before, but I knew that I could do it. Since I was what was called a minority, they would have one token in the office. At that time, I really didn't know what a token was; I didn't know that it looked good for them to have a variety. I went to work for Koslow's on October 20, 1979. They found out that I wasn't just a variety. I was very aggressive. They got more than they bargained for, but I had a good relationship with all of the sales reps, the managers, and so on. If they wanted something done, they'd tell me, and that was it.

Then on May 6, 1980, my world turned really upside down. That's when there was a fur robbery about three-and-a-half miles from our store. Fine Furs by Rubin was robbed and the owner was killed. Two Black females had walked in and committed this horrible crime, and the car was rented to a Joyce Ann Brown of Denver. My ex-husband at that time was living in Denver. The police investigator was showing a picture of me, and one of the guys says, "Oh, that's JB. Yeah, I know JB, but

JB wouldn't have done that." He said he left it at that. The next thing I knew, they had my picture out on the streets. At the same time they were showing the picture, police officers that knew me were calling my house, but I wasn't there to see what was happening. This was May 6; it was on a Wednesday.

By May 9, I received a call from my mother. She said that somebody said they were looking for me in connection with a robbery. I said, "Get out of here!" I thought somebody was playing a joke on her because that particular May 6, when we were alerted that there was a robbery in the area, I took the telephone call at work. We were all talking about what we would do if they came in our store, and that we were going to be on the alert; we weren't going to let it happen. I thought somebody was actually playing a joke and I told her that I was getting ready to go to work and I would talk to her later.

Five minutes later, my mother called back and said an elderly family friend had just called. The friend called and said she was reading in the paper that they were looking for me. At that time, I said, "Okay, let me get off the phone with you and call her." I was taught that I needed to listen when senior citizens speak because they normally knew what they were talking about. It wasn't so funny after that. When I called her, she told me what she was reading in the paper and just for a moment I wanted to think that maybe she didn't have her glasses, maybe she's senile. Can she read? Did she go to school? All of those thoughts went through my mind, but in my heart, I knew that she knew what she was talking about. I went out and got a paper and saw that they were looking for me. I thought that I would go down and straighten it out.

My picture wasn't in the paper. It said something like, "Fur robbery suspects have fled Dallas to avoid prosecution." Then it went on to say they were looking for Joyce Ann Brown, and listed my address. I thought, "Oh, my God." I wasn't really excited or worried. They made a mistake. Let me go down there and straighten this out. That's what I honestly thought. I called a friend because she had called the night before and asked me if I was all right. She said, "There was a police officer down here showing your picture in connection with the fur robbery." I told her I was getting ready to go there now and straighten it out. She told me not to go by myself and she called a lawyer that we knew. The lawyer said, "Well, Joyce, I can't give you any advice as a lawyer, because I'm not your lawyer. But as your friend, I would ask you not to go down by yourself." I asked him if he was crazy. I said I don't have anything to hide, because I didn't do anything. He said, "Joyce, this is serious." I didn't even know what capital murder was. All I wanted to do was go down and say, "Hey, I didn't do this. You've got the wrong Joyce Brown."

I called my lawyer and he said, "Go to my office. Don't talk to anybody else. Go to my office." Before I left, I called a friend at the police department but he wasn't in. I told the other officer I was coming down and would come directly to him. When I got to my attorney's office, he picked up a telephone, and he began telling these people that I'm coming in. "We don't have any guns, no knives, no weapon." I'm looking at him like . . . Is he crazy? He said, "This is capital murder, and this is serious." We got to the police department, and went to the lieutenant's office. When I walked in, the lieutenant said, "Joyce, I need to take your purse, and I need to read you your rights." I looked at him and he said, "Believe me, I don't want to do this, but we have to."

He started reading me my rights and I started getting angry then, because I got to crying. I'm crying because I came for help to straighten this out and he was reading me my rights. When he finished reading me my rights, he said, "I don't believe a word of it but I had to do that." Then he said, "I'll take you where you need to go, because they don't want us to question you, because we know you." He took me up to this room and I waited three-and-a-half hours before they came into that room. I was in the room by myself, my lawyer was in and out. At the time they heard I was on my way in, they went to my house and ransacked it. They found nothing because there was nothing there for them to find. They came in and asked me what was I doing on May 6. I told them I was at work and showed them a check stub. One of the guys said, "You're a liar." Oh! I almost came unglued, because a liar I was not. That's when I told him, "I don't have anything to say to you. I've told you where I was. I've told you what I was doing, and I've told you that I didn't commit this crime. So you can just book me, or you can let me go. You arrest me, or you let me go." We found out that they already had a warrant out for my arrest for capital murder. They booked me for capital murder and sent me to a cell. I guess around six o'clock that evening, I was arraigned. During that time, they came to me and asked me if I knew a White guy named Davey Shafer. I said no. They said they had found him working on a car in front of my house and that he had been positively identified as the lookout person. Still, I said that I didn't know him.

When we got to arraignment they called my name for capital murder, and they called Davey Shafer's name. Then, for the first time I saw this guy with this red beard that I've never seen before. They arraigned both of us on capital murder. Two days later, he was released; the charges were dropped. They said he had an alibi. His girlfriend said that they were together, pulling a boat down Northwest Highway, which was close to the scene of the killing. They said they were going by the dentist office, and then they went to the lake.

I had thirteen Anglos attest that I was at work. I had time cards that proved I was at work that day. I showed them check stubs, because the checks came in a day early, and that Wednesday, I had given a co-worker her check a day early. When my co-worker clocked back in, she thanked me because she had caught all those insufficient funds at the bank and they had not charged her. I accepted the call about the robbery in that area. I had all the paperwork to prove that my car had been at the car dealership for two days and that I was without a car. I had proof that my co-worker and I had clocked in. I clocked in at 8:58 A.M. that morning and didn't clock out till 4:12 P.M. I didn't take lunch, because my co-worker was taking me to pick my car up and we wanted to beat the evening traffic.

I had all kinds of alibis. It was checked; there were no flights out of Dallas to Denver in my name, and no record of me going up to pick up a car and coming back. In fact, because of the holidays, we had been working six days a week. So there was no way that I could leave six o'-clock in the evening, go to Denver, pick up a car, come back on a Sunday, and be at work on Monday morning. Still, at that time, I said, okay. I was refusing to believe that because I was Black, I was still there on this charge, and because he was White, he was gone. I didn't want that to enter my mind.

My bond was set at one million dollars. I stayed in jail for fifty-nine days. They lowered the bond. First of all, they dropped capital murder while I was in jail because they couldn't prove it. I was reindicted for aggravated robbery. After the aggravated robbery, my bail was dropped to $500,000. After the fifty-ninth day, bail was dropped to $25,000. My family made the bond and I went home.

They didn't check anything. They decided to carry me to court as soon as possible. We started to go to court on September 28, 1980. The trial lasted for eight days. For eight days, Anglo after Anglo after Anglo took that stand on my behalf. All of the paperwork put up before them was on my behalf. The young man that they claimed had said I rented the car in Denver came to Dallas and he told them that was a lie. He called the district attorney's office, and the district attorney's office told him that they didn't need him, and to stay in Denver. So he called my lawyer and said, "I didn't positively identify that woman. I didn't identify her at all." So he came down and he testified. The district attorney put the wife of the owner on the stand. She said I looked like the person that was with the person that committed the robbery on her husband. The district attorney put a jailhouse informant on the stand who said that I came in and confessed to her that I had committed that crime. Then there was the jury, which was all White, that came back with a guilty verdict. It shocked the courtroom completely, because nobody expected it.

My lawyer and I talked about the plea offer. My lawyer said that the district attorney was going to ask for life imprisonment if I was found guilty and that he might make a plea bargain. I told my attorney that if he was going to ask me to do that, I didn't need him as my attorney. I had nothing to plead for. Even if I had to spend the rest of my life in prison for something I didn't do, I wasn't going to plead.

We prepared to select the jury from the pool. I think that it was a pool of sixty-two. The district attorney has so many he can strike and the lawyer has so many that he can strike. It goes without saying that the district attorney in Dallas strikes African Americans first. There were three or four African Americans that actually were struck. One of the young men got himself removed because he said that he went to school with me and that he could not judge fairly because he knew me. I had never seen this man before in my life. He was lying, because he was a truck driver and he didn't want to be sequestered for a jury. Nobody questioned it. He said he knew me, and they let him go. That was that. The district attorney struck an elderly Black lady. I ended up with an all-White jury. At that time, that didn't puzzle me, because I had been taught that our system was fair.

I naturally assumed that when you went to court, they looked at the evidence, they looked at everything, and they judged you fairly. It never dawned on me that race was playing a part. That was one of the times that I said I would forever teach my child to always remember that when you're up against this system, no matter what anybody says, your race is the number one factor in going to court. I would have never started teaching that had it not happened to me. Like everybody else, I thought that because we had integrated, everything was all right, and that they judged fairly. That's not true.

Something else that I never questioned is the fact that before the trial ended, one of the jurors supposedly got sick and could not go on. We had to decide to go on or to start all over with new jurors. When she supposedly got sick, we decided to go on with the eleven, instead of starting all over again, because we thought we had a fair jury. That was my decision, and I take responsibility for that. But the juror that got sick had uncles and cousins in jail with pending cases. There were some other things they discussed with her, but they put her on the jury anyway. We didn't have a problem with her because we thought maybe she would be fair because she did have some relatives in. But at the very end, she was the one that supposedly got sick and couldn't go any further. I want to know what happened. Why her, of all people; why is it that she happened to have thrown her back out and could not come? My attorney didn't strike her because we thought that the state was going to strike her. My attorney couldn't believe that the state allowed her to stay on. But, they did, and just ironically, she got sick, and couldn't go on. And that's when they found me guilty.

I was found guilty of aggravated robbery, in which a murder occurred. Punishment was life imprisonment. I had to do twenty calendar years, not to make, but just simply talk about parole. I had gotten prepared for the verdict before they said it because when they first went in to deliberate, an hour passed by, two hours . . . I couldn't understand why it was taking them so long . . . three hours, four hours. For some reason, I just couldn't leave the courtroom. I was stuck to that chair at counsel table. The bailiff had to stay in with me because I didn't leave when everybody else went out. He went over and put his ear up to the door and they were just laughing and talking as if they were having a party. I have no idea what they were laughing about. The bailiff said, "I can't believe this. They sound like they're having a party."

When the jury knocked on the door about five minutes after they had gone back in, I had already prepared for what was going to happen. At that point, I was trying to look around and tell somebody to get my mother out. That was the first time that we had let her attend, but I couldn't get them to get her out. One other thing is when the jurors came back in, not one of them looked at me, or looked me in my eye. They all looked down as they filed in, so I kind of said to myself, "Those

bastards have screwed me. But I will not let them have the last laugh."
And that was it. They said, "Guilty."

They locked me up and the last thing I can remember is hearing my
mother scream. One of the bailiffs, the one that actually believed in me,
was going to allow me to come through and say something to her, but
the other one pushed me and made me go on, and wouldn't allow that
to happen. So I just heard my mother screaming. That was in October.
Every day, October, November, December, every day, I thought something would happen, and they would come get me, and they would say
they made a mistake. Then January, I pulled chain and I went to prison.

When they took me back to my cell after the verdict, I was in a daze.
I was out of it. I didn't know where I was. I couldn't believe it. One of
the girls in jail took Thyroxine, and one of the girls said, "If this happens, if she's found guilty, and they bring her in, she's going to be totally out of it." They somehow took half of her medication, and when
they brought me in, and I was crying and hysterical, they gave me that
pill. I'll never forget that. They kept telling me to go to sleep, but I kept
fighting it. Somebody said, "Ooh, she's strong, because she should be
knocked out by now." But I kept fighting it because I didn't realize what
they had given me, and I didn't want to buckle down to the medication.
I wanted to fight this on my own. I kept saying that I'm not going to let
it end like this. Eventually, I went to sleep.

On January 9, 1981, I heard my name called, and they were calling
more names. This young lady that I knew ran in and said, "Don't get
nervous. This is the chain. You're going down south." Then I heard
them say, "For the ladies that we've called, head them up and move
them out . . . like we were cattle." They put us all in this little room and
chained us together, and then they took us to this bus. I thought, "God,
I thought you would be here before now." Then I was on my way to
Mountain View. I kept saying to myself they picked the wrong person.
I just couldn't let them get away with it. I hadn't done anything. I just
didn't know why me.

When I first got there, I didn't want to deal with anything or anybody. I didn't want to talk to anybody. We had to go through the intake.
I remember being put in diagnostics. They were slapping that lice stuff
in your hair. Everybody was very rude. You have to go through all these
medical examinations before you went up to population. The nurse was
using the same stirrup to examine the women. You didn't see her scald-

ing it. In 1986, the *Ruiz*[1] ruling finally put a stop to it. Now they have to use the disposable kind.

When you were going up to population you had to make sure you walked on one side of the wall. It was unbelievable and I just kept saying to God that I know He did not put me here to do a life sentence for something that I didn't do. Why me? I think that over the years, He's answered that question. I went through the trials and tribulations so that nobody can tell me, "Oh, they lie? We don't do that. The prison system is run this way or that way." Not where I was. I think that I had to live it in order to feel it, in order to come back out and talk about it and educate people about it so that it would make a difference.

For the first year and a half, every time the phone rang in the dorm, I thought it was the call that they had made a mistake and I was going home. I received the first setback when the lawyers did the appeal, and the verdict was affirmed. In that appeal, it stated that the questions of my innocence were raised, but the courts of appeal were only interested in whether they took me to court fairly. I just couldn't believe that. So they screwed me fairly. I couldn't understand how they could even write that. But that's what our court system said, and they're still saying it today. They don't care whether you're innocent or guilty, just whether the procedures went right.

When I went into prison, I was not there to accept a life sentence that didn't belong to me. I was there until I could prove that I had not committed that crime. During that time in prison, I would not lose my dignity, my pride, or my respect. I would give it and I would demand it. I would not get institutionalized. Therefore, I didn't do what the others did. I didn't watch reruns on television. I became a sports fanatic, because if you look at golf, basketball, football, hockey, tennis, whatever the sport might be, that's today, not yesterday. That's not a rerun of what happened. You look at what they're wearing. You look at the way that they're speaking. You look at the commercials, and things that bring you up-to-date on today's technology and whatever, and you get used to what the world is still like.

I call it institutionalized when you know the routine and you automatically respond. For example, when everybody at the table holds up their hand in order to be excused. I was that person that said, "I'm going to get up when the rest of them get up. I'm not going to raise my hand. I'm not going to do that. You don't need for all of us to raise our hand.

The table is through eating. We're just going to get up." I've gotten pulled on the carpet. In order to not have to go through that hassle, I decided that I would not go to chow. I did everything that I could to avoid doing that. I guess three months passed by and I got a pass to come to the major's office. I went up and she said that she needed to talk to me about destroying state property.

By that time, I just wasn't going to be accused anymore of something that I didn't do. I said that I had not destroyed state property and that I didn't know what she was talking about. She looked at me and she kind of smiled, and she said, "You really don't. But what you're going to have to learn is that you are state property." That really pissed me off. She said, "You are state property and when you're not eating, we think that perhaps you're trying to starve yourself and we have to make sure. If I don't see you in that line at least once a day, I'm going to write you up for destroying state property." That's when I realized that I was only a piece of property, a piece of property that belonged to the state.

The most difficult aspect of incarceration was that the officers were trained that inmates were nothing. The inmates are not human, they all are liars, they are not to be believed, and that they are to be treated as such. Women are the forgotten creatures in prison. During the time I was there, if a woman was given fifty years in prison, and man was given fifty years in prison, the man would have paroled two or three times on that fifty and the woman would still be waiting in order to talk to parole.

Also, there is sexual abuse in the prison, by officers and by other inmates. There is physical abuse on the women's unit, the men's unit, all units. When the public is told about it, it's always the inmates who are at fault. That's not necessarily true. I was at the commissary once and I remember an African American sergeant who had come from the male unit. This young lady was angry and acting up. The captain, a White lady, was taking her to segregation. The sergeant was going with them, and the lady was cursing something terrible. The captain told the sergeant to take her to administrative segregation and lock her up. She was still cursing and going on, and the sergeant turned around and asked the captain, "What do you want me to do?" He said, "Do you want me to put her on the wall or put her on the floor? Where do you want me to . . .?" The captain said, "No, I want you to take her to administrative seg [segregation] and lock her up, with no harm."

This was a Black young lady who was doing all the cursing. Was she right? No. But had she charged them in order for them to abuse her? No. However, if the captain had said, "Kick her ass," that man would've kicked her butt. I could not sleep that night without asking him, "If that White woman had asked you to beat that girl because she was cursing, what would you have done?" He said, "Well, I would've had to do my job." I said, "Okay, so you're going to do the same thing to inmates that inmates have done on somebody to get here. There is no difference. But you are not held accountable." It's not that I think inmates should not follow rules. If you are in prison, you know that you're there and there are rules to follow. I simply think that if I don't touch you, if I'm not trying to hurt you, you should not have the opportunity to hurt me simply because I'm an inmate. Punish me, but don't punish me by beating me.

I don't care if you get a two-year or a life sentence, when you come back into society, you're still paying for that crime. When you come back, they don't have to give you a job, they don't have to give you a place to stay. If a person can't find a job or can't find a place to stay, then they're going to end up back into TDC [Texas Department of Corrections]. They are going to survive some kind of way. That's why our recidivism rate keeps going up and up. But they don't tell about the ones that get out and never come back. They tell you about the ones who have learned to play the system and keep coming back.

I made myself a promise, and I made God a promise, that when I was released from that bondage, I was going to spend the rest of my life doing something to help those that I left behind. I was going to create a mechanism that would give them an opportunity not to go back. Through the organization–M.A.S.S.–I think that I've done that. M.A.S.S. stands for Mothers (and Fathers) for the Advancement of Social Systems. I came home and started the organization with Brenda Overton. We're nonprofit and we've been in operation now for ten years. We've helped lots of inmates coming out to find housing and jobs, and to get them started back on their feet. We have a youth program for youth of incarcerated caregivers. We also assist the caregiver with that child. We do outreach. We have educational programs. We make sure that the children get to the prisons to see their parents because we want to make sure that the bond is there. A lot of the caregivers are grandmothers and aunts who have families and cannot afford to take the child to see their parent.

It's frustrating when you come out of prison and you're trying to do the right thing. You look for an apartment, they accept your application fee knowing all the time that they're going to turn you down because you've got an X on your back. A prime example: A young lady came to me, and she had this list of apartments that another agency had sent to her. She said, "Miss Brown, I'm trying. All of these that I've marked have turned me down because of the X." She had gone to sixteen places. She lost twenty-five dollars each time she went. I said, "Honey, just fill out the paperwork." I go out and talk to people and I get apartments to work with me. I screen people and send them to the apartments. So I have a list and send people to the apartments. We help pay the deposit and pay a portion of the rent for the first three months. They have to go through the educational components through the organization; they have to go through counseling. We've helped over a hundred ex-offenders find work and housing.

When I went in, I was stupid enough to believe that I was the only innocent person in prison. When I went in, I was stupid enough to think that I was the only one that had been abused by this system. It wasn't until I lived around them that I realized, "You are no more than they are." Yes, they might have committed a crime, but why? Prime example: A young lady named Margaret who became my friend in prison. She had three or four children. Margaret had been there for eight years before I got there. She had not received one letter from home and had not heard from her children because they were young when she went in. Her mother couldn't read or write and couldn't afford to bring them to see her. Margaret's crime was that she had been to prison once for theft. She didn't have a husband. During the Christmas holidays she did not have any food, didn't have a tree, didn't have anything for her children. As a mother, she went out to steal something to sell it, to get money in order to put some Christmas food on the table. She got caught. Knowing that her children were at home alone, she struggled to get away. She did not have a hairpin. She did not have a knife. She didn't have a gun. But because she struggled to get away, the district attorney was able to take a simple theft and change it into robbery. She got forty-five years! She was abused by this system.

I started to realize that there were different types of abuse. I looked at all of the women who were there for drugs. Black women had never been given any type of treatment. If they had a White counterpart, that person got treatment; they didn't even come to prison. There were others who weren't so innocent, but were abused in their own way. Some of them were coerced by their boyfriends to take a case, or to lie to say that he was at home. The women ended up with fifty years right along with him for actually lying, because they weren't with him when he did the crime.

I have found that African American women and some White women have a habit of accepting their sentence, accepting what happened to them. They just want to do their time and get it over with. They used to tell me I was crazy. "Why did you build yourself for all these let-downs? Don't you know you can't beat the system?" I would say, "I'm not trying to beat the system, I'm trying to prove that the system has wronged me." I continued and, yes, I got a lot of slaps in the face and I got hurt lots of times. When the appeals would come back "affirmed," there's not a hurt like it when it seems like all the walls are closing in on you. But my mother taught me about my foremothers and my forefathers. She said that if they had quit, we would still be in slavery. They figured out a way to meet secretly, to fight for our rights, for our freedom, and others died that we might have the opportunity to read and write. I did not have time to feel sorry for myself. I could read and write and I had to fight for my freedom. And that's what I did.

Centurion Ministries came in and did their investigation, and they found suppressed evidence. *60 Minutes* took that suppressed evidence and did their investigation and found there was no way that it was me and they aired all of it. The appeals court decided to overturn my case based on evidence that they had all along. The district attorney said that he was prepared to take me back to court. I wanted another jury and to be proven not guilty. I was a little bit disappointed when we did not go back to court.

On February 14, 1990, they dropped all charges. Four years later, in 1994, they expunged my record. I had to fight to get it expunged. The state didn't want to be saddled with an admission of guilt. The statute of limitations ran out in two years. By the time I got the expungement, there was an admission of guilt but there was no remedy for a lawsuit from the city, county, or state of Texas. I've never been paid a dime. I've had to work and struggle just like everybody else. I know that nine years, five months, and twenty-four days did one thing: it gave me patience. Over the years, things have always worked out for Joyce Brown. One day, the opportunities that I give others will be worth the nine years, five months, and twenty-four days that I spent in prison.

I I

BETTY TYSON

In 1973, an all-White jury convicted Betty Tyson of killing a business-man. She always maintained her innocence of the charge. In her trial defense and appeals, she claimed that she confessed after being beaten by detectives. After her conviction, one of two teenagers who testified against her signed a deposition that he was coerced into giving perjured testimony at her trial. Other discrepancies existed in the case against her. Her conviction was overturned in May 1998 and she was released from prison after serving twenty-five years. At the time of her release, Betty Tyson was the longest-serving woman inmate in the state of New York.

Betty Tyson

MY NAME IS Betty Tyson. I was born and raised in Rochester, New York. My family was very poor. I lived with my mother, brothers, and sisters. There were eight of us children—four girls and four boys—and I was the second oldest. Only my older sister and myself were the children of my father. The other children had one of four other fathers. I remember going to the store and filling up bags, stealing food, and when we came home, my mother never questioned where the food came from. At the time, I was about eight years old. We were literally starving. We ate peanut butter and jelly sandwiches for dinner and never had any meat. I remember stealing clothes from the stores downtown, so I could have something nice to wear like the other little kids in the neighborhood. After a while, I started stealing for my whole family.

The first time I was arrested, I was eight years old. My nine-year-old sister and I were arrested. My mother didn't know where we were, and when they put our pictures on the news she knew we were downtown. We were arrested for stealing a coat from a store for Mother's Day. We wouldn't talk to the police, so they put pictures of our faces on the news because they didn't know who we were. Nothing became of that case because we were too young. I didn't stop stealing after this whole incident. It felt good to steal, to get by the system and the store owners.

I went to school, but I didn't really pay attention and didn't really learn anything. I was too into playing and stealing. I thought I wanted to be a secretary, so when my mother was able to get enough money together she bought me a typewriter, but, of course, the typewriter just sat in a corner because I just pecked at it and looked at it. My future was already gloomy at that point. I felt like nobody could get out of my neighborhood and nobody could be anybody, because where we lived was so poor and we just stayed there. There was a lot of drinking and pot smoking. We lived across the street from a bar, so we saw this sort of stuff and saw people up late nights, fighting and stuff like that. There weren't any positive figures around and we barely watched TV because we didn't own a TV at that time. Sometimes when we went to see my grandmother, we would watch TV, but we would watch whatever she watched, and only when she watched.

My mother beat us a lot as children. She was very strict and if we didn't do what we were told, we were beaten. When I look back on it now, it was abuse. She would beat us until we bled. It was the only way she knew to punish us when we were bad. But, I still have scars from it—you can see them on my back, like zebra stripes. The beatings never deterred us from getting into the same trouble all over again. I think she really didn't know how to deal with children. She dealt with us in the same way as she dealt with her friends. This didn't change the way I felt about her, though—I still loved her and still do, now that she is gone.

I think I really could have used a mother who listened to me more or was really there for me. When I was little, family and friends teased me all of the time. They teased me because I had short hair, burned thighs, and raggedy clothes. People called me "bald-head," "pickaninny," and stuff like that. That really affected me, and I got in a lot of fights and became pretty aggressive. It was hard on me to come home and get beaten because my mother thought I was the aggressor, when I was defending myself.

My mother was very strict with us. We always had supervision, and if we didn't do what we were told, we would get a beating. My mother wanted us to have a better life, so we didn't have to be migrant workers. She wanted us to get an education, but I stopped going to school when I was about fifteen. At the time, my mother was on welfare, so she had to get the approval of a social worker each time she wanted something. I was sick of it, so I just thought I would get out of there and find a husband.

My parents came to Rochester from Sodus, New York, but originally came to New York from Florida. My father was an only child and my mother was one of sixteen children. When they first came to New York they did migrant work. They picked tomatoes, potatoes, and apples. I didn't want to work, but I ended up in a situation where I was forced to work. When I was young, it was fun. From about age thirteen to fifteen we would go out and pick strawberries, in a gang of kids, just going out and having fun. After I started smoking, one night I lit a cigarette and thought that I had put the match out, but the match didn't go out and my bedspread caught on fire and then the fire department came. The next day I was carted out on the farm and I said, "Well what am I gonna do?" My mother said "You're gonna' pick these two rows here." I looked at her and said, "That's a long row, Mother." She said, "But Betty, we have to eat." I said "Yes, Ma'am." Well I sat there for about twenty minutes and then said "Oh well . . . let me get up." By that time, my mother was halfway up the row. I just thought, "Oh my gosh!

She's picking too fast!" I started eating what I picked. I had my salt and pepper and just started eating the tomatoes I picked—all that I picked, I ate. This guy came by and said, "Are you gonna pick any? Your momma left two rows." I said, "What I'm eating, I'm picking." He said, "Do you want me to pick for you?" And I said, "Yeah!" So he picked for me, and soon he became my husband. I was seventeen.

My husband and I were both seventeen when we got married in October 1965. He was a farm and labor contractor; he had taken over his father's business. After we got married, I moved out in the country with him. That only lasted for about a month, because I decided I didn't want to be married. For me, the marriage was a convenience, something to get me away from my mother. I came back to the city because I missed being in the street. I couldn't deal with being so far from everything. I missed hanging out in the street, going to parties, going to different bars and different clubs. Out in the country, all I did was cook and clean, and really nothing—it was boring. It was after I was back in the city that I became a prostitute.

I always wondered why the people I hung out with had money, because I was the only one who never had any money. Then I watched my friends and I saw them jumping in different cars, talking to different men. I asked them, "Well, what do you all talk about?" They said, "Oh, you don't want to know." I said, "Yes, I do, too." They said, "Well, look, we're working. Look, we sell our bodies." I said, "You sell it?" I was seventeen, and my friends were between sixteen and twenty. I moved in with a family in town. I was so happy to live with them because I didn't have to cook or clean and didn't have to wash dishes; I ate in restaurants, and just did my thing. I was free. They were brought up in the street life, so the family was very different.

When I first got into prostitution, I thought, "Why give it away? Why not sell it?" I was very nervous the first time, and I think he knew it. After about the third or fourth one, I got the hang of it and I was out there all day long. I worked by myself—never used a pimp. The pimps would approach me and I would just say, "You know what, before I'd give you my money, I'd give it to my mammy, because you didn't do nothing for me."

As time went on, I just got deeper and deeper into it. I got robbed a couple of times. The first time, one took my sex and didn't pay me. He held a knife to my throat and I couldn't reach the knife hidden in my boot. After that, I robbed a few tricks, but I never liked doing it because it involved using force and I'm not that sort of person. I knew about the risks. One of my associates had her hand blown off. Some women were cut up by tricks. So, I started carrying my 007 knife in my boot. Even though it was dangerous, it was still exciting and gave me an adrenaline rush.

The pay was wonderful. I really got into a cycle. I'd go out at a certain hour and I was back. I'd go back up to the hotel, take my shower, and just sit up in my room and just shoot drugs. I wouldn't come out until the next day. The next day I'd go downtown and steal some new outfits. I'd take them back to my room, change, and go out and make some money. Then I'd come back and shoot up the money. Then I'd have to go back out again and turn some more tricks. After a while I started stealing larger and more expensive things to pay for drugs. I worked with this guy at a bar. He would take orders from people and I would go downtown and steal what they wanted. We would get a set price for the stuff.

I started using drugs when I was about seventeen. It was around the same time I started prostituting myself. I started with pills, CIBAs, red devils, red jackets, and cough medicine. I think I got into the pills when I was hanging out with the people in my little circle. They just offered me some and I started taking uppers and downers. Later on, I tried heroin. It started when a friend of the guy who was my best friend came in from Brooklyn. We were hanging out in a hotel and he shot up. I watched him shoot up and nod out. I wanted to try it, so I sat right there and waited for him to wake up. I had to try some. When he woke up I said, "Yo, what did you just do?" He said, "Um . . . shoot up."

I told him I wanted to try it, but he was hesitant—afraid that our other friend would kill him if he shot me up. After a while, I talked him into shooting me up. He cooked it up in a little bottle cap, and then drew some up in the syringe. I said, "That little bit?" He said, "Yeah." I told him I wanted more, so he let me draw up some more. Then I told him to hit me. He shot me up and after that, I don't remember anything else. I did remember the high, though. When I came to the next day, in a bathtub full of ice, I was still high. It was wonderful and I just wanted some more. The next day, I took some of his stuff and went down to the hospital and swiped some "works." It was so easy, because every room had syringes and all. After I started, I couldn't stop—I just wanted to get that same high again, but I never could get it. I would just keep on trying.

In 1969 I realized I was addicted. I was arrested and put in jail for a week while I was shuffled to and from court. While I was in there, I had a runny nose and stomach cramps. I couldn't figure out what was wrong—I was so sick feeling, but I wasn't sick. Then this junkie came up to me and said, "Betty, you got a habit." I went and shot up as soon as I got out of jail. It hurt both me and my mother. She would drive around the streets looking for me and then she would pick me up and take me home. As soon as I got home, I tried to get out. I even jumped out second-story windows. Whenever I saw her car, I would run and hide. Eventually, I had to start tricking in different neighborhoods because my mom and family were chasing me all the time. This is when I started tricking White men on Main Street, getting more money. But it is also when I was robbed a second time.

I never encountered too much racism on the streets and with my tricks. But at the county jail, I saw racism. The White women would get to speak to visitors first and for a longer period of time. There were only two spaces for women and their visitors; the rest of the spaces were for men. My mom had to wait about an hour and a half to see me.

The man I was charged with killing died on May 25, 1973. The police picked me up because they thought I was the sort of person who would commit such a crime—I was uneducated, an addict, and a prostitute. I didn't know that the police were doing sweeps, and didn't find out until Saturday because nobody was out on the street. I asked the bartender at the Grill, where everyone was, and he told me the police did a sweep. I said, "A sweep? What'd they do a sweep for?" He said, "'Cause some Cracker died." I just thought, "Oh, well, hey, it clears me." I was just going about my business, cutting some drugs, of course.

I left and went over to a friend's house and when I returned the bartender said, "Yo, they just came by and they had your picture." I said, "Had my picture?" I couldn't believe it, but I thought about it and went over to my mother's house around five o'clock that afternoon. From there, I called the police headquarters and said, "This is Betty Tyson." Instantly, the detective got on the phone. He wanted me to meet him somewhere, but I knew he would try to arrest me if I met him.

The police showed up at my house later on. They kicked down the door and were yelling into the house, "Come out, you Black bitch, 'cause we know you're in here." I hid out at a neighbor's house. The police were tipped off by somebody I knew, and the police chased me and my drug dealer and friend.

When the police arrested me, they started kicking me and beating me. Before the beating began, the police asked me if I wanted to go to the scene of the crime. I said yes, and thought that if they took me there, I could escape and get some drugs.

After I was hauled down to the police station, that's when the beatings started. They wanted me and my codefendant to confront each other. When they brought me back down, they told me that my codefendant was going to tell his side of the story. I said, "Then that'll be the only side you hear, 'cause I don't have a side." They said, "Well, you Black bitch, you know good and well that you got a story to tell." I said, "No, I don't either, 'cause I didn't do anything." The detective said, "Okay, well shut up, bitch." And that's pretty much how they addressed me. They sent in another detective and he came up to me and said, "Bitch, the next time you suck your daddy's dick make sure it's on a Sunday." I said to him, "You know what? Go fuck yourself." I said, "Because we don't have incest in our family. That's what Crackers do." He said, "Well, you lousy bitch," and he jumped up. I said, "Your mammy's a lousy bitch!" He jumped off the table and as he went to hit me I blocked his punch. My hand went around that tie and I started punching him with my right hand, and I guess all hell broke loose, because I was a whipped bitch by then. I was on the floor and they were pulling my hair, kicking, and stomping on me. They did everything to me. My so-called codefendant was standing right there.

At one point they wanted me to sign a statement that they typed up. I refused to sign, and they pulled my hair and hit me on the forehead. At the time I was handcuffed to the chair. Then one would hit me on the neck, then in my chest, and then one would kick me. There were eight of them in the room and they took turns doing different things while my codefendant stood over there and looked at me. They would ask me questions and I would say I didn't do anything and they would beat me again. The thing is, I didn't know the statement said I killed somebody. I thought I had traffic charges from when the police chased me before I was caught.

I didn't realize that I was charged with murder until May 27, the day of my arraignment. I was in shock. I didn't understand how they could charge me with murder when I was home sleeping at the time of the murder. My mom hired an attorney; he wasn't much help though, because he didn't prepare for my trial. I told him about my bruises and all from the beatings by the police and he took a look at them. He left and said he would bring back a camera, but he never did return. He never took the pictures and I only saw him four times around the time of my trial.

My trial took two weeks. I had a jury, but everybody on it was White and male. There was one African American man, but he was shot down by the prosecution. It was hard to sit there and listen to people testify—just lying on the stand. When the trial closed, it was close to Christmas. The judge told the jury that the trial might go beyond Christmas, and that it depended on the jurors, and how much time they took to deliberate. We charged the jury, and they went out, and then came back because they needed more information about some of the evidence. After they were charged I went back to the jail. Around 10 P.M. they called us back into the court and read the verdict. I looked at my mom and she said, "Let's just pray." When they read off the verdict, I just screamed at the top of my lungs. I couldn't believe it—Guilty!

They allowed my family to comfort me for about half an hour. Then I was transported back to the jail, where I just sobbed all night long. My sentencing was February 13. The judge gave me one hundred and eleven years. I thought I would faint. After the sentencing, I was sent to prison. When I first got there, I was bitter. I asked around and found some pills, and I would take those and just sleep all of the time. After a while, I began to think about how I would deal with everything. I just decided that God wasn't ready to kill me yet, so I just needed to go on living my life. I started talking to the older people that were in there and they got me back into the Bible. Over time, I became the person that everybody talked to about their problems. I guess I helped a lot of women, because I received so many letters from families.

I saw a lot of people go crazy in prison. They couldn't take the pressure, the "gayness," the racism, being called Black bitches, and being pushed around by the guards. The guards would treat women according to the manner in which the women carried themselves. If a person wanted to be respected, she had to carry herself in a respectable manner. There were also rapes of prisoners by guards. This was something I never had any problems with, though, because I had a wife that was an ex-boxer and looked out for me. Although, before I was with her, I still got a lot of respect.

I don't think it was hard to express my sexuality in prison. I realized I was bisexual when I first got out on the streets. One of the girls I grew up with was in prison at the same time I was, and we were on the same floor at some point. We started going together for about a year, until she went home and got into drugs. I had six relationships in prison and I still have my second wife. She's still inside, but we are hopeful that she will get out by 2005. Some lesbians experienced harassment from the guards. They would split couples up and put them in different blocks. But, where there is a will, there is a way. People would find ways of meeting up or sometimes the guard friends would arrange meetings.

I was in prison for twenty-five years. One of the hardest things about being in there was being away from my family. Even when I was on drugs, I would visit my family and remained close to my siblings. It was difficult for my family to visit me, but my mother could take the free bus once a month. This made a big difference, but birthdays and holidays were still hard.

There was also some racism in prison. The White women would speak up about something and something would be done about it. But, when the Black prisoners spoke up, their concerns were just swept under the carpet. The guards would also call us "Black bitches." They would say they were just kidding around, but I didn't find it funny.

Things changed as I was there over time. The program offerings were depleted from twenty vocational programs to about five. Vocational programs help people learn skills that they need once they leave prison; they help rehabilitate prisoners. The programs just kept getting cut. We would learn a skill and then work for a quarter a day. The most we made each week was two dollars and fifty cents. Taxpayers want to punish us, but what we really need are prisons that rehabilitate prisoners, teach them a skill and help them deal with their problems.

I was released from prison on May 28, 1998—twenty-five years to the day that I was arraigned. My conviction was overturned because a witness recanted, and it was found that the state withheld exculpatory evidence from my attorney. Right around the time they overturned my conviction, I was getting ready to serve two more years. I was in the prison garden when the call came in. My mother called me and I called her back. She told me the case was overturned, and I said, "For real?" I couldn't believe it. My mom asked why I wasn't excited and I said, "Because, you know what, I just did twenty-five years." I said, "My brain just got conditioned to do two more, because I know I have to do it. So I can't believe what you're saying until I see it." I was sent back upstate to jail in hand and leg irons. They took me in and fingerprinted me, and then I was free.

12

Karen Michelle Blakney

Two federal agents paid $2,800 to a dealer and $100 to Karen Blakney to "cook" the cocaine and convert it to crack. Karen faced a mandatory minimum sentence of ten years because the substance was crack-cocaine. The trial judge ruled that a mandatory ten-year sentence for a minor player like Karen would be "cruel and unusual" punishment. The judge also noted Karen's successful completion of drug treatment. He sentenced her to thirty-three months, the sentence she would have received if the substance were powder cocaine. The government appealed her sentence reduction and the judge was ordered to re-sentence Karen to the mandatory minimum. Ultimately, Karen pleaded to general conspiracy and was sentenced for time served.[1]

Karen Blakney

MY NAME IS Karen Michelle Blakney. I was born in 1960 in Washington, D.C. I grew up in Southeast D.C., where I went to elementary, junior high, and high school. I quit school in the twelfth grade when I got pregnant with my son. Later, I took some courses at Federal City College, but I stopped going there. After I got out of prison, I went back for my GED.

After I dropped out of school I had my son, and then my daughter. Around that time I started getting into the "street life." I started smoking weed and hustling. I was about fifteen or sixteen when I started smoking weed in junior high. The crowd I hung out with, kids from school, started smoking it. They were doing weed, angel dust, and other things. I saw them smoking and just wanted to try it. I would see people out there selling it, so we bought a bag and we started smoking it. We went up on the roof of the building, and then from there we started doing it up there and on the way to school and after lunch. I liked the feeling I got from smoking. It made me happy. It made me laugh and made me hungry. I knew I couldn't stop. My girlfriend and I just couldn't wait until we could get another bag and get high again. I never thought it would get out of control, but now I know it was only the beginning.

I started using cocaine after my son's godmother turned me onto it. I started hanging around her, smoking weed at her house. At first I didn't want to try the cocaine. I thought about the people I saw with all of those sores—I thought cocaine was like heroin. I didn't think cocaine was on the same level as weed and I tried PCP a few times, but never used it again. I didn't like the feeling of it—the high. Once she explained to me that cocaine wasn't the same as shooting dope, I tried it, but I didn't do it for a while after that first time.

I stayed away from my son's godmother for the next six months. At the time, I was about nineteen. I became addicted to cocaine, but didn't realize it at first and didn't want to face it. I felt like I was supporting myself. I was out there selling it and nobody was giving it to me. I started seeing people turning tricks for it, but I never went through that stage. I lied and stole, but I never turned tricks. I sold drugs and stole from my family and kids—I was spending their money on drugs, so really it was like stealing from them. I lived with my sisters and sometimes I'd take something from them. I was really out of control.

During this time I had a job as a nurse assistant. It started off as a summer job. My mom ran the recreation center at the community center. She told us to fill out some forms for a job and I was sent to the hospital. I worked there and some other places, but the deeper I got into my habit, the more I missed work. I wanted to hustle. I didn't have a job, but my kids' father worked; he hustled.

I have nine kids—seven girls and two boys. The youngest is three and the oldest is twenty-four. The first seven kids are by one father and the other two by a second father. I am good friends with them now.

My mom knew I was using drugs and I was addicted. She knew I smoked weed and did coke, but it was at the time when I didn't do it around my mom, and my mom couldn't really put her hands on it. She didn't see me, but I was taking care of the whole house and taking care of all of my brothers and sisters, doing the laundry. I got my sisters ready for school. I took my mom to the doctor and was always there for her. They say I was her favorite because I was always there for her.

There were nine children in my family: seven girls and two boys, with one set of twins. I had an older sister and an older brother. Then I was the third kid, but everybody thought I was the oldest. We all grew up together in D.C. My mom never allowed us to be separated, so we were very close. We all stayed around the house and people would come see my mom, who was like a community mom.

My mom didn't allow men to be around us. She didn't bring men around the house. She taught us not to sit on men's laps, even if it was a brother. I was brought up in a Christian home. My grandmother was very religious. My mother was into Black awareness and taught us morals, principals, and respect. She wanted us to be proud of who we were and wanted us to make the best of ourselves. She told us never to be ashamed to ask anything. She said, "If you don't know something, ask somebody." My mother taught us to respect ourselves as women. She also wanted us to remember that beauty is not only on the outside; it's on the inside too. She didn't want us to make fun of others, but instead think about what that person might have gone through. I've always tried to remain true to the convictions she instilled in me. I don't blame my mom for the things that happened to me. I chose to get into drugs and live the life I did because I wanted to grow up. I just ended up on the wrong path.

When I was a kid, I wanted to be a doctor or a teacher. I wanted to be a teacher because I really liked dealing with children, and I still do.

Now, I work at a clinic. I register the patients through the computer system, and I talk to them. When I think about it, I'm like my mom—a people person, a community mom.

Until I went to prison, I did not really know how much I hurt my family. When I was getting ready for court, I asked my daughter, who was nine at the time, to pray for me. She said "Mommy . . . I'll pray for you, but I pray that you don't come home if you're going to do the same thing." I asked why she said that. She said, "Because it hurts me when you do those things." That was when I realized I hurt my family. When I got out in 1991, I made a real effort to get off drugs and not to sell drugs.

My first drug charge was for possession of cocaine. I think it was in 1987. I jumped bond, and was sentenced on that charge; the drug possession charge was dropped. I was sentenced one to three years in federal prison on the bond violation. Then I was sentenced to probation for three years. I was charged with another cocaine charge, but it was dropped later. Later I was charged in district court with possession with intent to distribute cocaine, but was found innocent by a jury.

The 1991 charge occurred after a major incident in May, but they arrested me in September. I didn't know the co-defendants very well. They came over and wanted somebody else to cook the crack, and at the time my sister was on crack, so that's who they were looking for. They asked me to cook it up, but I didn't want to. When he asked again, I gave in, being the people pleaser. I thought it would just be one time and it wouldn't do any harm, but I ended up doing it twice in a couple of weeks. The second time, they weren't looking for my sister, they wanted me to cook it up for them. They brought some guys with them that they wanted to sell some crack to. They didn't know that the buyers were undercover DEA agents. The undercover agent gave me the drugs to cook up. When I was done, he gave me one hundred dollars, even though I didn't charge him. Later at the district court trial the undercover agents were asked, "Why did you want it turned into crack?" They said, "Because crack carries more time."

There is a skill to cooking crack. You have to know how to bring it back up to weight. Some people have to add more to bring it back up to the weight that the customer is paying for. If you don't do it right you might lose a gram or two. When the agent gave me the cocaine, there was no reason for me to suspect the man was an agent. Everybody in the neighborhood wanted crack. In the Black community people buy it as crack, because if you cook it yourself, you lose some of it. If he had wanted something else, then we would have known right away that he was an agent. The thing is, you can have a kilo of powder and get five years. Or, you can have a kilo of crack and you get 40 or 50 years. I knew this at the time because I'd done time before. But when the agents gave a piece of crack to me I didn't think I was dealing with DEAs, and besides, I didn't know I could get in so much trouble for only cooking it up. I had nothing to do with the sale; I just cooked it up.

I figured that I was arrested because they wanted me to be an informant. They thought they could lock me up and get me to snitch or something. This happens to a lot of women. They get locked up because they were riding along with their boyfriend, and the cops think that if they can get the woman to snitch on the boyfriend, their case will be much stronger. I think a lot of Black women are locked up because they don't know anything. The cops think that the women know something just because they are in the car with the boyfriend, but the boyfriends never tell the women what's going on. The cops wanted me to be a snitch, but I refused because I had morals and principles—loyalty. If I had agreed to snitch, they would have dropped the charges. Instead, I faced twenty years. It wasn't like somebody threatened me, in order to stop me from snitching—I'm just not that kind of person. As far as my family situation, it didn't affect my decision not to snitch and serve time instead.

There were four of us and our cases were consolidated, and each of us had our own attorney. The judge didn't feel that two of us played a major role. I faced twenty years, but the trial judge had a few lawyers from a big law firm investigate the case and determine how involved my co-defendant and I were in the crime. The judge cut my sentence down to ten years. Then, after some more investigation, he cut it down to thirty-six months. The government was mad. Immediately, they said they would appeal my case. In the meantime, I went home, and I came out of the halfway house, and started working and everything. Then, all of a sudden they said I had to go back to prison; the appeals court overturned the sentencing. The trial judge sentenced me again—to the same sentence: thirty-six months. The government appealed again and asked that the trial judge be removed from the sentencing. During this time, I just thought, "Praise God." I knew that God hadn't released me the first time so I could be sentenced a second time. I strongly believed that I would not be put back in again, so much so, that I had another baby. I just treated the situation as another test.

When I went before the next judge, the prosecution said, "In all my thirty years I have never seen anything like this happen." I said, "Maybe in all your thirty years you never met a person that believed that God would work it out." And that is how I left it. The judge asked me how I felt about the situation and I told her that I knew that God didn't make mistakes and that God brought me through. I thank the trial judge, but most of all, I thank and praise my God. The sentencing judge gave me five more years of probation to see if I stayed clean.

I served some of my time in D.C. Then I went to Connecticut for a year, and later to West Virginia for six months. Because I violated probation, I had to serve some time for D.C. So, I did twenty-four months for the feds and eighteen months for D.C. I spent the last six months in a halfway house in D.C. Some of the places were dirty and nasty, but others were nice and clean, not really like a prison. The time gave me a chance to realize I needed to change. I really put my mind to it and my faith in God. I had a baby girl while I was away. My sister took care of her until I came home. She was fourteen months when I got out. Prison was mainly what you made of it. In the federal prisons you have to go to school or work. It's almost like being on a college campus, its not all that bad. When you are in there, you know you were doing the wrong things and destroying yourself. You get to a point where you want to turn everything around.

There are a lot of Black women locked up, but sometimes we do it to ourselves. We want to stick with our men and do what our men say, but sometimes the men want to blame the women. The man isn't thinking about the woman and the woman gets in over her head without any way out until it's too late. A lot of the women in prison have been on crack, heroin, or other drugs. Some of them have been raped and abused by stepfathers, fathers, or brothers. Some of them have been pimped by their own mothers, so that their mothers could get drugs. So you have some women who just didn't care, and just went their own way, but you also have women who were set on the wrong path by those who were supposed to protect them.

For some people, prison presents a chance for them to turn their lives around. For others, it does not do a thing for them, and they spend their life getting out and going back. For so many Black women in prison, they don't even know why they are there. Many of them are babies—young women—that didn't know what was going on. This sort of situation doesn't just happen to Black women. I also met Latinas and White women that had similar experiences that led them down the same path I took to prison. I think we need to build rehabilitation centers where women can live and have visits from family. The violent criminals need to be separated from the women who committed nonviolent crimes. They have to be given a chance to better themselves, and to go to school. I know everyone has different beliefs about religion, but I think getting God into their lives would really make a difference. I think it helps people to have a program to help them turn their lives around. Prison cannot solve all of the problems. In cases where people are in prison for things they didn't do, the people become worse—their bad side is brought out. Particularly with young Black mothers, you have a woman locked up who is a mother of a very young child. The father is already locked up and he is responsible for her getting locked up. The woman won't snitch because the man is the father of her child. The man isn't going to defend the woman because he resents being imprisoned and feels that if he is in there, then there is no reason why she should be free.

I saw my youngest children when I was in prison in D.C., but I didn't see any of my children when I was in federal prison. This was mostly because they didn't have a way of coming to see me. I was in touch with my children, though; I called them. My relationship with my kids is beautiful now; it's a blessing. My drug addiction never came between me and my kids because they knew how strong our relationship was before drugs. When I would get high, they didn't want to be around me. I tried to stay out of their sight and out of the house when I got high, but when the oldest one saw me, he cried. After that I made sure I didn't get high when they were around. When I was in jail, my children wrote to me, even my youngest one, who was six. Even if they mailed off letters without stamps, they always made it to me. It was like the postman thought, "These kids are writing their mother who's in prison." It touched my spirit and heart each time. They always stayed in touch and to this day, they never throw that time in my face.

As I said before, I was raised in a Christian home. My mother instilled her beliefs in me. She would cry out and pray to God, so I knew He was real. So, when I was in prison, I just gave my life to God and I have stayed with Him since I left. For some people in prison, a program helps them get their life back, but for me it was God. The feds put me in a twelve-step program, but when it was my turn to participate, I stood up and said, "My name is Karen Blakney and I used to be a drug addict. Now I am a child of God." The man supervising us said I couldn't say that and I said, "Yes I can, because all God said when I gave my life to Him was all old things have passed away; behold all things become new." My probation officer took me out of the program because she knew how dedicated I was. Religion has helped me overcome a lot because I know that all people fall short of the glory of God. No matter what, God tells us we have to show each other love and respect.

13

Ida P. McCray

Ida McCray lived underground for sixteen years, as a fugitive from law enforcement. After being turned in by her son, she received a twenty-year sentence for her participation in an airplane hijacking. During nearly ten years in a federal prison, she witnessed racism, the increase of African American women's incarceration, and the lack of outside support for women in prison. Since her release in 1996, McCray has worked tirelessly to bring incarcerated women and their children together with prison visits through her organization, Families with a Future.

Ida McCray

I WENT TO PRISON at thirty-six years old, but it wasn't the first time I was incarcerated. I was incarcerated at thirteen years old for being "incorrigible and beyond parental control." Then, the system incarcerated youth for that. I went out with my girlfriend shoplifting. We both got charged with petty theft. For that, they locked me up for a year and a half. I didn't even see my fourteenth year. I had the misfortune of going to the California Youth Authority when they were building a new facility for girls. They of course needed bodies, so instead of sending me home, I was sent to this lock-up facility. They didn't release me until after my grandmother died, my fifteenth year.

At fifteen, I got married to Arnold-Ray Robinson. He wrote me each week I was in juvenile detention. I thought for sure I was "in love." Our marriage was fine, until he went to Vietnam. He said, "I've got to fight for my family name." And I was thinking, "What name does a nigger have? What are you talking about? Your last name is Robinson. That's not your last name." He went to Vietnam, and I became involved politically in the movement here at home. I read a lot about "US." I liked their philosophy. "If it ain't us, it's them." I wasn't an active participating member; I just liked what I read. I wasn't a joiner of any group. I don't like the group thang. I did not have the need to "belong" to any group.

I never joined any of the groups. If I had, I never would have gotten out of prison. When I got arrested, that was the first thing they asked me. That's the reason a lot of women inside right now are walking the circle—the prison compound—because they were part of a political organization. Those women and men are political prisoners. I have many ones I care for that were members of the Black Panther Party, and three decades later, they are still in prison.

After Ray returned, shot up and psychologically messed up, we never got back together. I was about eighteen years old then. I went to Louisiana with a bunch of college students. The then-H. Rap Brown was having trials down in Louisiana, and there was simply so much going on.[1] Living down South for the first time in my life was a big wake-up call. They were blatant about their racism, which was something I wasn't accustomed to.

I went to prison at thirty-six years old after being a fugitive for sixteen years. It was heartbreaking because of my very young children, my mother, and my older children, who I never spent any time with because I was running. In prison, I saw things I didn't want to see among our young people. The failure of our movements was thanks to the outside help of COINTELPRO, the U.S. government's counter intelligence program aimed at many groups during the '60s and '70s.[2]

During those years, I became part of something bigger than I could imagine. There was so much going on in this country. Civil disobedience, protests, street rebellions, and I just could not sit still and go to school. Inside meetings were very hush-hush. There simply were not a lot of questions asked by women to men, and I jumped on a plane thinking I was going to Los Angeles, when in fact, it was headed for Algeria. I became involved when I saw that taking of life could be avoided with my participation.

The plane could not make it to Algeria, so Cuba was the destination. The plane ride was scary. No one was hurt or killed, but my life in those moments changed dramatically. I lived in Cuba for four years. I was a single parent, pregnant with another baby on my hip. In Cuba, there was more community involvement in people's lives than there is here. There isn't the deep isolation of single parenting that you experience in the United States.

Later, I spent some time in the Caribbean. It was real hard to work there because I was considered a "Yankee." I wanted to scream to them and say, "Hey, I am from the diaspora. What happened to international solidarity?" But it was my illusion, not a reality. I wasn't able to survive there, so I came back to the States. That was hard and very dangerous considering the F.B.I. wanted me.

When I came back from Cuba, it was either go to jail or run. To me, it wasn't a choice. I ran. I had a three-year-old girl, born in Cuba, and a four-year-old boy. My mother took my two oldest kids, when I did come back to the States. I always thought the police were going to shoot me any minute. I ran.

English is such a limited language when it comes to feelings. It is hard for me to describe how you adapt to waking up automatically at every sound, rustle, boom, or thump. I was not able to sleep straight through the night as a fugitive, or underground, or in prison. I don't think anyone even imagines what it's like.

Nobody likes being hunted or feeling hunted and having it be a part of your everyday life. Try not seeing your family for a week, or anyone that you know or who knew you. Breaking off all connections is extremely isolating, and after a while you feel like death because you want to live and you live through other people remembering you. You live through other people knowing who you were, what you're about, knowing that you have credibility, or knowing that you don't. Once that community of people is not there, it's like you're just wind, nothing. I remember going to the park and watching people and their families interact. I would sit there (in the park) salivating, thinking, "Oh, my God, how nice it would be to be with a family now. Oh, look at them, they're arguing. Don't they know this is so precious?"

By 1987, my oldest son was staying with me in Sacramento. I came because my mom was having a hard time. She couldn't say it, but I could feel it in her voice. I took my son to live with me in Sacramento; my son and his father. My mom was still living in San Francisco. I felt that if I lived nearby, then maybe I could be of some assistance to her. My son ran away from Sacramento. He said he didn't want to live there, didn't want to wash dishes, the whole thing. He hated the place; he hated his father. I worked as a temp, and it was real important for me to have money to pay the phone bill, because without a phone, you can't work as a temp. My son stole my phone money and went to San Francisco. I went there and took his father with me, and we went looking for him.

The next morning, three of my tires were slashed, and the money was missing out of the glove compartment. I am super panicked because I'm wanted. I don't want the neighbors to see me and call the police on me, and I got three little babies that I'm taking care of at the same time. I tried to use Momma's credit card to get some more tires. When I went back to the house, his father had found him, and he beat him up. "What are you doing stealing?" For the first time, I did not take up for him because he was so wrong. I just said, "How could you do this?" He was sixteen. I told him to go in his room. He jumped out the window and called the police, and that's how I got arrested. He said, "My parents are trying to kill me, and, by the way, my mother's a wanted hijacker."

I never thought it would go down like that. I went back up to Sacramento, to get my car. I put the tires back on my car, and got out of there. Then, at three or four in the morning, boom, boom, boom, there they come, thirty-two officers surrounding the house, terrorizing my younger children, asking me, "Well, who are you? What's your name? Where's your I.D.?" and holding guns over me and my kids. That's how

I got busted, and that's how they took me to jail to start facing the charge for the crime that was committed sixteen years before. Low and behold, don't ever be at the mercy of a teenager who's going through their shit, being rebellious.

It felt like extreme betrayal, and it was extremely painful, extremely. It was like something had taken my heart and just turned it around, and I felt like that for about a year and a half. For about a year and a half I cried every day. I cried for the loss of my younger children. I cried for the betrayal that I felt. Then I cried for the future, because I didn't know what would happen to my mom. Mom survived two heart attacks. It is still painful, and my son and I have lived through it, and he regrets that spontaneous decision. We have reconciled and now he's my ally.

I was found guilty of air piracy. The mandatory minimum is twenty years, and that's what I got. What went through my head then was I was glad I didn't get fifty, but twenty years was a mighty long time. I would miss my children growing, but I was really glad it wasn't fifty. I cried and cried and cried, but I was still really glad it wasn't fifty. My mom and my kids and my sister were all there. My sister is dead now. She was dying of cancer, but she came down there at the trial. I had a barrage of people coming in there testifying against me. She was there to cuss them out in the hallway where I couldn't do it.

Hearing the sentence is like you hear but you don't want to hear it, and you don't believe it, and you don't really understand it. My mom didn't really get it, or didn't want to get it, because it was too much for her to think about. She had all of my children, plus my fourteen-year-old was pregnant.

There is a lot of hype about what people's charge is and how much that charge means. I say over and over, it doesn't matter what the person's charge is, because the charge doesn't make the person. There are a lot of people who are extremely political, who came to prison for social crimes, and could be more political than the people who came in for political reasons. People have to remember people are changeable, and that things change. I've known women to be in prison for shameful things that they wouldn't want to discuss or feel proud of, but who were extremely valiant and forthcoming in fighting for the rights of other women in prison, or taking care of other people. So people's charge doesn't mean much.

When I first started serving the time, I was serving more time than anybody. The first thing you say is, "Girl, how much time you doing?"

"Oh, five." "How much time you doing?" "Three." "How much time you doing?" And every time I said it, "Twenty." Twenty years! Ooohh! It stabbed me every time. Then they were kind of, "You're doing twenty years!" They'd kind of just move away from me. That was in the 1980s, but in the 1990s, when I came out of prison, Black women were bringing in more time than twenty years. Twenty-time didn't sound like shit compared to the women coming into the federal system with a lot of time. I'm seeing girls—and I have to say girls, because they're twenty or twenty-one—doing thirty years, two life sentences, two natural life sentences, sixty years. It's just a horrible, horrible amount of time. So my twenty years didn't sound like shit after that.

I did my time at Dublin. They didn't call it Dublin then; they called it Pleasanton. It was a co-ed prison when I went there. Then in 1989 they shipped the rest of the men out, so they could stuff more women in there. It was a gilded cage. "You see what a nice-looking prison this is. We have flowers and grass." It looks like a college campus, but it's a gilded cage, because no matter how pretty it looks—and there are no bars on the doors where the women are, and you had keys to your own rooms—it's still prison. You're still away from those you love, so it's a prison. People become institutionalized, in their own way. Inmates become like guards and become as inhumane as they are. They say negative things, do negative things, to each other. To me, that's what being institutionalized is about. You can get used to anything. But all of the negativity does *not* have to be accepted.

There is a lack of support for the women in prison. I know there are many men who don't have visits, but the whole society's attitude is, "Stand by your man." You see women with their babies, and they were fighting to get up there and the visiting room was full. When the men left the prison and there were just women there, the visiting room was barely ever full, ever. We're replaced in society. Not only women are replaced, Black women are replaced. If you're in a relationship, nine times out of ten, you will be replaced within a year, if that long. Year after year, you see people get sick, and you see women getting cancers and this, that, and the other, and nobody's really addressing it.

We have to extend our homes. With the end of welfare and food stamps, where in the hell are women going? "You don't have a bed? Come on." My mother comes from the South. They made pallets and you lived as a community. People lived together, and it wasn't even a question of sharing space, you just did it. But now, since everything is so broken up here, people don't think about that. They really should, because that's the only way they're going to be able to come out of this, is by some community, and we have to start building some community. There was no Black community to take over the raising of my kids when I fell. There was no Black community to take over for other women when they're out to lunch. We need this community, and we have to somehow figure out how to establish it.

Some of the worst moments when I was inside were with family shit. When my mother was having a heart attack, it would just kill me. It would just kill me inside. When my daughter ran away and I didn't know where she was, I couldn't call because in federal prison, you have to have money to call. Those who had money could call, and those who didn't, oh well. My daughter was twelve when she ran away. She got in a fight with her older sister and she ran away. I got my pen and paper and I wrote, wrote, wrote everywhere, and I found someone with open arms who took my daughter. Those were hard times, but that was a much better situation for her. Now she's in New York going to college.

The other thing that is difficult to endure is sickness, if there's something wrong. For years, I had bleeding and I didn't know what in the hell was wrong with me, but I did not trust going to the doctor. You have no rights, because you are the property of the feds. They don't have to explain to you what they're doing. And they didn't.

I'm still doing the twenty years of my sentence. I did half. I'm doing the rest out on parole. You may not see it, but I got a ball and chain. It's very limiting for me because I can't go out of the vicinity without getting permission. I was released in March of 1996. I was fortunate because I could've done more time, and I really came out just in time to get pieces of my family. I sat with my aunt who was dying from cancer for the last ten months of her life. If I hadn't been home, she would have gone to this old folks' home. So I came out just in time. She didn't have any children and I was the only one who was there for her, so that was really special. It was something I'd never done before, sit with the dying. It was a privilege.

Families with a Future helps to connect children with women who are serving long-term sentences, who would not otherwise have a visit. It's very hard because of money and not knowing how to get the money. It's hard, because of working with families who don't care whether or not the prisoner has a visit. The problem is, a lot of women give up.

They don't want to keep fighting, for whatever reason. I can only probably do ten or twelve visits a year.

I started this as soon as I got out. I work all day and night. It's an
ongoing thing. It's not something that you just leave alone at five o'-
clock. I had a lot of problems learning this nonprofit scene. I think that
a lot of women come out with a lot of fantastic ideas, and don't have any
help. If you don't have that help, you can't do it. If I didn't have any
help in my living situation, I couldn't have done it. I was fortunate. I
came out and I had a commune of people waiting for me. "I have a job
for you." That made the difference in me being able to help someone
else.

We got our first grant this year, $7,100. That will take care of some
visits. I am also going to send some kids to summer camp. You can't
erase all the stuff, but sometimes you can try to put a little light in their
life by exposing them to other ways of being, other people, and other
things. Two weeks ago, I just brought in two children from Arkansas
who lived in an orphanage, who only listened to Christian music, only
saw two movies all year, and hadn't seen their mother in almost three
years. They were just so grateful for every little thing that I did. It was
hard because they were raised in a racist community. I just hope that
maybe, that in seeing other parts of the world, seeing other people,
maybe it would open up their hearts. If someone wanted to drag another African American down the street, they would stand up to it.
They can't help the environment where they've grown up.

I get the stories, the mother writes me; she needs to see her children.
It's a process. It takes several months. I had one case that I wasn't able to
help at all, and that was a woman in New York whose one kid was deaf.
He was with one family member, and the other kids were with another
family member, and the two family members couldn't get together to let
the kids come. It's hard writing the prisoner back, but they know their
family better than I do. I try to keep my foot into the prisons here, so they
know who I am and tell other women. They're your greatest allies. The
administration generally doesn't care, but I have had a couple of officers
call the organization asking if I could assist in visitation.

We need to help women in transition. Women need a place to go.
Sometimes it's very hard for me to go back to the jails, but I believe it's
important for the women. I believe it's important for the children.
Sometimes you've got to walk through fire to get to the other side, so I
think about it, but I don't dwell on it.

14

Millicent Pierce

After serving time for the manslaughter of an abusive husband, Milli-
cent Pierce was released in 1996 and began to serve the community. She
began a program called "Count the Cost," a domestic violence preven-
tion program. After seeing how many women in prison are victims of
violence in relationships, she knew she had to be a part of the solution.

Millicent Pierce

I'M FROM LOS ANGELES, but I've lived in Georgia since 1979, off and on. I came to visit my brother when he was in college and I stayed. My first marriage was to a very young man. I have two teenage children from that marriage, my daughter and son. They live with their father, and I live around the corner from them. When I went to prison, they went to live with him, and they just continued to live with him when I got out in 1996. He's stable and I'm trying to rebuild my life. So I really love and appreciate him for just being a good father and a stable influence on their lives and mine.

I was responsible for my first divorce. I left that marriage, so I had guilt over that. My mother had married five times. She had three different children by three of her men, and none of those five husbands were any of our fathers. So I didn't want to follow in that same pattern of marrying and divorcing, and having different children by different men. I was very conscious of that.

Three years after my first marriage ended, I married my second husband. He was a psychiatrist. We met in 1988, and we married after three months. He was a wonderful man, creative, and funny, just a great guy all around. But I didn't know that he was a drug addict and had abusive behavior.

I was working and going to school when we met. I was studying to be a medical secretary and surgical nurse. He had finished his residency and had gone into private practice. So I fell right in with that relationship and began working with him and supporting him. He said, "Marry me and you won't have to work and struggle." He said that I could stay home and take care of the kids and he'd help me. It was just such a wonderful offer; it was just so hard to refuse.

We had gotten married on Valentine's Day, and the violence started shortly thereafter. His tirades and tantrums were over little things. I tried to calm him down and smooth things out, but it was a damned if you do, damned if you don't situation. It didn't matter if I was nice or if I argued about whatever the issue was, or if I didn't say anything at all. It was still just conflict.

Another problem was that he was always psychoanalyzing me, talking about my past and my guilt and my shame from my issues. I would listen and rationalize the things he said, which a lot of times were very good; but a lot of times, they were completely off base. You couldn't tell him that he was wrong about anything. I mean, he was a doctor and he knew what he was talking about. I was a high school dropout with a GED, so I certainly didn't know what the hell I was talking about. Sometimes he would say that; "What the hell do you know?" There was a lot of psychological and emotional abuse in the relationship.

I didn't listen to my intuition, and I did not read the signals, because there were signals all along. He was smoking reefer and drinking. He justified it as recreational. He would say that he just needed to release some stress. I didn't realize the enormity of his addiction. Addictive behavior leads to all kinds of other destructive behaviors and bad choices, and that impacts your relationship. I was trying to hang in there with my man and put up with his stuff and love him.

I was trying to love and be patient and kind, and all those wonderful biblical virtues that we're taught to be. That's why I teach the Count the Cost program now. Count the Cost—is this worth it? I found myself constantly compensating or overcompensating to my detriment. I learned how not to do that in a relationship now. That's a big lesson for a lot of women.

I think that he beat my self-esteem down so low, not that it was already at a high level at any given point. Even though I'm an attractive woman and I'm pleasant enough, I've got issues, too. I think that he did such a number on me psychologically, emotionally, and physically; it was just a recipe for disaster.

The original charge was murder. They offered a plea bargain, but I said no. I would rather go to a jury and have them convict me than to just admit it and be found guilty. I believe they offered me ten years for voluntary manslaughter. When I was convicted, they gave me twelve.

I didn't plan to do it. The jury even understood it. They said that they understood everything that happened to me. They knew that he was abusive and there was a whole history of it and all kinds of documentation. Nevertheless, they understood everything except the second shot. I shot him once in the chest and he was falling towards me. I thought he was going to fall on me, so I jumped off the bed and he fell. I thought he was getting back up, but the medical examiner said his movement was involuntary. I shot him again and they said that I killed him in cold blood, execution style. So, if it weren't for the second shot, I would have walked. But, I'm glad I didn't, because the enormous responsibility that I felt for having taken another human being's life was just too much for me to bear.

I had suicidal ideations up to the last day of trial. I felt that I was a life-giver. I'm a mother, I'm a woman; I brought life into the world. I killed another woman's son. Regardless of the circumstances, I had killed somebody. So having served time in prison was good for me because I needed to reconcile it. If you steal something or break it, it can be replaced or paid for, but you cannot replace a human life if you take it. That's why I'm really glad that I did that time. I spent four years, and it was long while I was doing it, but in hindsight, it was a mere four years. It was good for me.

Plus, my children understand, and they have a keener sense of justice too. If you do something, you have to be held accountable. In the course of feeling and reconciling, I was trying to deal with it on the highest level possible. I quickly tried to get out of the blame mode. I didn't need to blame the judge and the D.A. and the jury, because those people were not responsible for the choices I made in that relationship.

My attorneys came to see me in prison, and said that they were so sorry that they lost my case. I had already transitioned to a higher level. I said, "You didn't win my case, but you didn't lose it, because I'm here for a very important reason, and I need to be here." It wasn't because of him, actually, I need to be there for my own stuff.

I had two attorneys. One of them was a personal friend, who was a criminal defense attorney and a real irritant to the system. He took my case pro bono. He is wonderful and I love him. The second attorney was my neighbor. I didn't know anything about him, so when he came to see me in jail a day after it all happened, I asked what he was doing there. He said he was an attorney. He said not to worry about money, which I didn't have. Both of them came together to represent me. I think they did a good job. You never can predict the judge or the jury on how these things will go. Some women are acquitted quickly and easily, and others are convicted.

A lot of women's groups attended the trial. Here's the thing, I used to be a nude dancer and a call girl, and I met him under those circumstances. I met him in a club. I was working in a nude club, supporting myself by working and going to school. Therefore people knew that he had married this woman of ill repute. A lot of people were interested in advocating for me, but they weren't quite sure if it was politically correct to stand up for me because I was one of *those women*. Can you rape a prostitute? Can you abuse a woman like that? Once you have those stigmas, a lot of times people don't want to come help you because they figure you're getting what you deserve.

When I heard the verdict, I was suddenly flushed with a hot wave. I felt faint. They wanted to immediately escort me out, but I clung to the table for a minute. I had to absorb that. I needed some closure or something, so I hugged my attorneys and then they ushered me out. I looked at my family and they looked at me. Everybody was crying. Everyone was sad and bewildered.

Jail is hell, and that's where I began to see the wretchedness of the human condition. I understood then that everything going on in our jails and prisons is a microcosm of what's going on in society. I thought I understood social issues before I went to prison, but that's where I really began to get the big picture. It was so awful, the stench, the issues, the crimes, the struggles, the constant cursing and fighting, and phone calls to get bail, to find an attorney, and to find out the legalities of your case. There was constant cursing and fighting, and all the things that happen on the outside, 24 hours a day. Women were detoxing and there were health problems like TB and AIDS. Every conflict and drama goes on there.

After I was transferred to the prison, they took me to a minimum-security facility, and it looked like a beat-up old army barracks. They were just a bunch of trailers that were put together with a barbed wire fence around them. This place was in the middle of a glen or pasture. It was no man's land. I saw cows out there grazing, and I said to myself, "Wow, this is interesting." There was a nice cool breeze coming in. At that moment, I found a profound peace. There was a profound peace that came over me, and I felt as though God was saying to me, "I got you, honey; it's going to be okay." From that point on, I didn't resist the whole experience. I didn't fight, I didn't blame, I didn't externalize.

I wasn't mad at anybody. I realized, I had to figure out, how did I get myself into this mess, and more importantly, how am I going to get myself out of it. Then I began to work on myself. I started studying. I took some college classes, and I worked in the law library and began to study law. I immediately studied the homicide statute to understand the difference between murder and manslaughter. I learned about the terms for homicide and the difference between first degree and second degree murder. Now I understand the differences and why there are varying sentences for varying crimes.

I would see women who had the same type of scenario, an abusive relationship, yet I had a voluntary manslaughter conviction and this woman had a life sentence. So, I questioned why she got life and I got manslaughter. I looked at disparity in sentencing and questioned that.

As I got to know the women, I started to consider things differently, on a spiritual level. I learned that we have to work on our stuff individually. It is a spiritual thing. There's more to it than the judge, the jury system, and the White man. It goes beyond that. I think about the many ways that we are in bondage, and how it took me going to prison to get free of my thinking, because I didn't have the distractions and other problems to deal with. To me, prison was easy, but life is tough. In prison, you get up, you do what they tell you to do; it's a routine. It's not nice there, it's not pleasant and it's not comfortable, but you don't have to think. I took advantage of it by reading all the books that I wanted to read, and by working on my body and exercising.

The common denominators in women's experiences were violence and abuse in relationships, and substance abuse. Of course, there was economic deprivation. There were Whites and other ethnic groups, but the majority that I saw were African American women. It doesn't mean that we commit a higher ratio of crime; it's just the disparity in sentencing. The White girl gets the probation and the sister gets ten years. It's the same with the brothers. As women in prison, though, we're all the scum of the earth, we're throwaways.

If you commit a violent crime, you have to go to prison. But for nonviolent offenders, more community-based treatment is essential. First of all, it's cheaper. Second, it helps keep families together and helps women work on the issues in a healthier environment. Usually, when people go to prison, they come out more bitter and with greater disrespect for authority. They don't come out healthy. We must teach citizenship and what it means to be a member of the community.

I maintained contact with people on the outside basically through letter writing and collect phone calls. My children came, thank goodness. They came at least once a month through AIM (Aid to Incarcerated Mothers and Children), Sandra Barnhill's program. Sandra gave me love. I didn't know this woman from Adam's housecat. I found out about her program and I wrote, and she sent me a manual on prison and women and parental rights. I wrote a couple of letters and I signed up for the program. She hooked up with my first husband, and she would go and get my children, and bring them to the prison on the second Saturday of every month. Nobody wanted to take a two-hour-long drive one way, spend a couple of hours, and come all the way back. It's a burden on families. Many people don't have transportation, or someone elderly is keeping the children, and a lot of women don't even get to see their children when they're in prison. Sandra's program tries to help keep families together while Mom's in prison, because she's usually the primary caretaker, and when she goes to prison, Dad ain't even there. The grandmothers, we call them the guardian angels of foster care, happen to be responsible for taking care of the children.

I was released in 1996. We started our organization, Count the Cost, in 1994. Our warden allowed us to start our program while we were still in prison. She allowed us to do groups, and she brought in counselors and therapists to do some work with the women. Our group went to group homes and alternative schools. It was like *Scared Straight*, with twenty women who were there for different crimes. You can hardly scare kids these days. You have to talk and deal in real terms. Somebody has to help them process their issues and look at consequences of not making smart choices.

Then the new warden came on board and stopped the program. We got out in 1996 and dove right into it. We have to figure out ways to get funding and things like that, so that's the challenge of nonprofit work. But we love what we do, and we always get a great response. We're developing our own curriculum so that we can reach people effectively.

My advice to women is to know thyself and be true to thyself. We must know who we are as divine creatures, because if we're rooted and connected spiritually, that makes the path straight for the other stuff.

15

Joyce A. Logan

Joyce Logan was previously incarcerated in the Texas State Prison system for fifteen years as the result of a conviction for aggravated robbery. This was during the time when changes resulting from the Ruiz litigation were being implemented by the federal courts and when those changes faded and disappeared.[1] Unfortunately, the system reverted to the conditions prior to the decision. For example, Joyce and other female inmates encountered harassing pat searches by male officers, and the inmates initiated a lawsuit to end that procedure. Joyce also faced a very difficult transition in reentering the community after making parole. She is an advocate for education and rehabilitation and is opposed to the current system of punishment.

Joyce A. Logan

I AM FIFTY-SIX years old and grew up with my parents, six brothers and one sister. My father worked as a porter all his life, cleaning doctors' offices in North Dallas. My oldest brothers and I would sometimes go to work with him, and as I remember, this was my first experience with a vacuum cleaner. My mother was a homemaker and I had certain responsibilities to help care for my younger brothers and sister. My mother was a very generous lady, she loved cooking and sharing food with our neighbors. Everyone knew her, loved her, and called her "Sweets."

Apart from being one of the fastest track runners in junior high, school was not a good experience for me. I did not value education at that time. I was a little slow in learning and I don't remember anyone sitting down with me to make sure that my homework was done or identifying reading or spelling problems. Although my mother taught in elementary schools prior to being married, she somehow lost sight of the value of an education and failed to stress its importance. I shot hooky a lot. I finished eighth grade and maybe was promoted to the ninth, and that was it for me in public school.

At a very young age, I set myself up for a troublesome teenage life. I experimented with alcohol and cigarettes, which I took from my daddy. This led me to Juvenile Detention and Reform School at the age of sixteen. I was sent to Reform School for truancy. The education I got there made me "street wise" even before I had been exposed to "the streets." Reform School was just hearing and learning about everything that was illegal and unacceptable in the real world. For example, I never smoked marijuana or used drugs prior to going to Reform School.

A year later I returned home and knew that I needed to work. I tried several jobs, yet had no goals, direction, or motivation. My father continued to work to support the family; however, the invasion of alcoholism caused many of his hard-earned efforts to be tainted and surrounded by drunken evenings and fights with my mother. I saw a lot of violence, fighting, and alcohol drinking, not only between my parents, but my uncles—my mother's brothers—also fought a lot between themselves. In 1976, my father passed away after suffering from alcohol withdrawal and other complications.

My oldest brother was twenty-six when his girlfriend and her brother killed him. It was 1963, the same year that President Kennedy was killed. I was nineteen and my brothers and I wanted revenge for my brother's death. We swore that we would kill her, so we looked for her and her brother. Once we found her, we went into the apartment where she was in a pitiful state. Rather than revenge, we sympathized with her when we recognized that my brother's death had taken its toll on her as well. She sobbed, "I didn't mean to kill him." I guess that's when you know what's in your heart and what you are capable of doing and not capable of doing. We had all these emotions and feelings of hatred, but when we came face to face with this situation, our inner strength and compassion kicked in. At that moment we were able to turn and walk away.

In an attempt to recover from my grief, my mother sent me to East Texas to live with my aunt. Upon my return, there was a forgery check ring going on and I got involved in it as a way to make money. Needless to say, we were busted and I was sentenced to five years and six years probation. I was sent to the federal prison. While there, I kept trying to get an education but I felt I couldn't concentrate or just wasn't smart enough to learn. It took me a long time to complete my high school education, and I eventually did.

After serving five years in prison, I came home and tried to get work here and there. Again, with no goals, support, or motivation, I had little to rely on. My worst nightmare happened and I developed a heroin habit. I didn't realize it, because of the lack of knowledge I had about the drug. When I missed using it for one or two days, I thought I was sick with a cold or flu. Unfortunately, I was strung out and that led me to state prison.

I was released from state prison in 1976 and paroled to the Salvation Army Halfway House. I did well while residing there and was recognized for my success. I was offered a job and worked there for several years as a drug counselor. I was through with heroin and to this day have never used it again. I took my job very seriously, working with the desk and monitoring clients, some ex-offenders, which enhanced my spelling and gave me a sense of self-confidence. While there, I was able to act as an advocate for the clients and those who could not articulate their needs.

In the early 1980s, I decided to work for myself. I did interior and exterior residential painting, and I was doing okay. Then, in 1981, I lost my mother unexpectedly. She had diabetes. She passed away in her sleep. Behind the scenes it was clear to me that alcohol abuse played a part in her death. Her death was really hard for me and I wasn't able to function or work. I had no idea that I was speaking to her for the last time the night before she passed away. I started drinking beer and taking Valium, just trying to escape it all. Everything was beginning to crumble and fall apart. I lost my home because I stopped working and was on the verge of losing those that loved me, especially my best friend. When I lost my mother, I felt that if I didn't grieve for a long time and if I didn't hurt every day, it meant I didn't love her. I couldn't eat or sleep, I went from 135 pounds to 99 pounds in a matter of weeks. My best friend pointed out to me that I wasn't living for myself, and once I could grasp that, I would let my mother go.

Unfortunately it was too late. My grief and mood-altered state of mind had claimed its mark. I took part in a robbery that led to my arrest. I was charged with aggravated robbery. This means I had a gun. What a lie to be told and read throughout.

The officers were mean and rough when they searched under your breast, between your legs, thighs, and crotch. When male officers came into the women's dorms, they also did searches. We began to complain and filed grievances to no avail. Joyce Ann Brown, the founder and president of M.A.S.S., previously had been released from prison and got involved. This was one of the first things that she did for the Texas prison system as a whole. She and her lawyers negotiated with the state to stop the procedure. It was supposed to stop throughout the system, but to this day that was never the case.

When I went before the parole board, I was feeling very negative because I didn't think they were asking relevant questions and that they had predetermined that I wasn't going to be granted parole. It wasn't long, however, that I learned that I had in fact been granted parole. This was the highlight of my day. I started dreaming and planning to go home. I was released in November 1997.

After fifteen years in prison, I faced the challenge of my return to society. It was very, very scary. A lot had transpired. The city had changed a lot. Freeways are running through the neighborhood where I grew up. My old schools had been torn down, landmarks, theaters, and favorite barbeque hangouts were gone. Technology has changed so much that I didn't even know how to place a long distance telephone call. I had to learn how to use the microwave, not to mention a pager or cell phone.

Initially, I worked with Joyce Ann Brown at M.A.S.S. After that I went to work at a law firm. There were four attorneys in the office and

I worked as a receptionist. I learned a great deal from them; they are remarkable people. They knew my background and helped me through the technology transition, including paying for me to attend a computer literacy course. A stepping-stone for where I am today. Working with real "free world" lawyers surpassed all my dreams and job expectations. My interest in law started before I went to prison. During my trial, I felt that I was being railroaded so I began going to the County Jail law library. I didn't know my way around and had a difficult time reading the books. But I kept at it. When I arrived in prison, I found that some people knew even less than I did when it came to writing a letter to an attorney, filing a legal document, or filing a grievance to complain about prison living conditions or other unfair treatment.

Later, I decided it was time to explore. I wanted to be self-employed and started a cleaning service. I began doing subcontract work for home builders, private homes, and offices. This led to a position with one of the home builders as an administrative construction superintendent, which is my current job. This job is harder than any job I had in prison. The patience and tolerance I acquired in prison has enabled me to endure the multiple demands and responsibilities I face on a daily basis. I am an African American woman working in a field mainly reserved for Caucasian males.

I want people to know that African American women are very much discriminated against in the Texas prison system. It's real there and here at home. I want ex-offenders to know that they can overcome that discrimination with a lot of determination. In prison, when *Ruiz* was alive and well, and when the federal courts were monitoring the prison system, there had to be racial balance in all jobs and living areas. I don't believe that is the case in prison today, and I don't believe the federal courts are monitoring such things in this "free world" today.

Our society needs more alternatives to prison. We are incarcerating ourselves and prison is not the answer to all our criminal problems. The education of prisoners has all but stopped in prisons. I believe that a better education system, and a better understanding of ourselves will reduce even our most hideous crimes.

Education has become very important to me. If you have one hundred inmates and you educate twenty-five, there will be less recidivism and probably more productive citizens. So, I ask, what percentage of uneducated and poorly understood prisoners do you want released back into society?

16

Donna Hubbard Spearman

Donna Hubbard Spearman regained control of her life after several in-
carcerations in state and federal institutions for offenses primarily re-
lated to her drug use. She became an evangelist and started the organi-
zation Revelation Seed, which provides transitional housing and edu-
cational and employment skills to recently released incarcerated
women. The mother of seven children, she offers piercing insights about
her own life, her relationship with her family and children, and the so-
cial dynamics that affect African American women in prison and
throughout American society.

Donna Hubbard Spearman

I WISH I COULD SAY I came from a terrible family and had a terrible upbringing. I didn't. I came from what we'll call middle poverty. There is high poverty, middle poverty, and low poverty. I came from a middle-poverty family. I grew up in Pittsburgh, Pennsylvania. I had a pretty great childhood by all standards and purposes. However, there was the underlying alcoholism and the violence in my family.

We watched the violence that my mother experienced. One of the things I learned growing up in that environment that I didn't acknowledge then, but that I acknowledge now, is that anything that everybody does and nobody talks about is considered acceptable behavior. Twenty years or thirty years ago, that was how it was with domestic violence. Everybody did it, nobody talked about, so it was acceptable for that kind of behavior to go on. I also was sexually abused by a relative. Although there was some denial in my family, I know that it happened because I know what I remember.

Everybody's goal was to marry somebody, but I wanted to go to college. My mother had become a Muslim. She joined the Nation of Islam. Muslim girls didn't get educated; we got married and had babies. There was such a struggle for me to do that, to even talk about wanting to go away to college, and going out. That was out. I could leave home if I married somebody, but I couldn't leave home to get an education. So I ended up leaving home and marrying somebody who was twice my age. I was sixteen. We didn't even know the man. A week before I married him, we didn't know him.

I had a child by him. By the time I was twenty, I had three children by two different Muslim men and I realized that I was the most unhappy person in the world. The first one was emotionally abusive. The second one was physically and emotionally abusive. So, at age twenty-one and twenty-two, I found myself with children and very little education. Even then, I had a high motivation level. I was always motivated to do something and I knew that I always wanted to do something. So, I became a flight attendant, with three children.

At that point, I had left the second Muslim husband, had gone out on my own, and was trying to support my children. I was scared to death; I had been on welfare for most of my life at that time. I got a job at the airport and eventually was accepted as a flight attendant. Well, my life broke open. I was a flight attendant and had a great job, but I also had these children. I was in no way prepared to be a parent. I can talk about these things now and I can say, I loved being a mother, but I hated being a parent. It was more than I could tolerate because I didn't know how to do this thing, and I hadn't lived my own life. I'm the oldest of eight children and then I became a mother at sixteen. I had never lived my own life, I had never lived out on my own, with no responsibilities. Those years from sixteen to twenty-one are when a young girl finds out that she has her own identity and begins to think for herself. I never had that. I think I wrestled with that all those years and in the process neglected my children.

I can't say that drugs were the reason that I neglected my children. It was a whole life-style, a pattern that led me to using drugs, because I would say today that using drugs was not—is not—the problem with most women's lives. It's whatever process of thinking put us to where we think we can use drugs and live a normal life. It's impossible. But, I started using drugs. I was introduced to drugs because the life-style I started living as a flight attendant was very fast paced. A baseball player introduced me to using drugs on a much more sophisticated scale. I realize now that my drug use and that life-style cost me my job as a flight attendant.

At age twenty-three, I was raped again. At that point, a lot of stuff went through my mind. Most of it was that I put myself in that position because of my life-style and I never came forward to have anything done to him because I felt guilty. I repeated that later on in my life with the men that I became involved with, even down to where I was a prostitute. I became a prostitute in Los Angeles in the early 1980s.

I became promiscuous, and then when I started using drugs, I was promiscuous with a purpose, and that was to support my habits. When people say prostitution you think of one thing, but I understand prostitution as something totally different when you become an addict because before the addiction most of us are promiscuous. It's a life-style that we start living. Then you become promiscuous with a purpose and that purpose is to support a habit. By then, I had left my children, two of the children, in Washington, D.C. I had the other two children with me and literally began a transient life-style. I thank God I left the two in Washington, D.C., even though it was very hard for them, and in their minds I abandoned them. I now realize it was the best thing I could've done with them. I should've left all of them there. They would've been safer. The children were with my ex-husband's mother and my aunt—my mother's sister, my maternal aunt. They did the best they could with my children.

I lived like a transient and up until that point, I had been arrested on catch-as-catch-can things. I would be let out a few hours later for bad checks. The interesting thing is, by the time I moved to California the last time, when I was arrested, I had a habit but I don't think anyone ever recognized it. If they did, it wasn't as important as incarcerating me. I was arrested twenty-seven times and no one ever recommended drug treatment. Never!

Never drug treatment. Never. I didn't even know what drug treatment was. I had no idea. I didn't have a clue. When people started talking to me about it, it was 1987–88. This was through the period in Los Angeles of prostitution, heavy, heavy, heavy drug use, and a lot of violence. I had been beaten several times beyond recognition by men who I had picked up, or who had picked me up as a prostitute, men who were my friends, or who I thought were my friends.

I was so steeped in that life-style that I had stopped communicating with my family because I didn't want to bring them into it. I might call my mother every once in a while, but I had no other contact with them because I didn't want to drop them into what was happening to me. I lost the children, the last two children. I had taken them out in May 1986 and left them in a hotel. I went to go and work the streets and buy some drugs. When I came back the police had come and gotten them. The hotel had called them.

My daughter was born in 1987. I was addicted to cocaine during my pregnancy with her. Like I said, I was arrested and arrested and arrested and released and arrested and released. I would do three months, three weeks here and a month there and this went on and on. I was never sent to drug or substance abuse treatment, ever. But it was obvious by the arrests, where I was and how the arrests were done that I was steeped in an addiction. I needed help, but no one ever recommended that help. The interesting thing is that in the community I was in, nobody ever came out and told me about Jesus, either. Here I am today an evangelist. That's why they don't really like me most of the time because I often remind people in the church of what our real responsibility is, and how the church has been the last of the institutions to acknowledge the sick.

California was where I lost my identity, in Los Angeles. I lost my identity, who I was. I was ashamed of who I had become and forgotten who I was. I was too ashamed to go and get help and too proud to see I needed it. The last time I was arrested, the judge in the court said to me, "I would let you go, now, because we really don't have anything against you." It was a big drug sweep. I happened to be in the wrong place at the wrong time. But the judge said, "We're not going to let you give birth to a crack baby, so I'm going to put you somewhere." Now, anyone else would say that would be a place for substance-abuse treatment. Well, that treatment turned out to be a hospital bed in a women's hospital in downtown Los Angeles, with a chain to my ankle that would allow me to get up and go to the bathroom. I had no visitors, no television, nothing. I was allowed nothing to read. I stayed in there until my baby was born. She was born two months premature because of my addiction, and I remember very well that both of us almost died in giving birth to her. She was only two pounds and ten ounces. I call her my miracle baby. We both did survive.

When I gave birth, I wanted out. I wanted my baby, and I wanted my life. So, as sick as I was, I gave birth to her on that Friday, and I begged the marshals to take me back to the jail on Saturday or Sunday, so that I could go into court on Monday, go before that judge so that she could release us. That is exactly what happened. I went into the courtroom. The judge said, "I understand where you have a beautiful baby girl." Then she said, "I want you to go and get your daughter, and I don't want to see you in my courtroom ever again." My daughter was premature and could not leave the hospital so I left the courtroom and went back to the jail.

They released me in the middle of the night. I would get on the bus with my hospital wristband, and say, "I just got out of the hospital. I don't have any money." The bus driver would let me ride back to Venice, which was the only area I knew. I would walk the streets. I had just had a baby. I couldn't work. And I remember very well that no one that I knew would take me in, no one that I had been getting high with and that knew me very well, would allow me to come in. Four days later, they let me take my baby. My mother paid for an airplane ticket. I went to my mother, trying to save my life, and my baby's life.

I relapsed within four months. I still didn't know what drug treatment was, but I went into one-on-one therapy with a woman and that helped me to at least look at the fact that I was an addict. I went to NA meetings. I registered for school at the university. I was really working towards trying to get my life back together. I was abstinate from drugs, but I wasn't in recovery. I was a dry drunk. I just simply was not using, but I wasn't in recovery because I wasn't doing anything. You've got to do something to be in recovery. Within three weeks, I was using. Within three months, I was arrested. I found myself facing a judge and being sentenced to twenty-four years of federal prison. At that point, I knew that I had to make a choice to live or die, not physically, but emotionally and spiritually. I was going to live or die, because I was facing a long time in prison.

I was sentenced to the federal correctional institution in Lexington, Kentucky. The interesting thing is that I was in the midst of the mandatory minimum sentencing war with the Congress and the judges in the criminal justice system. I ended up being sentenced just nine days before mandatory minimums became constitutional. Therefore, I was eligible for parole, which was a big deal to my lawyer. I didn't know what it meant. I was barely sober. The first charge was aiding and abetting the possession of crack cocaine. The second charge was conspiracy to manufacture and distribute. I was sentenced to twenty-four years: two twelve year sentences. That devastated everyone.

Lexington was a whole different world for me. After all those years of being out on the streets in a lifestyle that was reckless and irresponsible, Lexington gave me a sense of security. I mean that it gave me a chance to sit down and work on Donna. Because my priority, the things that always occupied my mind were my children and my addiction; it was everything else but me. I was never comfortable taking care of me. Going to prison gave me a chance to take care of myself, to look deep inside of myself and pull on the strength that I had left, the faith that I had left, whatever piece of identity I had left and bring that to the altar of God, and ask God to help me put my life back together. I took every class, every AA, NA, CA, whatever, everything that they had to offer. I took yoga. I took everything. You name it, I took it. I also began to see the old Donna resurface.

I started making sure that I wrote my children once a week. I became accountable to myself, my peers, and to my family. I knew some of the things that they would write back would hurt me, but I did it anyway. I worked on the issue of commitment to my body because as an African American woman who was an addict, the first thing that women neglect is our body. That's the first thing, our health care. As an addict, there were times I didn't eat, and forget exercise or any of that. So I started my commitment right there. I made a commitment to get my body back in shape.

In 1990, the federal prison system brought men into Lexington and made it a co-ed prison. During that time, more than eighty women became pregnant. Now, I've always been a trendsetter. I became pregnant. I went to solitary confinement—segregation—for forty-five days. I was fortunate that I got out. My baby was born in 1991.

The second thing I did was, when I had my baby, I knew I had a long prison sentence to do, and I wanted to be able to get to know this child. Therefore, I wrote a letter to churches all over the city of Lexington, asking that someone open their heart and their home, and take my baby in, and be willing to bring my baby to visit me during my prison sentence. I never expected anyone to answer but someone did. This little old lady took my baby in, and for the next six weeks brought her to me every day. When that happened with me, other women started saying, "I want to bond with my baby. I want to breastfeed my baby." There was a Quaker home for severely disabled children in town who heard about what was happening at Lexington. Women were having babies, but no one was there to take them. If the children aren't picked up from the prison in seventy-two hours, they become wards of the state. This Quaker home decided to take the children of the women who were in Lexington Prison. That was another big step in the area of advocacy, that I felt I took part in. I understood I had found my niche.

I advocated for my transfer to a prison camp. I wanted to be closer to my children. During that time, I continued to stay in very close contact with my family. I think they knew by my letters that something about me was changing. Of course, it took them time. I was discriminated against many times. I met officers who were simply vicious and vindictive, and I would say that they were miserable in their own lives. They sought to make us miserable because we were the best victims they could find. I ended up being transferred to a prison camp, that was Alderson, West Virginia. Alderson was like a college campus. I thought, "Yeah, this is okay." But I also came face to face with my own vulnerability and realized that I was very close to getting out, even though I wasn't ready to leave. I was scared to death because, number one, I had become institutionalized. I had regained my identity, my integrity, my self-respect, and my self-esteem. I was saved, and I loved the Lord Jesus Christ, but I was also very aware that if I was released, I had the same challenges on the outside that I had faced before and not been able to deal with. How was I going to deal with them now? I realized that if I consistently began to work on becoming empowered and socialized, by the time that process was complete, I would be ready to leave prison. It was very difficult to get ready to leave prison because I had found a family in the women that were there. I was very close to them. Some of them got out before me, but it was really hard to leave others behind.

I want to go back say that the hardest part of my entire prison sentence was giving birth to my baby, having her taken out of my hands, being put back in shackles and taken back to prison, and leaving my baby in the hospital with strangers. It was the hardest thing I ever had to do. It was hard because I was sent back to a unit where there was nothing but pregnant women. The sad thing is that every time one of us would go away to have a baby, those of us that had had our babies knew the devastation she was going to feel leaving that baby there and coming back to the prison. We knew what she was going to be like when she hit the door coming back to the unit. I had begun to talk to other women about this. I said, "Let's be there for the women that were coming back. Let's do this thing together and comfort them and support them through their first week home without their baby." This became a very important part of my life during that time, helping other women through the process of separation from their babies.

I realized at that point that a large part of what I had to do when I got out was to work with making the process of motherhood easier to deal with during incarceration. This is where our organization's parenting program comes from. During my pregnancy, I talked to many women who were incarcerated about their experiences with their children. I actually took notes and I took all those experiences and put it into our program once I was released. We have a parenting program that directly addresses the challenges that incarcerated women face as mothers, and helps them to remain parents in spite of the incarceration. What I realized, as an addict myself, is that parenting wasn't presence, it's participation. Even when I was present in my children's lives, I didn't participate. For most of us, just before our prison sentence that was true.

In terms of African American women, the most common and most evident things to me are the lack of education and lack of job skills. I'd say probably two percent of them have education, and when I say education, I mean even a high school diploma. In Georgia, seventy-nine percent of the women in prison don't have a high school diploma. That limits how we can work and where we can work. If those two things are limited, how do you then support three, four, or five children? The other thing that was very obvious to me is that African American women are already subjected by a society that places us at the bottom of the totem pole. Within the prison system, not only are we placed at the bottom of the totem pole, but we are considered less than the average inmate. I don't know if that makes sense, except to say that we are given the worst details. We are considered last for special projects, for benefits, or privileges.

We have the stigma of going back into a community where African American men are almost made martyrs and heroes when they come out of prison and go back into the community. But when we go back into our communities, we are not only unfit people, now we're unfit mothers, and it's hard to trust us. I see that more in African American communities than I do in White communities, and I've worked in both of them. When you are living in an environment where you are constantly feeling that no one trusts you, it's hard to function, it's hard to regroup. It's hard to regain your integrity and your identity. It's hard to prove yourself. The communities want women who come back from prison to become gray shadows and to disappear, because if you are there, then we have to address you.

African American grandmothers are the care providers, the primary care providers for the children, when women go to prison. In the African American community, the grandmother has to go on welfare to support the children. The children, more often than not, will be passed around from place to place. I hear this more from African American mothers than I do with White mothers—"I don't know where my children are." I know that feeling because it happened to me. I didn't know where my children were for certain periods of time. The White women that have been in our program since we opened know who has their children even if the caretakers don't want to let the women see the children.

I think that it goes all the way back to slavery. We gave birth to children that were snatched from us and taken to do work at another plantation. We are seen as these breeders. We have all these babies, but we're not prepared to take care of them. We're not capable of taking care of them. When we go to prison and have to deal with being separated from our children, no matter how good a mother we were, it's perceived very differently when we start saying, "I want my kids back. I want to be a mother again." I felt very much like I was on a plantation many times when I was talking in a prison system to my counselors and others about being a mother again and about taking responsibility for my children. I did not see White women having that kind of problem when they wanted to make a phone call or to see about their kids. For us it was, "Well, they're better off without you, anyway." More often you heard Black women being told, "Don't you think you ought to consider adoption, since you have such a long period of time to do?" White women weren't told that.

I see that the solutions to recidivism, addiction, prostitution, in our inner cities, and the destruction of African American families, are going to come from within, not from without. It's not going to come from the criminal justice system making these changes, or legislators, even though eventually, they will have to do that. The real change has to start from within our communities, and it has to start from within ourselves as formerly incarcerated women. We need to begin to think of ourselves as survivors and not victims anymore. We need to think of ourselves and the power and the empowerment that we do have already. The strength that we have to be able to survive that experience is phenomenal. Truly, as Maya Angelou said, we're phenomenal women. Women whose greatest crime is addiction, who are convicted of nonviolent crimes, who have dependent children, need to have an opportunity that is supported by the community and the criminal justice system, to get their lives back together again and to reclaim their family.

It's going to take a community's support. It's going to take some innovative ideas. It's going to be criminal justice folks being willing to take some chances and take some risks. Granted, there are those of us that need to be in prison. I'm not going to lie, but there is a larger majority of women who don't need to be in prison and who would be better served by being in a program with their children. We're talking about rehabilitation. How about talking about *habilitation*. If you've never had a healthy life or a productive life, then you can't return somebody to something they never had.

C

CRIMINAL JUSTICE OFFICIALS AND SUPPORT NETWORKS

17

Judge Juanita Bing Newton

Judge Juanita Bing Newton worked as an assistant district attorney for eight years and served on a sentencing commission for New York State for two years prior to becoming a Supreme Court judge in 1987. It was in this position that she met Angela Thompson. Judge Newton presided over Thompson's trial, and despite believing that Thompson was more a victim than a criminal, she had no choice but to give her a mandatory fifteen-to-life sentence for her minor role in a drug operation. Judge Newton was one of Thompson's supporters in her successful fight for clemency.

Judge Juanita Bing Newton

I GREW UP in the South Bronx, a product of a New York City housing project. I came from what is the greatest value in society, a loving, intact family. I once said to someone, "You know, we weren't the Huckstables, but we weren't *Good Times*, either." We were the very typical result of the migration from the South to the North. My father's parents come from humble beginnings. My father was a farmer, a sharecropper. To paraphrase Stevie Wonder, in those days they didn't educate colored people, so he never went beyond the fourth grade in formal education. After coming to New York City, he worked in the garment district. My mother was a school crossing guard, and then she became a paraprofessional in the public schools. She was a very resourceful woman.

We were a very close family. My father and mother both came from big families, so we had a lot of aunts and uncles. My parents were very active in the community. People went to work every day. Integration was not true in the North. There was de facto segregation and we lived separate lives. So, Sundays were not spent shopping and they weren't spent going to restaurants. They were spent in church and going to somebody else's house, usually aunts and uncles.

I'm a product of the parochial Catholic school, elementary and high school. I went away to college to Northwestern University, in Chicago. Then, I really didn't know what I wanted to do. I finished school a bit early, and did what was obligatory in those days for women to do; I got my teaching license. My last quarter in school was spent doing student teaching. After a vacancy at the Evanston Township high school, I took over the class. I have a great respect for teachers, having had six months of experience. I taught high school social studies to ninth and tenth graders. It was interesting; the ninth graders were more diverse. The tenth graders were all problem kids. I think it was my first opportunity to look at young women, African American women, who may have been troubled. There was a large affluent African American population, but there are difficult kids everywhere. There was a particular government class that had only two girls and about eighteen or nineteen guys. Both of the girls, arguably, were troubled girls, but in their own way they also were very sweet. They had issues, but they were teenagers.

I think those girls were grappling with the kinds of things kids are always grappling with. They wanted to do what they thought the popular kids did. They really weren't interested in an education for academic virtue. They weren't interested in thinking great thoughts; they just wanted to get out of high school. They had issues with boys even though this was the early 1970s, which were interesting times. These girls were a little tough in the sense of being a bit slow socially. Clearly their vocabulary was peppered with expletives deleted. But we made it through the year. It was endearing also; in their own way, even the worst among them wanted to succeed. That's the lesson that I took—no one really wants to fail. But it was enough for me to know that I didn't want to do this right away. It was also a time that I was given a wonderful opportunity for a full scholarship to go to Catholic University in Washington, D.C., so I went. I no longer remember how I got involved in the law. I think that you go through the "what do you want to be when you grow up" kind of fear of the process. I know that I made applications to a couple of law schools, and I also had applications to rehabilitation therapy programs. I didn't take that track; I went to law school. Also, I think it may have been an extension of school, as opposed to a determination of a future occupation. That's why I tell people in law school that it's a good thing, in that it teaches you a lot of information. It teaches you how to think, and you can develop transferable skills that are very valuable.

I really didn't like law school in the beginning. I did all right in law school, but I went to law school and found people so hell bent on using it as a career enhancement. They had these great ideas about what they were going to do and they wanted to go to law school, or they wanted to go to big firms, or they wanted to go to the city. That was sort of interesting to me because that was not my sense of what this was for. I went to law school ignorant of what to expect, except maybe that people were thinking about important issues. Of course, you always gravitate to what is interesting to you. I can remember that the first time I was tempted to say something in law school was in my constitutional law class. It was about the Japanese internment case. I'm sure it wasn't said with great eloquence, but I had to shake my head and say, "I can't believe this."

I wasn't the first person in my family to go to college. My brother had gone to college and most of my cousins had gone to college. But I was the first person to go to law school. I didn't know any lawyers personally, there were no lawyers in my family and we had no wealth. I sat in corporations class and they talked about debentures, and I didn't know what these people were talking about. It was foreign to me. I said that the only thing that I would learn in corporations was Rule 10(b), and someone told me that if you knew that you somehow could work it into the bar exam.

I worked for the Legal Aid Society after my first year in law school. Afterwards, I worked for the Justice Department and the Law Enforcement Assistance Administration (LEAA), in my last year of school and during the summer. All of that took place in D.C. Then, I came back home to New York and got a job with the D.A.'s office, literally down the street from the housing project where I grew up. I did not intend to stay there for more than my three-year commitment, and ended up staying there for eight years.

I really enjoyed the work. I enjoyed being in the courtroom. I tell my son, my nieces, and other young people, "We all have some talent and it's always there on the surface." I also say, "I still don't know what my talent is, but I do know that I was a pretty good litigator." I had success as a litigator and I enjoyed the work. I think it was the first time it was clear to me that most of the victims of crimes, particularly violent crime, are poor African American people. I guess that probably is not as unusual as we think, and probably is a historical thing. It was interesting work, and worthwhile work.

District Attorney Merola was a wonderful person. Women were accepted and permitted to do the same thing that men were permitted to do. That sounds so odd to young women today, but in 1975 it was still very new. I remember that he once said, "I don't know why all you women want to do this, but you make wonderful employees and you're hard working and you're good at it, so that's all I require." He was sort of an old-fashioned guy who was smart and lived in the real world.

After eight years in the D.A.'s office, I was looking for a change. An excellent opportunity was presented to work on a sentencing commission. It was a temporary commission that was created by the laws in 1984. The purpose was similar to the efforts of the Federal Sentencing Guidelines Commission. We were to look into sentencing policy in order to make recommendations for alternative sentencing, particularly determinant sentencing as opposed to indeterminate felony sentencing. I was asked to come on as deputy counsel. I worked with them for two years. Governor Cuomo took an all or nothing approach to the legislature. He said, "Listen, I can live with this and so I will take this report and I will put it in legislation. If the legislature agrees to it, I will sign it."

I never had thought about all of those issues in a "think-tank" way before. As a prosecutor, I was more of a hands-on, get-it-done, case-by-case type of person. So this was a very interesting opportunity to look at these issues from a multidimensional perspective. I began to understand a lot of the philosophy and theories of sentencing and punishment, and computer models, and how we were going to increase the prison population. At that time, I met Jonathan Gradess, who was executive director of the New York State Defenders Association. Of course, sentencing from his perspective was very different. I worked with Michael Smith, who now is a law professor but then was head of the Vera Institute. His views were always practical in one sense, because he didn't want to see the prison population increase dramatically; but he also was very philosophical in a sense.

We are a product of our experiences, so I'm sure that a lot of what I think about sentencing or feel about sentencing probably came from those two big chunks of my life: the D.A.'s office and the Sentencing Commission. After the commission, I was invited to come and work for the Office of Court Administration. Two significant mentors from the Sentencing Guidelines committee were Judges Joseph Bellacosa and Milton Williams. Judge Bellacosa had become the chief administrative judge, and Judge Williams was the deputy chief administrative judge. I worked for Judge Williams, and part of that job was also to work for Judge Bellacosa, doing court administrative work. I did that for two years.

It's a fascinating business. In a sense, the courts are so uniquely different that we merit being a separate branch of government. Our concerns are different, and our approaches are different. The ultimate end product that we seek is both ethereal and tangible. We have to resolve the case, but we have to understand that it has to be done with justice. The bottom line is that there is a business side to the courts. There are widgets that we make in that sense, in that we have the constitutional imperative of resolving cases-in-controversy, but it matters that we cannot let them languish.

During that time, we were becoming swamped by the narcotics crack epidemic in the City, in the 1980s. The courts, as part of our legislative program, urged the legislature and the governor to create twenty-three new judgeships to help address the court system problem. I had just the requisite number of years since admission to the bar to become a judge, and it dawned on me that perhaps this was a golden opportunity. I spoke to Judge Williams and Judge Bellacosa, and both of them encouraged me. The position was a gubernatorial appointment to the Court of Claims, in 1986. I was one of twenty-three who were named, and I took the bench in January 1987.

I have been a judge longer than I have held any other position in my legal career. Although when I speak at programs from time to time, I do say that I think that thirty-six is too young to become a judge. I say that not because I don't think I did a good job; I think I've been a good judge. However, there are things that you can't do. For example, you can't be political. Also, there are things that you will never learn from a different venue that you arguably could bring to the judiciary. So there are pluses and minuses.

I sat as a trial judge in Manhattan from January 1987 to January 1995. I'm going to come back to the trial bench eventually, but I don't know when. I found trial work fascinating. I love being in the courtroom and I miss it. I even liked jury selection, as long as it didn't take too long or was too repetitive. I liked the interpersonal dynamic in trials. The trial, criminal or civil, is one of the most unique procedures that we have in our system of government. Mostly, juries want to do the right thing in the worst way. It is an incredible experience. They want to hear what you have to say, and they want to understand. When it comes together, it's a wonderful thing.

I remember the *Thompson* case very well, in large measure because of the outcome.[1] The interesting thing about the *Thompson* case is that in the end, twelve judges heard this case and had to give an opinion one way or the other. They were evenly divided six to six, although the six on the winning side obviously were more potent. I believe in the appellate process and I have no quarrel with the decision. It's just one of those things about being a lawyer.

Angela Thompson was indicted with her uncle. It was a multi-count indictment and she was included on just one count, literally the last count on the tail end. For the most part, all of them were A-1 felony drug counts, and it was clear that this was a case where the special narcotics units had information and were making a series of buys from this operation. I remember that I also did something that I rarely do, but it was appropriate. We did some pretrial hearings on the case, and I actually severed her count from her uncle's count. It was requested and I granted the motion for severance because it appeared to me that her case was never going to go anywhere in the short run.

The uncle's case was never tried. He pled guilty, so her case went to trial.

There was a plea offer of three to life; actually, at one point it was probably lower than that. It may have been one to three. They weren't really out to get her; they could care less about her. This was Specialty Narcotics and they were not your typical hard-nosed prosecutors, in that respect. They had a pretty liberal plea policy. It is interesting that I read someplace that Angela Thompson felt that she couldn't plead guilty because somehow she would have been disloyal to her uncle, or been a snitch, or had to testify against her uncle. I wasn't quite sure about that because I don't recall any condition to her pleading guilty that would require her to testify or give any information or statement against her uncle. However, what typically happens when an accomplice admits guilt in the allocution, more as a shield than as a sword for prosecution, is that they ask the accomplice to admit that the person they were acting with was the named person in the indictment. You can't use this in court as evidence against the other person for confrontational purposes, but it does prohibit the pleading defendant from taking the stand at the trial of the co-defendant and saying, "Yes, I admitted to doing all that, but it wasn't with this person." I don't know if that was explained to her or not, but I read that she felt that the result would require her to give up her uncle.

She should have taken the plea but she gambled. I used to say to defendants, and I'm sure I said it to Ms. Thompson, "You know, this plea offer is too high if you're not guilty, or it's too high if you expect that even if you're not guilty, you will be convicted. But if you have done this, then you really have to search your soul and decide what it is you are going to do." Some people, like veteran defendants, come in and plead guilty, and their goal is to get the best deal. For others, there are real dilemmas. I suspect the greatest dilemma for a person who knows he or she committed the act but somehow feels it was justified, or the sentence is inappropriate, or he or she should be given a different chance, or should have a better offer, is to make this choice. Making this choice especially is hard if your counsel had advised that you have a certain probability of winning. Angela Thompson did not have a public defender; she had privately retained counsel who was a very good lawyer.

I don't think that there was anyone in the courtroom who knew the consequences who didn't say this was a tough case. I remember reading the probation report and saying, "My goodness, this is a tough case." This is why I am a tremendous advocate of probation and probation reports, which I say as a footnote, because now in New York City where there are mandatory jail sentences, you're not getting full-view probation reports. Instead, you're getting what I call "fill-in-the-blank" probation reports. There is a sense that they don't need to tell you a lot about the person because they have to go to jail, anyway. It was through this wonderful probation report that I found out who Angela Thompson was, what had happened in her life, and the fact that there were extenuating circumstances, in my opinion.

We send mixed messages to people. We all know and understand that selling and using illicit drugs is illegal, but you wouldn't know it if you looked at television every day. I couldn't be more against the legalization of drugs because I see what drugs to do people and their lives. I saw, for example, how my Bronx community was turned into a hellhole over the introduction of heroin into the community in the 1960s. We got hit with the Vietnam War, but home-side we got hit with the heroin wars. We are the product of our information. I guess it was very touching to me that Angela was raised in the family business, which happened to be an illicit business. Nonetheless, this was what she was involved in, and I'm sure she did it knowingly. On the other hand, when you're seventeen and you have these kind of circumstances, what do you do? What should she have done? Should she have picked up and gone out and lived on the street? And if that's not what she should have done, where should she have gone? Do you know? I don't know. She was seventeen years old. What should she have done, where should she have gone, to whom should she have gone to free herself from this environment? Those are the larger questions of the lives of children.

My sense is that she was seventeen, and I meant it. These were critical times in her life. I'm not a Pollyanna. I grew up as tough as anyone. In my view, she should have been studying to go to college, preparing to go to the prom, and looking towards her future. As I sit here today, I think the message we need to get out in our community is that jail is not really an alternate life-style option. I don't know that people understand that anymore. Instead, it seems to me that the notion of going to jail is not as horrible and unacceptable to young people as I think it should be. It seems that it's almost the life experience that everyone is supposed to have. Where did that idea come from? I was on a visit to Bedford Hills about two years ago when I was on the governor's commission on domestic violence fatalities. We held a public hearing at Bedford Hills for women to offer testimony. Many of the women who testified were there, at least in their minds if not objectively, because they were victims of domestic violence. They either had injured or killed their abuser or had been abused and subjected to a kind of abuse that led them to participate in criminal acts. It was interesting to hear these women, particularly the ones who were there because they did a "favor" for their boyfriends. They were "mules" in the classic sense of being asked to "carry this" or "hold that." These are the things that you have to tell your children: you tell your sons not to ride in cars; you tell your daughters not to hold anything for anybody.

Substance abuse certainly is one of the reasons why we're having so many African American women in jail. Crack caused a tremendous change in the population. Even though crime is down overall, we still see a lot of people in the court relative to the increase in narcotics crime. In a place like Manhattan, felonies are narcotics based, as in possession and sale of narcotics. There are more women in that range because more women are using narcotics, and it is a natural segue from using to selling.

Another case that comes to mind involved a young woman, who was sixteen or seventeen, and a man who was a little older. The thing that struck me was that she was in on bail of $5,000, and it was her first arrest. He was also in on bail. Her case was called first. There was a classic African American mother in the audience. This woman was on the edge of her seat from the time I came out. She was in a sea of people and she stood out. When the attorney came and the case was called, she was so anxious. The young lady had spent three weeks at Rikers Island, and she was seventeen years old, and she was beyond scared.

The lawyer came up and said, "Judge, I want to talk to you about bail." And I said, "I don't want to hear that. I want to hear something else." He said, "Judge, I want to talk about bail." I said, "Do you think I'm going to keep this girl in jail? Please, give me a break. That's her mother over there?" He said, "Yes." I said, "She is going home with Mom. We have to talk about something else because she has to get her attitude adjusted." When we called the case, I told the young lady to look at her mother. I said, "Turn around and look at her. Now what is your problem? You're going to stand on a corner and hold some penny ante drugs for somebody. Your mother is here crying her heart out for what? You have everything; you probably have too much."

It was fascinating to me. I saw embarrassment and a sense of confusion because she could not explain this in a rational world. Maybe she could explain it in her world, but she couldn't explain this, and she certainly understood that this rite of passage was not all that the people on the block said it was. So she pled guilty. We gave her youthful offender treatment. We got her in this program where she got her GED, and also a special program with Hunter College.

Over time, I increasingly realized that there couldn't be a great disconnect between the judiciary and the community it serves. We can't look at cases only as numbers and as opportunities for great legal discourse. We really have to look critically at what we do and what the outcomes will be. This is not to say that we make it up as we go along. As I tell jurors, "When I rule, I rule based on the law." I'm very proud that in all the years I've been on the bench, I've never been reversed for an evidentiary mistake. But, I have had some sentencing issues that have caused me some problems. I think that when you come to the bench, you have an obligation to apply the law and to exercise discretion. I don't know how you exercise discretion if you don't consider the body of knowledge that you bring with you, including who you are and what you think. This affects your sense of what is just and fair. So I think it is appropriate to bring the perspective that you've acquired, coupled with learning from the community, your reading and your learning, and your application of the law.

One of my very first reversals was in a sentencing case, in which I sentenced an older White man who had sold several kilos of drugs. The negotiated sentence was six to life. His greatest mitigating factor was that he was ill. I believe it was a heart condition or something involving a major system. I was reversed in the interest of justice by the appellate division, and they reduced it to three to life. Now, in that brief decision, they spoke in terms of a factor that made it appropriate for them to reduce the sentence because of his illness. And that's fine. That's an objective factor, and I'm sure that an underpinning among the court members was that they were knowledgeable about what it meant to have this illness, and that's fine.

Similarly, with the Angela Thompson case, I found that it fit within the *Broadie* criteria by objectively looking at the issues with respect to her and for the larger population.[2] I looked at what we could expect and should expect in terms of what the sentencing should mean to her. I got involved in the case simply to decide what was the best thing for

Angela Thompson. It was done in open court one day without the intention of making a cause célèbre. I never intended or expected that to happen.

There were several factors in my sentencing opinion. They included her youth, her situation, the fact that she was an orphan, and the fact that her choices were limited. It wasn't just her youth as a number, but her youth as a basis for her not having any options. How many options do you have when you're young, you're an orphan, and you're left in a household without direction or real choices? While she consciously did what she did, which was criminal and inappropriate, she never had many options to put herself in a different place and a different time. Those were big factors for me. Frequently, I hear, "Judge, this person comes from a good home and will never do this again." And I say, "Well, if you come from a bad home, should you be treated worse than if you come from a good home?" That analysis escapes me. It almost should be, "Judge, he comes from a good home and we should punish him more harshly because he knew better."

Once I promised a young African American male youthful offender treatment. The D.A. objected to it and the defendant wanted to speak on the record. We let the young man speak. In fact, I closed the courtroom, even to his mother for at least a time, because there was something that he wanted to tell me. There is nothing harder than for kids who are basically good kids to say that they've done something bad in front of their parents. He spoke about how he got into trouble because his father left his mother and the family, and there was domestic violence. The father burned down the house; it was just a horrible tale. The kid was basically a good kid and he was going to school. He was selling drugs on the side to help Mom.

Then we opened the courtroom again and proceeded to sentence the young man. I said to the D.A. who had been so angry with me, "And what would you like to say?" And she said, "Nothing, Judge; I'll rely on the court." Afterward, she came up to me and said, "Judge Newton, that was pretty amazing. I didn't know anything about this kid. In some respects because of the press of business, we look at them as 'cases.'" She said, "I promise you I will never pick up a file and look at it as a case. I will always look to see the person and the humanity if I can." I think my talent is that I ask good questions and I'm curious about people. In the law, facts and information matter, for lawyers and judges. Informed decision making is the only kind that is acceptable, and it was the facts, all of the facts in Ms. Thompson's case that affected me.

I would be less than truthful, though, if I didn't say that her being African American didn't affect me personally. As an African American woman, I look at the world from where I come, from where I stand, from where I sit. My view is not the same as the view of others, and this is why it is important to have diversity on the bench. Diversity on the bench is essential because you are a product of your background, your history, your ceremonies, and your life-style. All of that is important in decision making that affects the community and that speaks for the community in a thoughtful, rational way. We shouldn't miss the opportunity to do what is fundamentally right. One of my favorite stories is the whole story of *Gideon*, where from nothing came a whole wealth of information and change that affected our approach to the issues of fundamental fairness and justice.[3] Gideon's little note that "I was convicted because I didn't have any money, and I couldn't get a lawyer" is a wonderful story for all students who go into law because they are convinced that justice is an important feature of what we do in this country. You never know when we have that story of the litigant whose needs are not just an answer to that little case or problem that they have, but affect a much broader level of justice.

I think one of the reasons the *Thompson* case and some of the other cases I see are touching to me is because of my sense that this is not how it has to be. One of the problems about poor people and African American people when they come into court is that the expectations are so low. There are people that have the attitude of "let's negotiate" because there is no expectation that any of these people will go someplace further. It is fascinating to see that and to see how people look at these people. I think the most telling case I ever had on this issue was a robbery case in which I had read the file so I knew the defendants were incarcerated.

In this case, three twenty-something African American male defendants came out from the jail holding area. Their attorneys were anxious to step up to the bench to have a private conference about the case before going on the record, which is typical in New York. One of the attorneys said something like, "Judge, we want to make a bail application because the defendants are really not what they look like." I looked at the attorneys, and I said, "What do you see? The bad thing is that you look at your clients and see all that's bad. What is worse is that you come to me and you're assuming that I see all that is bad, and that is very scary to me. It means that this is what you say to my other colleagues on the bench. I don't know what you see when you look at them, but I see three young men."

In my current position as deputy chief administrative judge, my task is to focus on justice initiatives. I am looking at the court systems statewide, in civil and criminal spheres, to develop programs that will provide meaningful access to justice for all people, regardless of their economic or social status, or race, creed, or color. Wherever I go, I ask people for ideas about local practices for perspectives that we can use as we continue this evolving process of the judiciary and the legal system. We want to eliminate barriers to justice, particularly for poor people. We are working on it. It is an interesting task.

18

Assistant Warden Gerald Clay

Gerald Clay is an assistant warden at Franklin Pre-Release Center, an Ohio State Prison. He has held various positions in law enforcement, and has worked in male and female correctional institutions. At FPRC, he deals with grievances against prison employees and determines disciplinary actions. His discussion here provides a glimpse into the views of prison personnel toward the prison system.

Gerald Clay

I HAVE BEEN at Franklin almost two years and I've been in the department for almost twelve years. I began my career in 1985 as a corrections officer. First of all, in 1985, I started as a correction officer at Southern Ohio Correctional Facility. I later resigned, and in 1987, I came back into the department, as a correction officer at Ross Correctional Institution, otherwise known as RCI, in Chilocothe, Ohio. I was a correction officer about nine years at that penitentiary. During the course of those nine years, I functioned in the capacity of officer, case manager, unit manager, inspector, and went over into labor relations.

As a labor relations officer, I respond to grievances from the employees. We have three unions: ASME, 1199, and OEA. Our ASME employees are the majority of our correction officers. Union 1199 is the majority of the nursing and treatment type staff. The Ohio Education Association (OEA) basically centers around our teaching staff. I'm involved in what's pretty much the final say on disciplinary actions of the employees. I also respond to kites from inmates. A kite is a system established in the department where an inmate can formally make correspondence with an appropriate staff member, and get a response back, otherwise known as a formal correspondence. The majority of the kites need to be referred to another area sometimes.

I think that one of the first similarities between the male institutions and the female institutions is the issue of confinement itself. Confinement is just that, it's confinement. As staff, we go in and out every day, while the inmate is here until the end of their sentence. When I look at similarity, that is one of the main things. The biggest shocker for me was not realizing all the needs that the female inmates actually have. I mean, you've got your personal needs and pregnancies, which is a big thing. Obviously, we did not have to deal with that at a male facility. Pregnancy is, and has been, probably the major difference that I see. I think this would have to put a tremendous amount of stress on the inmate. It gets to a point that they're not able to perform their jobs, but they're still considered an inmate. Pregnant inmates are treated medically. We have prenatal programs and things like that set up here at the institution for those inmates that are preparing to birth a child. Other than that we treat them pretty much as any other inmate that is here.

I've learned to deal with it this way—an inmate is an inmate, whether you're female, whether you're a male. You're incarcerated; you committed a crime. I don't think that a female can convince someone better than a male can that she did not really commit the crime, because she's a female. I don't look at things that way. To me you're an individual, you just happen to be female. It doesn't mean that you are more slick or more sly than the male inmates. I see the equivalence. An inmate is an inmate. I think some people who have stereotypes could say, "Female inmates whine a little bit more, they press to get their way, they keep pushing and pushing and pushing, or they cry." There are men that are that way. That is a view that I have heard, but that's a view you hear on the street. You know, "Females want to get her way." Not all the time. I don't see it like that. This is my profession and I've seen both sides. I don't do that stereotyping. There are a few differences, and a lot of those concern the personal needs that they have. And, that's solely it. I don't get much into the emotional things that others might.

In general, the thing that keeps us in check is that first of all, we are all professionals, or we should be. Also, we have audits, just like we're preparing for right now. They are very in-depth audits, which keep us in check. We're also an accredited institution. We're nationally accredited by the American Correctional Association, and there are standards that we have to meet. If things are not going right, you're going to know it. If it's not running right, more or less the inmate somehow is going to let you know.

For example, inmates have said on occasion that the food is bad. We check into it. We check to see what was served. When someone says food is bad, it could be that it was too cold, or that the meal that was supposed to be served was not served. Things like that become issues in a correctional setting. The food temperature is another example. In the opinion of some inmates, it is not adequate. Well, we check it. We go right to the food service line, and we get a hold of the food service manager, and we check it. In pretty much all your institutions, you have supervisory staff who are normally in the chow hall area during the time that chow is being served. That's because we consider the chow hall one of the more hot spots, since that's where larger gatherings occur three times throughout the course of the day. You just immediately check things that relate to food. I have found in my career that if you immediately check things out, you can normally get resolution to the matter.

I was not interested in corrections before I knew friends that worked in corrections. A steady job is a steady job, regardless of what state you're in. The benefits are more than adequate here, and I just thought I'd give it a shot. When I was nineteen years old, I went to Lucasville. At that time, that was the "toughest penitentiary going." I think people that have not worked at a maximum facility really don't know what it's like to actually deal with the hard-core criminal. The job can be dangerous, as can anything else in dealing with the criminal justice field. I didn't know what I was getting into when I first got in, but after being employed there, I found out. It was really challenging.

I left the correctional setting in 1985. During that time period, I was in and out of college. I played college ball at Wright State University, Dayton. Then I played for, actually, three schools. I didn't really know where I was going and all that. I mean, I was confused, I didn't know what I wanted to do. I went in and out of the state highway patrol and decided that's not what I wanted to do.

When I came back in 1987, I knew what I was getting into. I did not want to go back to a beginning career in Lucasville Correctional Institution at that time, because I wanted a more medium security style penitentiary. I'm thirty-four now. At that time, it was a much more stressful environment. In the summertime, it was just unbearably hot in those units. I remember going in there in my uniform, and I'd leave at the end of the second shift just sweating. I came back to corrections with the intent of going back into OSP (Ohio Patrol State Police), but I wanted them to see that I had stabilized for about a year or so. It all went the way I had planned it. They readmitted me back into the academy, which was not the norm. I got good reports from my supervisors and the warden at the penitentiary that I was currently working at, which was RCI. They accepted me back into the patrol. During that time, I had put in for a promotion within the department, for a case manager's job. I was awarded the case manager's job, so I had to decide, am I going to stay in DRC, or am I going to go into Ohio State Patrol. I opted to stay in corrections.

There's consistency in this work. Life is dependent on a paycheck because you're not going to make it without a paycheck. And the pay for corrections, compared to maybe some other things in Ohio, is very, very good. I've been blessed and fortunate enough to be at this particular level, financially. Benefits are hard to come by these days, even in some private organizations. Private employees don't necessarily have the good benefits that a state of Ohio employee would have. I know that I've got a job to come to. I know the job's going to be there. I don't have to worry about layoffs. I think consistency is the biggest thing that I've gotten out of this.

I've had the opportunity to work for three wardens directly. They all three have different styles. Two males, one female. Two Black wardens, one White. The institution has a pulse and that pulse is that of the managing officer of the institution. If the warden is more laid back and lenient, sometimes your staff have the tendency to be so. Then because of the leniency, you still have to hope that there is not the possible risk of things maybe occurring on the compound that you wouldn't want, because the staff has become a little bit more relaxed. In general, the other pulse would be the level of status of the security of the institution. I mean, obviously, a minimum-security penitentiary is not going to be the same risk level as a maximum or a closed penitentiary, for that matter. So security status of the penitentiary also plays an important part. Those are the two biggest things: the status of the penitentiary, and the style of the managing officer.

I do not have an aspiration of becoming a warden at this time. I am pretty much happy with what I'm doing. I'm very involved in my personal life and I don't want anything that's going to interfere with that, at all. The next level for me would be a deputy warden. There's another level of responsibility that would come with that. Sometimes you find a niche and you stay in it. I moved so fast there for a while, that, sometimes I just want to rest and enjoy it.

I've never really talked to anyone about how they feel when they come in the fence and in the gate and come to work and punch in. For myself, it has no effect. It has no effect at all. It's almost as though I'm going into a factory. You go in and do what you've got to do, and clock out and you go home. The biggest thing for me is that I've got a life outside of corrections. I'm going to come in and give you a hard 8 hours, I'm going to eat my lunch, and then I'm going to go home. And that's pretty much the way I've got it set. I enjoy my Saturday and my Sunday off. Hopefully, I don't get paged for any unforeseen circumstances. But I'm dedicated; if I were paged, I would be here, but you have to remember that the higher up you go in this rank, the more you are accessible to the needs of the department and the institution. In my opinion, that involves much more of a commitment.

If I would allow myself to think about the sentences people were serving, then I'd be entangling myself too much into the atmosphere; that is, the obvious atmosphere that's behind the wall, or behind the fence, or behind the gate. I don't like to think of it as that; I like to think that I'm walking into an executive building downtown and I'm coming in to perform a job for a company, and to perform it to the best of my ability. Our primary duty is to house the inmate for the duration of their time that they were sentenced to. So I don't allow myself to get really wrapped up into, "Wow, I wonder what's going through their mind?" or "I wonder why they committed that crime?" I think one of the first things you learn in the academy, through your experiences and from the onset of being an officer, is that you're not concerned about what they did. It's irrelevant. What crime they committed is irrelevant. I keep that in mind—because I don't want to become prejudiced.

In the FPRC there are substance abuse programs, school, GED programs, parenting, and prenatal. I also believe they have crafts, computers, education classes, those sorts of things. In general, the substance-abuse programs and education programs are pretty much the same in all institutions. I think that's a continual program. But you have to understand, the aspects of a program sometimes are dependent on the people that you have.

I think, just in general, the demands that the public makes on legislatures and politicians are the cause of the increase in incarcerated numbers. FPRC was designed to house maybe one or two inmates per unit, and we've been able to put beds in there for four. That has been a common thing across the board. I believe every penitentiary has more than what they're built to have, and I don't know of any legal issues or court issues at this institution regarding overcrowding right now.

When the inmate files an appeal, it is my determination to decide whether or not I'm going to agree with the findings of the Rule Infraction Board, or decide if I want them to rehear the case, or modify the penalty, or dismiss the case in its entirety. I decide this on the merits of the case. I get a whole packet, I get the full packet of the whole thing that took place, and I review it thoroughly.

I sent a letter to the warden two weeks ago because of my background in music, and I'm involved in that on the street. I am proposing a chorus here at the institution, which I'm formulating under, quote, "a program." That means there will be guidelines I'm going to establish. It's not going to be centered around spirituality. I'm not going to preach spirituality, but I'm going to do gospel songs. I'm volunteering to do it, which means it wouldn't necessarily come under my job description. So I set the rules.

There are all types of gospel music. The purpose of the choir is to be a gospel choir. A choir in general would mean you could sing a variety of songs, but this is going to be the FPRC Gospel Choir.   That's   what we will be known as. The warden knew my music background and all, and mentioned that he wants to get a choir started. Well, I don't do rock music, I don't do rap and I don't do this and I don't do that. My style might sound jazzy, and my style might sound classical, but the basis of my music is gospel. So, under that, we'll do gospel music.

19

Grace House Administrators

Rochelle Bowles, Mary Dolan,
Annie González, and Kathy Nolan

Grace House is a transitional residence for women just released from prison. This interview with some of the Grace House administrators provides an in-depth look into the programs and efforts of this inspirational institution. One of the goals of Grace House is to help women reach their potential and establish a new life in the community, one they can take pride in living.

Left to right: Kathy Nolan, Rochelle Bowles, Annie González, and Mary Dolan

MARY: I try to keep the place running. I'm the administrator. I do the liaison work with the founding agency, St. Leonard's Ministries. I pay the bills and make sure that we have a budget every year, and coordinate all of the physical accoutrements of the house. I make sure that the house is well run and the cook is here, and that we have three meals a day. I also work with the women on their savings accounts, which we help them set up. I work with the staff in terms of making sure that we have adequate staffing. I also do all of the funding proposals, and attend meetings with the city to make sure that our finances are in order. The one thing I like about my job is that every day is different.

Basically, my background is that I've been an elementary school teacher and principal, and then I was a community organizer for about twenty years. I wanted a situation where I could work directly with people as individuals rather than with large community groups and neighborhood organizations. I had no history at all of working with anyone in prison ministry. When we talked about this idea, it was of creating a community here in a homelike atmosphere, where women could feel safe and secure, and could do some simple everyday things, like celebrate holidays, birthdays, and the like. We wanted to create that kind of atmosphere, where people could come and try to find themselves again.

KATHY: I'm the program counselor, and my job is to provide for the mental health needs of the women. Each woman will have an individual counselor during the time that she's here. Sometimes the women have needs for medications or are seen by a psychiatrist, and they may need to continue with that. I make sure that there's follow-up for that kind of thing. Adler's School of Professional Psychology provides many of our counseling services, both individual and group. They do our parenting classes. They also run several groups on self-esteem, anger management, and relationships. I do the remainder of the individual counseling that they don't provide.

We do an initial interview to get some background and find out if they've had any previous treatment, and what kind of treatment they've had. This way, we are able to get some idea of their mental health status when they come in. I also work with the women who have children in the Department of Children and Family Services, in the foster-care system. I work with them in building a relationship with their caseworker, making sure that they are following their service plan, going to court with them, and advocating for them in that system.

I had never worked with women in prison, but the idea of what we could do in terms of creating a homelike atmosphere appealed to me.

MARY: What has always struck me is that the women that come in are decent, nice women. If anybody were to walk in here on any given day or afternoon, I think it would take them awhile to figure out that they have a history of incarceration. Kathy and I have lived in convents, and the same kind of thing goes on; people are ironing and they're cooking. They're just ordinary folk, in terms of their expectations and their hopes. Something happened along the way and they got screwed up, or life handed them a plate that was pretty heavy, and they just tried their best.

ANNIE: I'm the aftercare director here. I work with the women as they get ready to leave the program, and after their two-month evaluation, I help find mentors for the women. I also recruit mentors and do presentations at churches to recruit the mentor population. In addition, I work with the women to find housing, generally second-stage housing, where they would pay 30 percent of their income and be able to participate in supportive services.

Grace House has built relationships with the supportive housing programs in the area, and some up north on the other side of Chicago. I work with the women in terms of areas where they might want to live, whether or not they want to go into supportive housing, and whether they are making enough income that they feel that they can go into market apartments. Sometimes, women choose to find apartments on their own.

In most second-stage housing programs, one of the criteria is homelessness. So we have to send a letter verifying that they have lived here and are, in fact, homeless. Many times, the programs will want a recommendation from someone here so that they can get an idea of how the women will live in a residential setting. Second-stage housing is basically like apartment living; it's not communal, like it is here. But there are supportive services.

ROCHELLE: My work begins with interviewing the women prior to the time that they come to Grace House. They fill out an application, so at least we are aware of what issues they have before they arrive. I can get their mental health records, find out how many children they have in the system, and find out their educational level. During the year, I spend a few months on the road going to the prisons to interview women directly. Therefore, when they get here, we have an idea of what their service plan should look like.

Once they come on board, my job is to make sure that they get the services that they need so they are able to move through our program, coordinate treatment between programs, and leave benchmarks. Sometimes a person may have to stay in the program longer than someone else because her issues have not been addressed. This is a holistic program. I try to make sure the women are getting what they need; if they are not, I try to put those things in place.

About 99 percent of our women have drug abuse problems. The second highest characteristic is the sexual abuse. We find that most women have difficulty because of unhealthy relationships. They're very needy and want to be loved. They have a lot of emotional issues. As they become clean, they think they can get involved in relationships, and it usually doesn't work out. That tends to lead them back into the drug community.

KATHY: As Rochelle said, the women have a lot of abuse issues, both sexual abuse, from an early childhood, as well as abuse in relationships with men. I think that their drug addiction speaks more to coping with the consequences of abuse. We see a lot of women who are depressed and have been for a long time. Oftentimes, the drug use is more about self-medication, and then it becomes an addiction. They have low self-esteem, and absolutely no sense of worth as a human being. I think they come in with a lot of shame and a lot of guilt around their addiction, around the loss of their children, and around the fact that they have not been good mothers.

A number of women have told me that they were sexually abused by a family member and were afraid to report it. When they did report it, their mothers denied it, or didn't accept it, or said they were lying, or in one case, one woman said that she was slapped down the stairs. We have a number of women whose mothers were addicted themselves. Several women even have mothers that were in prison, so they were raised by their grandparents, or an aunt. Sometimes they were not accepted in that family, or were looked down on because of what happened to their mothers. I think the kinds of things that get misdiagnosed or go untreated are the posttraumatic stress disorder kinds of things. A lot of the women are suffering from posttraumatic stress because of the traumas they've experienced in childhood, and often, they are diagnosed as borderline or antisocial. If they are having severe trauma reactions, sometimes they get to the point where it may mask or look like some psychosis, in extreme cases. Also, there's a tendency to criminalize the drug addiction, rather than look at it as a symptom rather than the problem. For many of the women, it is a symptom of these underlying issues, which go back to the violence and the abuse that they've been exposed to from early childhood.

ROCHELLE: I was really surprised at the number of women that had been sexually abused, either through incest or mothers' boyfriends, uncles, brothers, or cousins. I also was surprised by the anger that the women had at their moms, and their feelings of abandonment because of the abuse. They were very angry because they had experienced it, and often this was the first time they had told anybody. Any time you ask, "What is your relationship with your mother?" they would burst into tears or get angry. I began to see a pattern, and I began to understand. I knew what was coming next. Either they had been sexually abused and had never told anyone, or they felt abandoned by their mother because their mother knew about it and chose the male over them.

When I would ask, "Where was your mom?" they would say, "She was out working. She worked two jobs to take care of us." So there was this love-hate relationship, because even though they understood that their mothers were doing what was necessary to take care of them, even as adults, that little girl in them said, "I needed my mother to protect me." I saw that the women began using drugs because of the sexual abuse, often at an early age, like eight or nine years old.

As a Black woman, I was appalled. I had no idea. And it makes you think, "Where have I been all of my life, with all of this stuff happening to other Black women?" The sexual abuse also has an impact on their sexual identity. There are some women who are very confused about whether or not they are homosexual, heterosexual, or bisexual. If they were sexually abused as a young child, and some of the sexual abuse was with other women, there can be a lot of confusion down the road regarding their own sexuality.

MARY: I think we experience homophobia here, too. Sometimes the reaction to a lesbian resident is overreaction. Perhaps it comes out of some of their own experiences or issues. We say to women, "Wait a second. This is nothing new for you. You have been exposed to this. You know it exists. What's going on here that you would be so upset by someone else's behavior?" We don't shy away from it. We try to deal with it.

ROCHELLE: We also have discussed when women make the decision whether or not to regain custody of their children. There's guilt there, when they really don't feel they are equipped to raise their children. It's difficult for them to say, "It's not in my best interest." In the Black community, we've always raised our children, even if it was a grandmother, great-grandmother, or an aunt. The guilt arises when they come to the realization that "my child would probably be better off left where they are. I'm not equipped to take responsibility for this child."

We must help that woman understand that's okay, because it is. That is very difficult for Black women, because of our history and the guilt that's associated with that. I think the counseling has been helpful, so they understand who they are, their ability, with whatever limited resources or education they have, to really provide adequate housing, education, clothing, or whatever for their children and say, "No, where they are is the best place for them to be." It is difficult to release that child without any guilt but still have an active part in the child's life.

KATHY: Sometimes it can be very difficult. Often, these are women who started in the system when they were in their addiction, so they don't have a very positive track record with the system. First of all, it involves getting the system to sit back and start working with them and give them a chance. The women often have very negative attitudes toward the system, so I'm trying to help them to step back and say, "Okay, this is a new time. I'm going to build some kind of relationship with them." There's a lot of animosity on both sides.

The other thing is that the women don't understand that if they don't ask a question, they're not going to be told. So I'm helping them to take a little more initiative in their interactions with DCFS, because they do have rights. Their rights as parents have not been terminated. I try to help them know what those rights are, and in a respectful and positive manner, see that their rights are respected. We have found that when DCFS knows that some professionals are working with these women, they start to pay a little more attention and start to work with us. I think that's been pretty successful.

ROCHELLE: We bring in speakers, and have lots of workshops. For instance, we have women who need to be tested for HIV, so different agencies will talk to them about different diseases. Also, many women do not know a lot about their bodies, and do not know how to take care of themselves. So our workshops have a lot of medical and education information. We also had someone from the DuSable Museum talk to the women. She brought materials that other women had written in prison, and read stories to the women in Grace House. We take them on trips to the zoo, and horseback riding. We want them to be exposed to things they've never been exposed to before.

ANNIE: Our programming also includes a computer class. We have a computer tutor, who is very good. She's also one of our mentors, and she's very dedicated. She did the introductory class, and then some of the women chose to do the second part of that. They were getting more advanced, and got used to doing real work at the computer. Everyone seemed very interested. We broke the groups into two classes, because we have so many. We don't have enough computers to allow everyone to sit down and work on a computer at a given time.

We also have monthly meetings for former residents. Speakers at those meetings have talked about finance and issues related to credit and investment. For instance, women want to know how to establish a bank account, how to clean up their credit records and those sorts of things. We're trying to explore new ways of figuring out what we can offer former residents. It's a slow process, unfortunately. What we've found out is that they are very busy, especially if they're doing their programs, going to work, and doing everything they have to do. To try to get them to come back, even once a month, is very difficult.

ROCHELLE: If we had to name any particular weaknesses in our program, I would say employment is probably one of them. Most of the women do not have a high school education, and their levels of math and reading are very, very low. If they dropped out in the eighth or ninth grade, which is the average, their reading and math levels are at the fourth or fifth grade level. They would have to go to school for several years in order to get their GED. Sometimes they get discouraged.

Their experience has been that they've either been on welfare for a number of years or never held a job, or they've done work with fast foods or in a health-care community. So, we have seen overall that they do not have the adequate training available to become economically self-sufficient. Consequently, they work in fast-food chains, telemarketing, or manufacturing. The pay is minimal, and the hours are very, very long, which is not conducive to them being at home with their children.

We try to get employers to know who Grace House and St. Leonard's House are, what we have to offer, and how the women and men are prepared in our programs. We ask that employers step out and take a chance, by either giving them internships or training them for employment. Right now, though, we find that it's very difficult for women to become and remain self-sufficient.

MARY: I think that second-stage housing is our future goal. It will provide us a longer period of time to work with a resident. Right now, the average stay is six to eight months, and it's amazing what gets accomplished in that time. But, realistically, when you think of a pattern of living for fifteen or twenty years, in a very self-destructive and negative environment, it doesn't go away in six or eight months. So we would see a lot of changes in people's lives if we could offer a supportive environment for maybe as long as two or three years. They would achieve stability and self-sufficiency.

ANNIE: I definitely would echo the need for second-stage housing in the future. I work with housing programs, and as I call around I find that there are no openings. I also have dreams of enlarging our computer lab, and doing more with that. With technology going the way that it is, there is a lot to be done, including working on the computer and repairing computers. I hope that we can expand the number of computers and the kind of classes that we offer.

KATHY: I think it's important for us to be role models, and to bring in women who can be role models for the women. I think the whole issue of relationships for women is very significant. The women, in general, are disconnected from other people. One of the things that women learn here is how to be in a relationship with other women in a positive and healthy way.

ROCHELLE: I think they watch how we interact with one another. There's a genuine caring between the staff here. We have been role models for them in terms of how to have a relationship with a woman that was not necessarily anything sexual or physical.

ANNIE: We're also modeling cultural diversity by working together, and doing that very well. It's really easy for us to stay in our own groups. You can do that if you want to, but there is so much more to do and see, and places to grow when you move outside your own individual and group boundaries. To work on a team of all women is great. I haven't had that opportunity very often, and I really appreciate it.

MARY: Because we are all committed Christians, the first thing is that we believe in people's absolute goodness. Good people do bad things, but the people are good. Every person that walks in this door deserves to be respected, and deserves to be cared for. I think that's the way we treat each other, and that's the way we treat the residents.

We're not preachy. We're not here to evangelize. But we are open to allowing individuals to express whatever is their relationship with their God, their Higher Power, however they want to express that.

KATHY: The other important thing is forgiveness. In our understanding, our Christian understanding of who God is, every day is a new beginning. No matter what you do or how you do it, or what you've been in the past, each day can be a new beginning.

20

Sandra Barnhill, Director, Aid to Children of Imprisoned Mothers (AIM)

Sandra Barnhill is the executive director of Aid to Children of Impris-
oned Mothers, Inc. (AIM), an Atlanta-based advocacy organization for
incarcerated women, their children, and the children's caregivers. She is
an attorney and practiced death penalty defense and prison conditions
litigation prior to creating AIM in 1987. Among AIM's unique contri-
butions in advocacy was the creation of a support program for grand-
mothers, who are the main caretakers of imprisoned mothers' children.
In addition, most of the families served by AIM's intergenerational
programming are African American. She discusses her motivation and
the organization's approaches to advocacy on behalf of incarcerated
mothers, their children, and grandmothers.

Sandra Barnhill

I ATTENDED the University of Texas (Austin) Law School. I practiced law for about four and a half years, but most of that time, I did death penalty work and a number of prison condition cases. One day I looked up and realized that we weren't doing anything at women's prisons, and so I said to my boss at that time, a White male, "Don't you think we ought to do something?" He said, "Hey, yeah. Fine. You find the money to do it and we'll litigate it." Along with another woman in the office, we began to put a call out to women in southern prisons who had written the office and some women in Alabama. One woman in particular wrote a real compelling letter to me. I went down to Montgomery and spent eighteen months doing an investigation. We finally filed suit. Before the ink was dry on the consent decree, the prison was in violation of everything. The primary issues were parity between men and women in terms of the vocational and educational opportunities. We also included Eighth Amendment cruel-and-unusual-punishment issues, as well as issues regarding visitation.

After all of that happened, I was very disillusioned. The woman who initially wrote to us was a woman in her fifties and a strong warrior. She too—all of us—were sort of disillusioned. It became clear that the law is not the answer. It's a part of the answer, but the real answer is people claiming and using the power in their own lives. So, I quit practicing law. I started this organization in 1987, and we've been around for about fifteen years. I really started it to do two things. One, to work on my own personal empowerment as an African American woman. We all live in a society that constantly says, "I can't." We internalize some of that, and so I wanted to say, "I can, I will, I must." Therefore, I started AIM. I also wanted to be active in the empowerment of women because I think we have to learn how to be sisters and allies. I wanted AIM to be a place for our voices, so the way we figured out what work we do, is we ask the women. When I first started AIM, I went to see women in jail and in prison and said, "What is it that we can do for you?" They said, "Bring my kids. Help me take care of and see about my kids." So, those are the ways in which we try to do the work.

I think that, as African American women, there is no place for us in American society. I think we carve out little enclaves, but this is not a safe place for us. It doesn't make a bit of difference whether you're locked up in prison, or whether you're out here on the outside, because we're still locked out regardless of where you are. I think it's doing the work and just seeing that in some ways, there is a lot of joy about the work, but there is a lot of pain about the work, too. As I look at my sisters inside, it speaks so clearly about my own life, in that prison is the end product of the racism, sexism, homophobia, and antifamily that converges in a place called prison. That's the most extreme manifestation of it, but there are manifestations of it every day in our lives as Black women.

We take a phrase from the battered women's movement. We always believe the women, and the reality of their lives is different. They are not bad women. I think that's a lot about how the racism plays out because there are two predominant images of women in our society. One is what I call "the bad girl," and that's primarily associated with White women—that they are susceptible and easily tempted and swayed. They've fallen off, but they can be redeemed. Then there is the "evil woman," which is the predominant image, in this culture, of African American women, as beyond redemption.

I am really proud that our work is intergenerational: the kids, the moms, and their grandmothers. In a five-year period, we moved to do more mostly for the kids and the grandmoms. In order to do that, we decreased what we did for the women. I'm happy that we're moving to a place where we can hold those three balls because we have to work on each of those fronts.

The kids are writing books about their lives. One of the young women said she was going to be a millionaire, and I forgot all that she was going to do. That's what I mean, that untouched spirit. They haven't figured out that in this world, there are no constraints. They haven't figured that out yet, and I think that is really good, particularly based on the situation that they are in. Because if anything about the reality of life would smack you quick, it would be that your mama's locked up. Yet what came out of that is that kids are normal; what's not normal is the situation. The kids developed coping mechanisms, and some of the mechanisms that they develop to cope get them through the short term. They survive through that. However, over the long term, those are not the best coping skills. I see a couple of things in the kids. I see resilience. I see vulnerability. I see what I call the untouched spirit.

What kids understand about their situation depends on the age of the kids. When they're very young, they just kind of understand that their mother's in prison, she's away. I think that as they begin to get older, the analysis is different. What we put forth here is that the children need to know, we need to tell. Then you also need to talk about how you're being held accountable, because I think having kids think that this is just a set-up or a frame-up and that kind of thing is not good. Now, some of that may be involved, but each of us has choices that we have to make.

Some women are locked up because when they looked at the array of choices, first of all, all of them were bad. That was the first thing. Then, out of the bad ones, they just picked the one they thought was the least bad. That's true of some women, but it is also true of women that they looked at the choices, and some were good and some were bad. But they picked the bad choice. There are issues around personal decision making and we think it's very important to share that with the kids because kids see what you live and that's how they learn. We talk a lot here. So many women are incarcerated for drugs. But, we have house rules here: no drugs. We don't steal from one another. This is a community. This way, kids are developing their principles about living.

The grandmothers in our support group are in the forties to late fifties. They talk about the reality of their lives, their frustration, and their feelings. Sometimes they say that their daughter had been in prison before, and out and in, and "When is she going to get her life together so I can live my life?" One of the things that hit me in a real poignant way is that most of the grandmothers that come have health issues. I think that's a manifestation of the stress, the "dis"-ease in their life, struggling with a lot of stress issues. The therapist who runs the meeting for them talks a lot about wellness and stress management. A lot of women in our community have high blood pressure, hypertension, and diabetes.

We support whoever the caregiver is. In most cases, it's the grandmother, but also there are a lot of maternal aunts and cousins. Women fill up the gaps in society. When the mom's gone, the women in that family take up the space. I've been doing this work for fifteen years, and I've only worked with two fathers who had the kids. Statistics and research show us that men get far more visits than women when they go to prison because there is a female in his life: his mother, his sister, his lover, whomever, will bring the kids. Women get very, very few visits and women struggle more with the issue of who really is going to take care of my kids. What if the grandmother is ill or can't take care of them?

A woman once called, and she was talking about who could take her kids. She had very young infants and nobody in the family wanted to do it. It was about punishing her. That's the way our society is. Men make mistakes, but somehow they're still men. We definitely don't want to punish them or we don't hold them accountable. But the level of our rage or anger at women is much more profound. That goes back to the images of the "evil woman" and the "bad girl." When a woman falls, she really falls.

I hear a couple of different things about the issues of drugs in women's lives, particularly in Black women's lives. A lot of women are involved with drugs because they are involved with a man who's involved with drugs. He's either selling it out of the house, or she's being in a sense a "mule" for him by carrying and delivering packages. Sometimes it starts like that. Sometimes women are trying to medicate themselves against the pain of this world. I mean, in terms of society, I'm educated, and some days I want to get away from it, to escape from it. I don't have anybody I have to care for but me; no children or spouse. Some days I find life to be overwhelming. What if I had a couple of kids that I was caring for?

What I'm saying is I don't justify it, I understand it. I understand that we live in a society that basically is woman-hating, and also, in many ways, threatened by people of color. It becomes very difficult to negotiate your way in the world. And when the world has also said, "I don't care what you do, you have no place . . ." I think all of the realities of that are very, very painful. That doesn't excuse what the women have done, not in any way, because I think ultimately each of us has to be accountable for our own life and how we live in the world.

I remember when I represented a man on death row. One of my clients said, you know, "The first time I ever thought about my future was once I got here." I mean, locked up, waiting to be executed. Hello! In some ways, life is so fast that there isn't a chance to think about what could the future look like? How could it be different? As we have these kids write their autobiography, we tell them to "write whatever ending you want." What I found to be real for some of them, and some of their mothers too, and even the grandmothers, is that the ending that they see is very, very bleak.

Yes, it's hard to parent in prison, not impossible, but it is difficult because there are so many issues. You're locked up. There's somebody else who is playing the primary caregiver role. How do you support that person, when your philosophy around parenting or discipline may be different? When your kids get older, as teens—and part of what adolescents do is challenge their parents and challenge the system—then what place does that put you in, because they could very easily say, "Why should I listen to anything you have to say? Look where you are?" All of those issues come up for women. One of the things that I've noticed over the years—and a lot of people don't agree with me on this, but I really feel strongly about it—I feel that when a woman comes out, she should not be with her children for the first six months. That's my personal opinion.

She gets out of prison with a bus ticket and twenty-five dollars, and she has to find a job. She has to report to parole. In an institution everything is structured. You're told when to get up, when to go to sleep, when to go to work, when to eat. So now, a woman is out and she has to reconstruct her life. I think that kids deserve and that mothers want to give their kids their best self. And I think there ought to be some way for us to support the creation, or re-creation of the best self. Sometimes when women get out, the next day they're at their mom's house and they're all living together. She's trying to find a job, and she's trying to interact with the kids. I think the best self doesn't have a chance to come forth.

The women told us they want this—we just don't have the money for it—it is counseling when they come out, for them and the kids and the grandmother. I think in that six months that kind of intensive stuff ought to go on. Women ought to be helped with getting a job. There ought to be a family plan to be developed, a family mission statement. All of those kinds of things need to happen in that time frame. I think women need to see and spend time with their kids, but I fundamentally think they need to see and spend time with themselves. It is hard in this world, whether you are locked up or free, to see and spend time with yourself. That's what I think needs to happen.

Prison is antifamily, and it doesn't have to be. I understand the issues around safety, security, and custody. I also acknowledge that being a correctional official, and a guard, and all of that are difficult jobs. I understand all of that. But I do believe that as bright as we are as a society, we ought to be able to find a way to hold people accountable, but work towards their restoration as a human being, the dignity of the human spirit, and a reconciliation with the community, where they have to live. Until we figure all of that out, I think things are going to be more and more screwed up.

21

Rhodessa Jones, Director, Medea Theater Project

Rhodessa Jones became involved in the prison system in the early 1990s when she agreed to teach aerobics at a local jail. Her activities with the women have increased significantly and have culminated in a theater program for incarcerated women called the Medea Project: Theater for Incarcerated Women. She is the artistic director and founder. The theater process has allowed women to discuss their struggles and to express their thoughts and emotions in a safe environment with people who are sympathetic and supportive, as well as with people who have had similar experiences.

Rhodessa Jones

THE MEDEA PROJECT is theater for incarcerated women. The project began out of an invitation from the California Council for the Arts, through a program in the jails called Programs for People. I've been working with the California Arts Council for a very long time. I got a call from this woman who had gotten my name and wanted me to consider replacing an artist that they had at the city jail. They had a belly dancer at the city jail. I was totally mystified. I thought, "Wow! Working with incarcerated women, belly dancing!" In that moment I thought, "This must be really new territory. They have no idea what to do, but, bless their hearts, the California Arts Council wants to do something."

Programs for People asked me to teach aerobics to the women at the city jail. I thought that was kind of odd, being that I wasn't an aerobics teacher. But, again I was thinking, "Well, they want to do something." So, I agreed, and I started working two days a week at the city jail in San Francisco. This was 1989 or 1990.

After about a month or so, I realized that I had to get really creative if I was going to impact these women's lives because they weren't interested in aerobics, and I wasn't an aerobics teacher. The women would be corraled every morning that I came, and they would be made to go to the gym with me and work out. But they would go to the gym and just sit around, and they'd listen to—I had a beat box and some tapes—and they liked that. They would talk with me a little bit. I started to think about how to engage them really. So, I started to dress in a somewhat provocative way. I was imitating television, cable television at the time, which had the early aerobics stuff on TV, which was really a lot like soft porn—really skin-tight unitards.

The women were just fascinated. I would move, and at that time I was turning forty, and I talked about turning forty, and an aging body. I talked about the possibility of being a grandmother. They were just entranced that I could stand on my hands, walk over, because I'd been a performing artist for a long time, and I'd been a gymnast for many years. Most of the women were African American or Latin women. They were just amazed at me talking and moving, so they started bringing other people just to look at this "crazy gym teacher," as they called me.

Most of the women were in jail for prostitution, drug addictions, drug sales, writing bad checks, welfare fraud. So, I started talking about looking for love in all the wrong places. I started talking about my own narrow escapes around drugs and men. I started talking about being Black and being a woman. I started talking about being a teenage mother. They were just more and more fascinated because they can relate to all these things. Finally, one woman said to me, "Why are you telling us your business?" And I said, "Well, I'm an artist." She said, "What's that?" with no malice whatsoever, total innocence. And, that was my entry. I thought that I will give myself this problem to solve in this environment: How, and what is an artist in jail? What is a woman artist? What is an African American woman artist in jail? And how do I impact the lives of these women, as an artist? I'm not a psychotherapist, I'm not a social worker, but I am a womanist. I did come of age during the great cultural revolution in America which was the '60s, and I did have a baby when I was sixteen.

They said, "Well, can we talk?" And I said, "As long as you're willing to participate in the truth, and as long as you're willing to agree that what is said here stays here. And you have to be willing to agree that no one person has a greater pain than another person." And then we began to have some dialogue, especially the older women.

At the same time, I was still working on physical stuff, so the girls who had been cheerleaders, the girls who had been African dancers, and the girls who had been really active in their youth started to surface. People started taking leadership positions. Some of them really wanted to compete with me, because I was just this old bitch, and if this old bitch could do it, then they could do it. All that was fine with me. So I had two heavy components: I had the girls who wanted to move, who remembered movement, and then I had the older women who wanted to participate in a conversation about our lives.

Then I went back to my improvisational handbook by Viola Spolin, *Improvisation for the Theater*. I took that handbook in, and I started to use games in that book to get us to play. If we could play, we would relax, and then we could get into the deep stuff. They started to tell me their stories. I realized that if I could get really basic with games like blind man's bluff, red light green light, and volleyball, everybody would warm up, and everybody would start to breathe. Once they could play, their defenses came down, and they felt lighter. A lot of people weren't that old really; they just had been doing drugs since they were very young. When you start doing drugs and you're very young, your childhood disappears rapidly. I was able to tap into that kind of memory.

I'm an artist in my own right, who's always taken my own story and made theater, because a long time ago, I decided I wanted a place on the stage—we're talking the late 1960s, 1970s. I realized early on that if I was going to create, if I was going to perform, I had to create my own work. Then I read a piece by Toni Morrison, and she was talking about why she writes. And she said, "I write the kind of books that I like to read." I thought, "I want to make the kind of theater that I like to see, and that I think other people should see."

I came to the jail with a body of work already. I had taught science and math and history with theater, with Kindergarten through six, before I even started to work in the jails. So I had that ability when I arrived. Also, the politics of the experience, and reminding those women-of-color that it was by no small act that they were in jail. Trying to create a real laboratory to explore the reality of their lives and the context of jail was one of the first things that happened, but I wasn't allowed by the authorities to videotape, to record, or to photograph. So I would go home every night, and I would write down as much of what I remembered that I heard, because the language interested me. Their thought processes interested me. The ages of women interested me, there were babies with babies, the old con, the matron, the virgin, all those. So, I started to look at the ages of women in jail, and it was fascinating to me, because I was not prepared for how immense that population was, because we always hear about men in jail. All of a sudden, there were just so many women in jail, and so many women were weary with it already, and as they talked, a loss always came up.

They didn't even know that it was about sexual abuse or sexual violation. A loss of faith, a loss of a structure or family. Their mothers might've been in the life. With their mothers' boyfriends, it became open season on them, and there was nowhere for them to go. There was no protection. They would fight back, and they would consequently end up being victimized as well as being incarcerated, because they were fighting back. They were running away from home. They were running away from a system that didn't work. They had lost a sense of their selves, their families. Also, around them, people had died, people had OD'd, daddies had gone to prison, daddies had left, mothers had left. Loss plays an amazing part. Abandonment, anger. At the same time, you're always being hauled before some juvenile system, and because you are female, I believe you get a worse slapping than if you're a boy doing this. All of these things would come up in the conversations, and a lot of tears, and a lot of rage. There was also betrayal.

I realized what these women would inform me of was that if I'm losing on this end, I'm losing families, church, school structures, I've got to go out and find a family. I've got to go and find love. Most people think that women become addicted and then they are prostitutes. Whereas usually, you start out being a prostitute because he says, "Ooh, baby, you're so fine. We can make a lot of money." Or, your kids are hungry, and then you have to anesthetize yourself to go out and turn the tricks, and be in that life. And then, the next thing you know, you've got a heavy habit, and you're dealing with the police, and they've got your number. So all that stuff came up in conversations.

I talked about us, not them versus me, but "What are we going to do? What are we going to do about our children? What are we going to do about this system? What are we going to do about our daughters?" I'd have to go home and write down the curve of the languages, the music, the rage, the incredible humanism that surrounded everything. Humor.

I made a piece entitled *Big Butt Girls, Hard-Headed Women.* It was a one-woman show about jail, based on my interviews and interactions with these women. Everybody across the country wanted to see it. I've done that piece in Rome. I will probably do that piece in Greece next May. That sort of informed me that the country really wanted to know. I was interested in how to put these women center stage. I thought, how do I as an artist make the culture remember or know that our sisters are going to jail in such numbers?

Big Butt Girls, Hard-Headed Women—the title was such a communal thing with African American people. I'd go somewhere and they'd see that title, and they would say, "Ooh, I've got to go see this." And they thought it was going to be a booty show. Or, women my age would say, "Ooh, girl," or "Girl, why you chose that title?" It was because growing up, we were always admonished to not be so hard-headed, and to "sit your big butt down." And I would look at women in jail, and I'd think, "Boy, I'm glad I was raised in the house that I was raised in." I'd hear my father and my mother say this. Then other sisters would say, "Yeah, you know, my daddy used to say that too."

I've been doing this piece for more than ten years now. As the piece grew and matured, and I started to travel all over the place, I started to ask that they connect with halfway houses because I wanted the women that I was talking about to come and see this work. I needed their response, and that was just magical for me. To have them out there "amen-ing," and also to have the arts community realize the person sitting next to me has been through this.

In the piece, I made an altar, a place of concrete memory, which is the
only real set piece in the show. It's made up of photographs, bits and
pieces of mythology around being Black, or things that the women made
in jail and gave me. The altar became this place for the public, where,
after the show, people would come up and they would just tell me the
most amazing things about their lives. Really bourgeois Blacks, Blacks
who were living the good life. I remember one woman in particular
when I was in San Diego, California, and she had heard about the piece,
and she had come from Arizona. She was real CEO material, just really
put together, educated, beautifully coiffed, gorgeous sister. But, she had
a twin sister who was just the opposite. Since they were fifteen, her twin
sister had been in and out of jail. Her parents had since died. She was in
her late forties, and she had sort of written her sister off. She said, "You
know, I just decided I couldn't know her." She said, "And tonight, your
piece made me want to claim her. To try to understand what's happening, and to know that she is my sister. She is my family." And that was a
pretty amazing thing, for somebody to lay their burdens down.

I started working at the county jail, and the first year was all babies;
I mean nineteen and twenty-year-olds. I wanted to reinterpret *Medea*,
the story of *Medea*. They didn't like to read, but they loved story-telling.
So I would tell them the story of *Medea*, and how *Medea* killed her children in revenge. They got very upset, and they said Medea was a dumb
bitch. It is so funny how faith is, how spirit is, because always, we
would get into one of these conversations, and prior to that, somebody
would be flipping out because their kids had just been taken away, or
their man had gone to jail, and so another baby was lost to the system.

I remember the first day I said, "Wait a minute, how different are we
than Medea? Your mother may have your children, your grandmother
may have your children, but they're not with you. And this coming and
going in jail, who is trying to explain to the little ones what's going on?
What kind of murder is that to the spirit of a child whose mommy's
there one day, and then mommy's not there? When mommy's there,
mommy's like in an altered state." And, they started to get it.

I talked about how *Medea* was all about giving over your power to
men. I started to see them connect with the story, and I said, "I want you
to take this story, and I want you to write your own version of it from
your own experiences." And that's how the text begins for the play.

First, we just had a group of women in jail who were doing this piece for all the different groups, men too. They were performing for the different classes: GED, mechanics, poetry. So they were performing. I started to notice also that they were feeling protective about this group. This belonged to them. This was something that they had made. All this stuff, for me, was like a part of my idea of the new model in jail. What is rehabilitation? What do we expect from rehabilitation? How can art be effective? This was what I was learning as I flew by the seat of my pants.

All of a sudden, there was a group of girls who came to me and said, "You know, this is our show. This is our project. You can't just let people come in. We want to have something to say about who comes in." They said, "We going to talk to them, like you be talking to us." And I said, "Okay." And so they would set up their own little orals, and would ask, "Why do you want to be in the group?" "Are you going to tell the truth?" "What's the worst thing you've done? What should we know about you?" I would just sit back and be like the consultant on the side. And they would decide, "Well, okay, she can be in it."

Since then, it's gotten really big. I go in now every four to six months. I've been trying to do four months, because my own life just took off in a certain way with the Medea Project, and I do national shows. With the help of Sheriff Hennessey, we got clearance for these women to come out under guard. They got to come out and do their show, and they'd have to go back to jail each night. Then next time it was two weeks. So now, we get a two-week run with the sheriff's blessings. There's also a bunch of guards who have been with us for a long time.

The women's communities are the ones that took it over the top, just word of mouth. So many really fine technical artists came on board for no money, and did the sets, the costumes, the lighting. We just killed, because I was really interested in a state-of-the-art work. I didn't want to do community theater. I wanted it to be run like anything else that was going on in the city, and it is.

As the women began to dance again, they started to understand the discipline that was required. People claimed their space inside of the group. People participated in the choreography. Some people said, "Well, why don't we do this?" It was a great awakening for all of us that this was a collaboration.

We talked about our names. We talked about matrilineage. One of the exercises was to organize your matrilineage as a part of the show, like, "I am Rhodessa, the daughter of Estella, the granddaughter of

Flossie and Anna, the mother of Saundra, the grandmother of Chaz Nicole." Everybody had to do that. For people who say, "Well, I don't know," I would say, "Well, next time you get a visit, part of your visit's going to be finding out as much as you can about where you come from." Then you would get another kind of story. That's how you would introduce abandonment, loss, in a safe way. It was all about gathering material. It was all about examining our lives, and exploring and investigating grief, anger, pain.

There also was a lot of touching, though. I taught a lot of group lifts and ways for handling each other. The "womb circle" is one of the things that we do. [In the womb circle, women move in as close as possible to encircle a woman who may be leaving or who is in great pain. Everyone will touch her.] It is also touching in a nonsexual way. It's a way to establish community and camaraderie amongst women.

I think through the Medea Project, we help to get the women standing on their feet. Then the question is, "Do you want to live or do you want to die?" Some people have said they don't know. I say, "Well then you better figure it out, because none of this other stuff's going to work if you don't want to live." The other side of that is, I feel there are certain aspects of other treatments that are counterproductive. In jails, it's like, "Well, they're not ready to be in a theater company, because they've got to work on their real issues," or "Well, you're spending too much time with this theater group." Part of the national consciousness is that theater is something over here. Also, I feel like it's a plantation. So we're competing with all the other overseers, all the other people who—a lot of White folks—want these people to belong to them. They're people of color, and that really goes on, but that conversation has not been had, yet.

I feel that I'm a success when I can say to somebody, "It's your story. Your story is greater and bigger than most of that crap on TV. If you really want to do something fabulous, write a book so you'll be on *Oprah*, versus watching *Oprah*, because your story would blow Oprah's hair back." The women in jail used to love to read Jackie Collins, and I said, "Well, what's that got to do with us, though? How many Black folks are in these books? Or Latino folks in these books?" They said, "Well, I still like it." I said, "Well, fine. But there's a whole lot of other stuff." That's when I introduced Alice Walker, Toni Morrison, and Fannie Lou Hamer, because you're dealing with people that don't have a lot of information on a lot of levels. Which is why they're in jail.

The Medea Project is a mixture of intensive social and political science projects. It's a real exploration of the justice system, and our places in it, racially, culturally, and socially. It is, as well, an art project, a theater project. I think that what the Medea Project, myself, and other people have brought is a consciousness that was not there surrounding the female populations. I've grown a lot working in the jails. I've learned to be really thankful about my position as somebody that didn't fall through the cracks, or that the relationship I do have with my mother is special and I shouldn't take it for granted.

My family was always performing for each other and telling stories. My father was a great storyteller. My mother is a wonderful storyteller, and a wonderful singer. We were rural people. My mother and father were migrant workers, so we ended up in upstate New York because my father had been doing that migration forever. Then, at some point, he decided that it was time to do something else, so we were going to have different lives than they did. So my father and mother bought a little old plot of land with a house on it, way up in the country, outside of a place called Wayland, New York, which is like sixty miles south of Rochester, New York. We settled there, and my mother and father wanted us to get a good education, which for those two Black people was simply finishing high school. My mother and father were not really educated people, but we always had a ton of books. I always saw my father reading. My mother and father both read the Bible all the time.

I always begin by telling people that theater saved my life; the art making, being a part of the theater community, saved this colored girl's life. Like I said, I had a baby at sixteen, and then I met up with a theater group when I was probably seventeen or eighteen. They were like a hippie commune. I started out as a gopher. It was there in the theater that I really felt acceptance, or felt that I had a greater mission. I sensed that there were more possibilities to life than to be weighed down with a lot of children, or even to just be some man's wife. I felt the possibility that the world could and would really open up for me. It wasn't like, "Oh, now I'm going to go to art school." It's just that everything started happening, and I would say "yes" to things, and that's a great game in theater.

It was coming to San Francisco, in the late 1960s, early 1970s that I started to really train for theater. I danced with Theresa Dickinsen, and Theresa was one of the original Twyla Tharp dancers out of New York, and Theresa came to California. I really wanted to make theater that informed as well as educated.

22

Professor Brenda V. Smith

Brenda V. Smith is an associate professor at the Washington College of Law at American University. Prior to teaching, she was senior counsel for economic security at the National Women's Law Center and director of the center's Women in Prison Project. In 1993, she successfully litigated a class action lawsuit on behalf of women inmates in Washington, D.C. The case involved sexual abuse of female inmates in the District of Columbia prisons.[1]

Professor Brenda V. Smith

I GUESS I HAVE BEEN going in and out of prisons all of my life. I come from a huge family. When I was a kid, I went into prisons to visit cousins and uncles. I didn't have the traditional fear and separateness that people have about prisons, because some of the best people I knew were in prison. My parents were migrant workers, and I grew up doing migrant work. A lot of the people who we worked with went back and forth between the community and prison and jail, particularly in the South. Generally, contractors would pay people's bail, and they would work off their bail. They might get arrested again, and they would come back out. So, I had a very intimate knowledge of prisons and jails.

When I went to law school, I participated in the juvenile justice clinic. I liked the clinic and I felt very comfortable with my clients. I wasn't uncomfortable going to my clients' homes and neighborhoods or the institutions because I had been in and out of the institutions all my life. I was recruited for the D.C. Public Defender Service out of the law school clinic. But I didn't go directly to PDS. I clerked for two years with a judge on the D.C. Superior Court. After clerking for two years, I worked at PDS for two years.

I left PDS because I felt that my intervention wasn't really effective. It was effective in some ways, but it wasn't doing anything long term. I left PDS to do policy work. I wanted to intervene in a way that would prevent people from coming into the criminal justice system. While I was at PDS, I became the specialist in cases involving women clients. I saw that there was a certain connection that women clients wanted, whether they were girls or adults, which wasn't really part of the standard representation that was provided for people. Often, the particular charge was the least of their concerns. They were concerned about a child, someone in a relationship, or trying to piece their lives together. Therefore, I went to the National Women's Law Center to learn more about policy issues affecting girls and women.

I went to the National Women' Law Center in 1988, and did policy work for a year. The funny thing was that I missed my clients. Also, I found that there were not many women's organizations, certainly not national women's organizations, that did anything with regard to women in prison. Partly, I believe this was because these organizations were so accustomed to looking at women as victims in regard to the criminal justice system. The organizations did not understand that there was an entirely different group of potential clients within the criminal justice system. I also think that the women's rights community felt an uneasy fit between its alliance with law enforcement, particularly around the issues of domestic violence, on one hand, and work with people who were in the criminal justice system, on the other hand. But it didn't feel uncomfortable to me.

I pitched an idea to develop a project that would bring together all of the center's resources to work with this particular group of poor and disenfranchised women. Women in prison had to be seen in the larger context of a particular disenfranchised group who happen to be in prison. Prison presented another barrier. Around 1989, I did a series of focus groups with women inmates at the D.C. jail at the Lorton Minimum Security Annex. I said to them, "Look, I cannot assist you with your underlying criminal charge or appeal, but if we could bring you the information and resources on anything that you wanted, what would it be?" The women listed about forty-two things, and a lot of them were issues related to family, public benefits, housing, employment, health, issues related to kids, and mental health services.

Initially, this was solely my project at the National Women's Law Center. I was able to get the Georgetown Women's Law Public Policy Fellowship Program to allow eight fellows to work on this as their project. I did focus groups with the fellows, and I started seminar groups at the prison with them. Mostly, I coordinated it. The idea was pretty simple—to get local and national experts to commit two hours a week to the women in prison. For example, if someone was an expert in child abuse and neglect, they would come and talk to the women about their work and answer the women's questions.

I thought a seminar series would be noncontroversial because the prison was very sensitive about people coming in. As it happened, just teaching people about their rights and about resources was controversial. After the first month or two, we were on a collision course with the prison because the women were saying, "I'm losing my kids because I'm not allowed to go to court for the abuse and neglect proceedings." We had judges come in and say, "Well, all you have to do is tell your lawyer that you want a 'come-up' to come to court." Later, the judge would say to women, "You mean, you didn't know that you could get a 'come-up' for court?" So, it was educational on many levels.

Typically, the speakers were more educated by the women, than the women were educated by the speakers. Sometimes people would see people and say, "What happened to you?" And the person would say, "I've been in jail." This speaks to the invisibility of prison. People disappear once they go into the system and no one bothers to check for them. For example, at the typical abuse and neglect proceeding, the lawyer doesn't do anything until a week or two before the hearing. They can't find the client and they say, "Miss X has not been in contact with me." The social worker does the same thing, "There has been no contact with this writer since X date, and X hasn't expressed any interest in getting back together with her kids. I suggest that we initiate termination of rights or whatever, at this point."

When courts began to understand that lawyers were not checking to find out where their clients were, and the social workers weren't checking, and even if they did know where the women were, they weren't asking for come-ups, it became controversial. The prison system was angry, because it had to send people up to court hearings. Lawyers were angry because they felt that we were making them look bad in front of their clients and the court.

In a number of situations, women were—and still are—released from prison with no money, no clothes, and just an armband to show the bus driver to take them someplace. That should not be the case. People should not be released to homelessness. Therefore, we brought in people from the transitional housing community to say, "Oh, yeah, we have beds. We have great places for people to come and work with people on employment and on health issues." Of course, the women would say, "Well, why isn't my case manager making this referral before it's time for me to go out?" So the case managers got angry with us as well.

After a year, we began to put the legal services piece together. There was a cadre of community-based providers and local and national experts who did this work. We made many referrals for housing. We began to know the drug treatment system and the parole system. We also did a lot of child custody work. In January 1993, it became very clear that we had to sue the Department of Corrections; there was no way around it. We had informed people about their rights and at every turn, they were not able to vindicate those rights in the system. In October 1993, along with Covington and Burling law firm, we filed suit against the D.C. Department of Corrections, alleging that the prison conditions violated women's constitutional rights under the Eighth Amendment, Title IX, and the Equal Protection clause.

We alleged that the residences were roach and rat-infested, and that women had unequal access to educational and vocational programs compared to men. For example, while men could get a four-year college degree, women could only get a GED. The only apprentice program available for women was an apprenticeship in housekeeping, where the practicum was to clean the jail.

We also sued about the pervasive pattern of sexual abuse and misconduct in prisons. We weren't going to raise this, but as we interviewed women about the education and vocational programs, the women said, "Well, you know, the way to get ahead here is to have sex." It was a sort of dance that everybody knew, and the dance differed from institution to institution. In some instances, a whole economy developed around sex—sex for cigarettes, sex for food, or sex for phone calls. We were able to certify a class with regard to this conduct because everybody would say, "Yes, I've had this experience."

I was doing a lot of work with women who became pregnant while they were incarcerated. I tried to get the women before the parole board before they delivered. I also provided legal services for women who wanted to terminate their pregnancies, which is a very tricky issue in the District, since we cannot use any of our funds for abortions for low-income women. D.C. General Hospital provides medical care for women in prison and they stopped doing abortions. In order for women to obtain abortions, they had to contact the local Planned Parenthood, get the money together, get a private escort and go out into the community, in shackles, to have the abortion. I also was doing a lot of work to set up custody agreements for people who had delivered. So, I knew what was going on, but I don't think that we ever thought about the magnitude.

As we started interviewing women for the complaint, it became clear that I personally knew fifteen to twenty women who had conceived while they were in prison. When we started interviewing people, everybody started talking about it. Then we started asking people whether they had experienced sexual harassment or misconduct while they had been in prison. Most of the women would say yes. The women were housed in co-ed facilities, which contributed to the problem. At the annex, the women had to run a gauntlet of male prisoners every day. They would leave the facility and walk down the hill through a row of men to go eat their meals on the men's compound. The men would yell obscenities about the women's bodies and the staff would just look away when that happened. This happened every time they had a meal, and there were three meals a day. It was a highly sexualized environment, which the court discussed in its opinion.

When we talked to them, individual women said different things. Some women said that they felt demeaned by the way that the staff talked to them, calling them bitches and "hoes," and that the staff allowed the men to speak to them that way. Another group of women felt that they were *all* viewed as being sexually available because *some* women were available sexually. Another group of women said, "There are no jobs here. There is nothing to do in order to get money in order to buy food. I can't eat the food here because it's so bad. If I have to have sex with someone in order to get some food, I'll do it. I don't have anybody in the community to take care of me." Some women really felt that they had developed a relationship with the other person. They craved intimacy. Also, it increased their status in the institution. They got tapes, new sneakers, perfume, or jewelry; things that made them feel valued.

There also were those situations where men in some institutions were predators who preyed upon particular types of women, particularly women with mental health problems, very young women, and women with drug addiction problems. More often than not, this was unprotected sex. This is particularly troubling because the rates of HIV infection in the District, and in the prison population, are astonishing.

Another piece of the litigation was on obstetrical and gynecological care, not all of which was abysmal. Basically, as stated in the Amnesty report,[2] women who were in advanced stages of pregnancy were shackled. Women could not get basic prenatal care in the institution, so they had to be transported to D.C. General Hospital. The only way that they would be transported was in leg shackles and arm shackles with a belt. Some women would just refuse to go for prenatal care. Also, women were shackled in labor; they were handcuffed by an arm or a leg or both while they were giving birth. Often, their medical-care complaints were ignored.

Another big issue in the lawsuit involved work training, which permitted inmates to work in the community within six months of being released. They would work during the day and return to prison at night. There never had been more than one woman at a time on work training, while there had been sixty or more men in the program. They could not work in highly paid industries, which helped foster their dependence and need to have sex to subsist. For a time, the District of Columbia had a college program that men could participate in. One year, the valedictorian for the undergraduate class was a male prisoner. Women could not get into those classes. The women were outraged about it, especially since they were in mostly for drug offenses, while men may have more violent offenses.

Ninety-nine percent of my clients were African American women. It was very unusual to see White women in the system, and White women who were in the system were treated differently. They were viewed as smarter. It was so paradoxical that they received better treatment, even in a system primarily run by African Americans. There are many issues for African American women. One is that because of our detachment from the economy, we tend to be poor. We tend to be underemployed and unpaid. That sets up situations for us to lapse into the criminal justice system. A lot of African American women end up in prison primarily because of drugs. Women typically are low-level in these drug operations, and so they are very vulnerable to law enforcement. A lot of women come into this country from Africa, the Caribbean, and other parts of the diaspora, and they come in carrying drugs for men. They don't have habits themselves, but they are mules for men.

Often, women will not turn men in because of faithfulness or the men saying, "You know, I'm going to get much more time than you would get. If you do this, I'll support you." But it doesn't happen. Also, there is a lot of fear because many of the women have been physically and sexually abused in these relationships; therefore, they won't turn them in.

I have seen some improvement in the lack of inclusion in the domestic violence movement, regarding perspectives of communities of color. Still, there is more to do. For instance, if your primary response to the domestic violence is the criminal justice response, you must understand that these are communities that have a healthy and justified distrust of the police. Many African American women felt that taking action to protect themselves was totally justifiable. Some women said, "I hurt this person. Either I killed him, or I hurt him really bad. But that's what I had to do in order to be alive today. I'm alive today, even though I'm locked up here. And I'm willing to do the time for it." I didn't see women making a lot of excuses. Instead, they would say, "I did it. I wish this time wasn't so hard." Women are willing to take responsibility for what they have done.

I believe that there are still a lot of legal battles out there to be waged. But I also think that women have to become whole in order to thrive. They also have to understand how to connect with resources and how to use them. No one resolves anything on their own. I find a real sense of deprivation and despair with a lot of my clients, so they fill their lives with drugs, men, and bad schemes. But they also have a quality of resilience that allows them to acknowledge what they did, to balance things in their lives, and to move on.

Kito

Judy

Debbie

23

A Family Story

Renay, Judy, Debbie, and Kito

Many women who have been incarcerated say that a supportive family is one of the most important pieces to surviving their sentences. Judy, Debbie, and Kito are such a family. Their sister-mother Renay is serving a twenty-five years to life sentence for the killing of an elderly woman in upstate New York. Renay asserts that the confession used to obtain her conviction was gained coercively while she was under the influence of drugs. She maintains her innocence and her family supports her continuing efforts to fight for her release.

Left to right:
Debbie, Judy, and Kito

Renay

RENAY: I am presently incarcerated with a twenty-five years to life sentence. I am innocent and wrongfully imprisoned. I must believe that God's justice will prevail. My vision is one of hope, not despair, one of faith, not fear.

Using drugs and lying was the biggest mistake of my life and now I wonder if it has actually cost me my life. My conviction rested upon my statement and the testimony of a jailhouse snitch. Had I not been addicted to crack cocaine, I would not have told this lie to police.

I have been denied all my state appeals. Legal Aid represented me through this process. Now, I represent myself *in forma pauperis*—as a poor person. I have a writ of habeas corpus pending in federal court.

My family's endless love and support for my freedom is truly a blessing from God. Their fighting for my freedom every step of the way keeps my hope alive. Nevertheless, I do get exhausted, and the road I have been traveling has led to many blind alleys.

I do realize at this point in my life that life is serious and one misstep can cost you years of regret and grief. I'm aware that prison will either bring out the best in a woman or ruin her entirely. I'm through with weakness. I stand firm in my faith and fighting for my freedom.

JUDY: Renay is my sister and I love her. I never believed that she had anything to do with this murder, and I never will. I want to support her 100 percent. I've never known my sister to be a violent person in my life, that's why I will do whatever I can do to help her. The rest of the family knows the situation, and when they heard about it, they also didn't believe that Renay was capable of doing this.

Our mother and father are deceased. My father was a laborer and my mother was a housewife, although she worked in the laundry. We had five sisters and four brothers. One of our brothers is deceased, so eight of us are living. Everybody grew up in upstate New York. Renay is the middle child.

DEBBIE: I love my sister dearly. I know that she didn't do what she was charged with. We grew up in a large family. Momma had simple, basic rules for us. My father passed away when I was two, so I didn't get a chance to meet him. But I've heard stories about him, that he was a loving and supportive father. We were taught that we could do anything. We believed and strived for it. There was some fighting among us, but not with Renay. They say I'm the no-nonsense sister. I'm nurturing and loving, but I'll turn to the other side in a heartbeat. But Renay was the peacemaker. She would shy away from the violent aspect of anything.

KITO: I'm Renay's daughter. I'm supporting her because I feel in my heart that she is not capable of any physical harm. No matter what pitfalls she may have come across, that does not make her a murderer. At the same time, I want to shed some light that there is hope. There are a lot of strong things in my character that I would not have if not for the special ingredients that I got from my mother.

JUDY: Renay has always been my protector. I have polio, and she wouldn't let anybody do anything to hurt me, even to this day. She's always been there for whatever we've gone through in life. As kids, when they used to play and jump off roofs, Renay always said, "Come on, Judy, you can do it." Anything they did, I did. I jumped off roofs, I slid down poles, and I got in a lot of trouble, but I was right there and she was right there. She wasn't going to leave me in those situations.

When she was about fifteen, Renay told me that she wanted to be a race car driver. She loves to drive. When she was younger, she had a boyfriend who had these different cars, all fast cars, and Renay loved to drive them. She also wanted to be a model. She was a runway model, and she didn't really pursue that. She was too short to be a model and that kind of crushed her.

DEBBIE: Our mother was an alcoholic, so we grew up in an alcoholic home. We all masked our true selves and true feelings because we didn't know other avenues. A lot of things that led Renay on the path that she chose stemmed from childhood and issues that were never addressed. We always had some kind of mind-altering device in our lives. If it wasn't alcohol, it was cigarettes, or a man or a

woman. There was always something to divert us from
ourselves.

Renay and I have a very different, very special relationship. We shared something in common as sisters, and I can
tell Renay a lot of things that I don't tell anyone else. I am a
recovering addict, and she and I have used together, and
that's the bond that we share. That's why, in my heart, I know
she's innocent. I've seen a side of my sister that the others did
not see. We were caught up in getting high, and the extremes
that you go through are not a pretty sight. Once she inhaled
that crack cocaine, Renay was scared of her own shadow.
When she was sober and not on drugs, Renay would give
you whatever you wanted. She would give you a bag of
clothes, or give you all the dope, just to keep the peace.

That's why I miss Renay—not being able to talk to her.
When I came into recovery, just having someone to confide
in was important, and she was that person for me. She's the
one who saved me, even though she was an addict herself.
My sister came and got me and my son when I was at my
lowest. Being an addict, she knew where I was coming from,
and she was standing with me no matter what. When I
slipped, she came and got me and said, "It's going to be all
right, Debbie."

Now me, I would not let no drug boy or anyone think
they were going to ramrod my sister. That's how it was
going to be with me, but Renay would just say, "Debbie, it
ain't worth it. Here take this shit. I'll go out and get it again."
And she did.

JUDY: Renay was fine throughout high school; she never had a
problem. She graduated from high school. When she was in
her twenties, she met this man who was much older than she
was. I do not believe she was taking drugs before that time.
I believe after that relationship, it went downhill for her. He
was a major drug dealer. He could get anything he wanted
or do anything he wanted. It was the excitement. She was
young, she was beautiful, and she liked the nightlife. He had
the cars, and she could drive anything she wanted. People
recognized her and she liked all of that.

I believe it was the crack. Everybody has experimented with marijuana before, and I don't think that was a problem for her. The crack might not have been a problem for her at first, but if you can get so much of whatever you want and you keep doing this on a seven-day basis, eventually it will get to you. I believe that's what happened to her. That's when it really went downhill. She started acting different, not caring too much about the kids. When that happened, I knew something was going on, because when it came to the kids, she went all out for them.

When he wouldn't supply her anymore, she just did it herself. She had gotten started at that point, and she was back and forth, incarcerated for crimes like petit larceny, boosting, and grand larceny. Nothing violent. She didn't care; it was like she was in another world. You would have to protect her because people would take advantage of her. In her drug state, she wasn't violent; she was real paranoid. When she wasn't on drugs, she was always quiet.

DEBBIE: Renay was arrested for boosting, and she whined and she cried. Back then, we really didn't know about the crack and how it affected the individual. So Judy and I went to bail her out. We brought her back to my house. We were in the house trying to talk to her, and she said, "Okay, okay, I'm going on the porch." One of her kids was out there, and we heard, "Mamma, where are you going?" We all ran out there, and all I saw was Renay cutting the corner, and I didn't see her for a week or so after that. That sealed it; we knew there was a problem.

KITO: I left my mother and lived with my Aunt Judy for about eight months, and then my father made me go to his house. I was fourteen. Every day when I was in eighth grade, she would not be there when I would come home. The house would be empty, barely any food in there, the phone cut off, cable turned off, just going to an empty house. I tried to hold on because I knew I had my little brother and I had to make sure that we got to school, because my mother always told us that we had to go to school. So I was trying to hang in there.

I would wash her clothes, I would iron them, I would do my homework, and I would be there to comfort my little brother like everything was normal. But it wasn't, and then I thought I'd leave and she'll get it together; maybe I'll scare her straight. Because her kids were her life, I thought that was the only way I'd get her to be a mother. But it just kept getting worse. I'd come home the next day and the T.V. would be gone. I'd come home the next day and the furniture would be gone. The next day, the stove was pulled out of its place; she just couldn't get it out of the house.

My father wasn't involved in the drug life. He was doing the opposite. He was trying to make a change in his life to set an example for me because I'm his only child. After I had been at my Aunt Judy's house for about eight months, he figured that he had to be a man and take care of his child. My brother wasn't his child, but being the kind of man that he is, my father always made sure that my brother was all right, and he kept us together. My Aunt Judy and my father really supported me. My father always told me to do the right thing. Regardless of what was happening and the heavy burden that I was feeling, he always told me that I could get out of it. I was naturally smart in school, so I did well. He stayed on me about going to school. He is the major reason why I went to a special high school. He and my mother always told me that I could be anything I wanted to be no matter where I came from.

JUDY: When the drug problem got really bad, and the kids came to stay with me, all of us talked to her. We said, "Renay, you're at the end of your rope now. Come on, leave the drugs. Your home is destroying itself." Even when the kids left, Renay was still getting high. The drug had just completely taken over. We suggested different types of programs and counseling. She would go, but it really wasn't working. When she got back on the street and the drug addicts would say, "Hey, come on Renay, I got some crack," she could say no for a while before eventually giving in. I know drugs are difficult things. She wanted that drug so bad that she was going back out there to get it, and that was as simple as that.

KITO: Social Services did offer some help to her and to me, because I was the oldest and I was affected. I recall going to see
a counselor for about six months, and I did deal with a lot of
the anger that I had. Then they sent me off to some kind of
summer camp; they were trying to show me a normal summer. They focused on me, but they never focused on the family. There have to be programs in place that have real follow-
up. There was no real follow-up. It was like the system said,
"Okay, we did it." Closed the case, boom. But it was never really over with; there were still more problems that just kept
escalating and escalating.

I just believe in my heart that if they had identified the
real problem, which was the boyfriend, things would have
been different. When she went to the emergency room to get
a busted eye sewn back together, the system should have
come in and said, "If you're not going to press charges, we're
going to press charges." I can only imagine how many
young women are still experiencing what she went through,
because it was well known what kind of man he was. My
mother wore black eyes like they were sunglasses. He almost
killed her once. She had a punctured lung. The system did-
n't do anything then. I remember that they put her in protective custody, but that was it. He still swindled a way to get
up in the hospital.

She probably felt that there was no way out. She had
taken everything that you could think of, emotionally and
physically, and there was no way out for her. So drugs were
the outlet for her. When I became a mother and started experiencing that unconditional love for your child, I started to
reflect on some of the things that she told me about some of
the pain that she experienced. That's why I refuse to be in an
abusive relationship, because she always told me that if they
do it once, they'll do it again and they'll almost kill you. I've
seen that with my own eyes. I saw this man walk in the
house and just flip on her. He would just start beating her
with whatever was there, fireplace equipment and stuff like
that. No woman deserves that. She would take the beating
and then he would find a way to get back in her life.

JUDY: She's real. If she's got it, she's going to give it to you. If she doesn't have it, she's going to get it. Renay was a professional booster. If she needed money, that's how she got it. When she was out there, my sister could make money within an hour if she wanted to. That's just a part of her past. She might have gone into department stores and done it, but she did not go into anyone's home and take it.

KITO: She knew how to get money and she never did anything harmful to anyone to get her money. She was always honest. She told me that she was a thief, and I saw my mother steal. Then, the relationship with this drug dealer added to the life-style. We lived a wealthy life-style until the drugs took over. Everybody wanted to be at our house. When the drugs took over, all of the material things disappeared. She would replace them, and they would disappear again. My whole senior year was so rocky for me because I was eighteen years old, and I was trying to come to grips with everything and people were saying crude things about my mother.

After I graduated, I left the area altogether to live with another aunt. While I was away, I found out that Social Services was going to get my brother. I told them, "No, I'll come and get him." I don't know how I did it, but I came back and got my brother.

DEBBIE: I believe that Renay is the scapegoat in this killing. The area where it occurred is predominantly White. There's no way that something that awful happened and no one saw or heard anything. Somebody would have reported seeing a Black face over there.

JUDY: I was not living in the area when it happened. When we heard it, we couldn't believe it. We came back home. We thought it was going to blow over because there was no evidence. It was a big case, because the victim was elderly and had standing in the community.

Renay was not the immediate suspect in the case; someone else was the main suspect. There was a two-year-long case, and they still hadn't arrested her. For two years, nothing came about. They had questioned her, and she passed two polygraphs. At the time she was arrested, it was for a separate theft offense, not the murder. When she was in there, apparently the murder came up in some way. When they arrested her, Renay had just come down off a two-week binge from getting high, and she was real jittery and shaky. They said that Renay said, "Well, if you let me go, I know something about some particular murder." They claimed that Renay told them about this murder in detail and told them all the details of the murder. They claimed that she confessed in three different statements that she made. To this day, the only evidence that they have is that confession. Also, there was a guy that said that Renay did it. They went out of state to question him. He said he didn't know what Renay was talking about. That was the end of that and nothing else was said about him.

We retained a private attorney at the beginning. But that was for the theft; when it turned into the murder charge, he dropped us. He said we didn't have enough money. His attorney's fees had already wiped her out. So, then we got a court-appointed lawyer. Renay had difficulty with him from the start. I think he could have shown more initiative in her case. He represented her at trial. As the trial went on, they portrayed her as a liar, a thief, a prostitute, and a drug addict who would do anything for drugs.

KITO: Her defense attorney won't even talk to us. I called him. I left a message at his home. I even called the original attorney to schedule an appointment to get any records that he had on my mother. He won't even return my call. It's like we're the plague. Whenever we call someone and ask for more information, they say, "Oh, no. You know what you know, and that's all you need to know. She's got twenty-five years to life and that's all you need to know." Well, that's not all I need to know, and that's not all I want to know. If you're going to have her take a hit like this, then I want the missing links to be filled. No one ever filled the missing links.

JUDY: We were there for the summation, and then the jury went out. They came back two or three days after that. All of us were there, but they still didn't have a verdict at that time; they had to come back again. They wanted a clarification on something. It was late in the day, so a lot of us had left and were going to come back. I came back, but by the time I got up there, the jury had come back; they never called us. I went back because Renay had said, "Judy, please come back." But I didn't even get a chance to get up there. I saw a stenographer in the hallway and I asked her. She said, "I'm sorry, but she got twenty-five years to life." I just couldn't believe it. I wasn't actually in court; Renay was there by herself. It was absolutely terrible. After the verdict, no one asked us how we felt. The media just interviewed the district attorney.

Renay went straight to the law library when she went to prison. She has had two appeals and she lost both. We're going to keep on trying. People can say, "Well, you would say anything for your sister." But most of Renay's friends would say that she is not a violent person. Whatever she needed, she would get by boosting. If she has any downfalls, that would be it, that and taking drugs. On this charge, she really was in the wrong place at the wrong time. They gave her twenty-five years to life and we've been working ever since to get her out. It really was an injustice.

KITO: It's refreshing for me to visit my mother. It's like the strength that I need to keep on keeping on. I enjoy the visits. It's tough at the end when we're saying goodbye, but I have the faith of seeing her again the next month. Then I have the hope of overcoming this nightmare, so it keeps me going.

JUDY: I go to visit Renay every month, or every chance I get. The church sponsors a program with a free bus ride to the prison for visits. Renay loves the visits. Her son goes a lot of times with me. He talks to his mother when we go for the visit, but he really doesn't talk about it with her. The grandkids always go. We try our best to send her what she needs. Everybody tries to chip in and we send a food box or we take it to her because it's cheaper. We just try to support her.

DEBBIE: I don't get up there to see her. I went once. I can't take that road trip, but I correspond with letters, and if she needs anything, I'll send it through the others. I'll give anything. I can't see Renay in there. I don't like to be locked up, that caged feeling. But that's not it. I don't want to see my sister in that place, and I can't cope with it.

KITO: My mother instilled in me the strength and courage to make something of myself. She always told me, "It doesn't have to be this way." Each day that I make it now is because of my family, my Aunt Judy, my Aunt Debbie, my boyfriend and his family, and my father and his wife. A lot of times, people get on me if they feel that I'm not doing enough. A lot of times, I just get heavily wrapped up into my children. But my family keeps me balanced. I'm doing what my mother would do for me, what she would expect of me.

I want to open up a home for women and their children, because I can sit down and get on my knees and cry with them because I can relate to their experiences. I think it's important for twenty-four-hour service to be available. Someone has to be available at any time of the night for people that are dealing with mental abuse, because living through my mother's drug addiction was mental abuse for me. I had inner strength, but everyone does not have that. A lot of people need encouragement; they need people. They need an example like me. They need to see that my mother's in jail, doing twenty-five years to life, but I'm still a productive citizen. I still get up every day and go to work. I'm still pursuing my education, and I'm still there for my children and my family.

One day we will wake up from this; the evidence will be revealed soon enough. I hope that people understand that there's a transition period that people have to go through in life. In my heart, I believe that this is just one of the transitions that saved my mother's life.

PART III

CONCLUSIONS AND RECOMMENDATIONS

> As one reads history . . . one is absolutely sickened not by the crimes the wicked have committed, but by the punishments the good have inflicted.
>
> —Oscar Wilde

SUMMARY OF *INNER LIVES* NARRATIVES

The American approach to crime and punishment is severe for its over-reliance on imprisonment to sanction criminal conduct. "Only in the U.S.," notes Professor Michael Tonry, "are constitutional and other safe-guards of criminal defendants systematically being reduced."[1] The harsh punitive thrust of current criminal law doctrine and policy adversely affects many African American women whose poverty, physical and sexual victimization, and drug-related problems are substantial contributing factors in their incarceration.

As the analyses and narratives in the preceding sections reveal, African American women are treated in disparate and disparaging ways at virtually all stages of criminal justice system operation. Automatically suspect as criminals, women such as Denise Pullian and Janneral Denson were subjected to humiliating, intrusive bodily searches, and were further dehumanized by being referred to as inanimate objects—"that thing"—by government workers. As Joyce Ann Brown and Betty Tyson's circumstances starkly illustrate, through criminal justice apparatus, U.S. society willingly incarcerates African American women despite overwhelming evidence of their innocence.

Karen Blakney's experience highlights the gross injustice of drug laws and prosecutions. Her encouragement by undercover DEA agents to "cook" powdered cocaine was expressly induced to trigger the harsher mandatory penalty for crack cocaine. Despite the trial judge's

273

resistance to institute the statutory sentence, successful government appeals overturned his sound determination that long imprisonment was not warranted based on Karen's minor role in the offense and the major turn-around in her life. Although Karen's situation ultimately was resolved positively, many similarly situated women and men languish in prison as "collateral damage" in these misdirected wars. Martha's experience similarly epitomizes the inherent injustice in drug-sentencing laws. A first offender who sold drugs for less than a year, she now serves a maximum life sentence for arranging a buy for a former customer who worked as a police informant. Surely society is not made safer nor whole by the sentences meted out of proportion with the offenses in such cases.

Rae Ann and Donna exemplify poor initial decision making and unfortunate personal allegiances. Events stemming from these choices dramatically changed the course of their lives. These adverse consequences resulted in prostitution, drug use, and drug-related offenses, all of which had a deleterious impact on their self-worth and ability to extricate themselves from criminal offending. Nevertheless, prison seems an inappropriate place to address their level of wrongdoing, particularly without giving effective attention to their underlying emotional needs. With Donna, for instance, issues of self-esteem, past abuse, and sobriety must be addressed to end the cycle of recidivism.

Questions of accountability and culpability, of course, are central to criminal adjudication and sentencing. The resolution of these issues is complex, frequently involving varying degrees of acceptance or denial of responsibility by those accused of criminal offenses. As we also have seen, however, resolution of criminal cases is further complicated by frequently being fraught with conscious or unconscious race, gender, and class biases.[2] In Mamie's situation, for example, long abused and neglected herself, her conviction results from perplexing unanswered questions surrounding her daughter's death, including questions about Mamie's alleged involvement, the rigorousness of her legal representation, and her understanding or lack thereof of the charges and legal proceedings against her. Thus, issues of structural inequality in society and unequal treatment in criminal justice proceedings render the ultimate determinations as suspect in many such circumstances.

Difficult issues regarding culpability are raised by situations involving women's responses to violence in their lives. Women such as

DonAlda and Millicent Pierce, for example, waged ultimate struggles to defend their lives after chronic abuse by male partners. Their stories highlight the pervasive violence in women's lives and the lack of preventative measures to ensure women's safety. Perversely, women who act to prioritize their own lives over the lives of their abusers often are punished more severely for taking such life-saving measures. This irony should prompt greater examination of legal concepts of self-defense, particularly where abuse is endemic in the relationship and where the racial backgrounds of the parties are implicated.

Moreover, Marilyn, DonAlda, and Cynthia's experiences raise serious issues about incarcerated women's access to mental health care, as well as concerns about ethics and efficacy regarding prescription drug use for inmates and inmate autonomy regarding decisions about their health care.

For some women, prison raised their consciousness about the circumstances of women's lives, with particular regard to the criminal justice system, whether or not they shared economic, educational, or sexual orientation backgrounds, or particular experiences related to their incarceration. In prison, they found value in their own lives and the lives of other women despite such differences and became advocates for individual and common concerns. For example, even where women such as Cynthia acknowledge the grave harms they have caused, they insist on fair treatment within the prison institution. Thus, overcoming feelings of worthlessness and demanding recognition of their human dignity occur after much introspection and self-forgiveness. For Elizabeth and Joyce Logan, new-found awareness and self-worth in prison provided the impetus to become self-educated about the law. This enabled them to challenge prison policies and assert their rights to humane treatment and conditions, including necessary health care and prevention of abusive cross-gender body searches.

Upon release, other African American women who are former inmates, and organizations like Grace House and Aid to Children of Incarcerated Mothers (AIM), can support women in the reclamation of their lives and human potential, particularly if such assistance was not available or effective in prison. Bettie Gibson, a former Grace House resident, shows that such structured support in transition from prison can enable women to develop skills for self-sufficiency as well as skills to understand and cope with past histories of physical or sexual abuse, and of substance abuse. With renewed motivation, professional assistance, and peer support, the women can redirect their energies toward positive life changes.

Thus, as Joyce Logan and other women have emphasized, educational and vocational skills opportunities are key to the realization of their potential as productive citizens. Further, as Donna Hubbard Spearman particularly emphasized, the spiritual dimension of the women's lives cannot be ignored in their journey toward personal fulfillment and human development.

Significantly, ex-inmates themselves are providing the assistance that incarcerated and formerly incarcerated women need. Joyce Brown, Ida McCray, Donna Hubbard Spearman, and Millicent Pierce demonstrate the importance of engaging formerly incarcerated women who recognize the particular needs of women inmates and their families to work to meet those needs.

Notably, irrespective of geographical location or variations in their individual circumstances, in their narratives the incarcerated and formerly incarcerated women reported experiences or observations of unfair treatment of African American women inmates within the prisons. These women resisted the stultifying effects of institutionalization by taking advantage of available programs within correctional facilities and demanding human dignity inside and outside of prison environments. Their reports of subtle and overt bias against African American women warrant greater attention by correctional administrators, including a greater diversity within correctional staff employees and greater training on cultural diversity for all prison staff.

Finally, in this book, officials from the judiciary and prison administration have explained precepts of the criminal justice and correctional systems, while members of supportive networks lent valuable insights into the complexities of the women's lives. The depth of Judge Newton's knowledge and sensitivity confirm the importance of having professionals of diverse backgrounds and experiences on the bench, in law enforcement, and throughout the legal profession. Judge Newton's cogent decision in *Thompson v. New York*,[3] a case that was considered by twelve justices of the New York appellate courts, surely contributed rationality to the current debate to reform New York's severe drug laws. Gerald Clay, an assistant warden, approaches his work with equanimity in a professional, no-nonsense, and seemingly detached manner. Conspicuously, however, he volunteered to direct a gospel choir as an expressive outlet for women inmates at his institution. Thus, like many correctional administrators who view themselves as more than jailers, his actions evince more concern than his exterior veneer would suggest.

The importance of community volunteers and involvement of others who are external to the institution, cannot be overstated. Such involvement reduces isolation from members of the larger community and exposes the women to a variety of perspectives. In this regard, artistic director Rhodessa Jones and the Medea Theater Project bring life-saving theater into the prison, helping to restore incarcerated women to wholeness and psychic well-being through connections to classical works and the creation of their own stories. Through the dramatic process, the women develop skills and safe spaces to cope with pain and loss and begin to envision brighter futures for themselves.

For women, one of the most difficult aspects of imprisonment is separation from family. The geographical location of women's prisons and prohibitive transportation costs for many family members make regular visits rare for incarcerated women, assuming, of course, an inclination by family members to visit. It is not unusual for incarcerated women to lose contact with family and friends. This is in stark contrast to incarcerated men, who frequently have visitors and receive mail and care packages. This is why the relationship between Renay and her family bears recognition. Judy, Debbie, and Kito are steadfast in their love for their sister and mother, Renay, currently serving twenty-five years to life for murder. Disbelieving claims that Renay's confession about the killing was truthful and voluntary, they maintain her innocence and continue to support efforts to overturn her conviction. Their regular visits and correspondence are lifelines that sustain all of them.

Sandra Barnhill and her organization, Aid to Children of Incarcerated Mothers (AIM), provide the vital function of helping incarcerated women maintain contact with their families. Thus, critical ties between mothers and children are facilitated through these efforts, as Millicent Pierce and Donna Hubbard Spearman attest. Equally important, AIM supports caretakers, usually African American grandmothers who often assume custody of their incarcerated daughters' (and sons') minor children. Often on the margins of physical health and economic well-being themselves, caretakers require tangible resources and emotional outlets for their unique frustrations and concerns. Similarly, AIM addresses the needs of incarcerated mothers' children by providing counseling, support groups, and special activities for them. Supported in this way, the children have avenues through which to express their fears and frustrations over their family circumstances and can establish foundations to reach their aspirations.

The women of Grace House—Rochelle, Kathy, Annie, and Mary— are lifesavers, too. Women often leave prison with little more than that with which they entered, in terms of material goods or life skills. Thus, Grace House offers women released from prison much-needed housing and the opportunity to become stable and self-actualized. They model sisterhood within a supportive and challenging environment in which released women learn self-sufficiency and a healthy regard for themselves and others. A cadre of professionals and volunteers in educational, occupational, medical, and mental-health fields work with the Grace House residents to redirect the women to more positive alternatives in their lives in the larger society.

Lastly, Brenda Smith shows the power and importance of inspired and effective legal advocacy on behalf of female inmates who are vulnerable to sexual abuse and poor conditions in prison. Her work on behalf of women in the District of Columbia prison system and her continuing efforts to improve prison conditions nationally and internationally infuse meaning into the principle of equal justice under the law. The realization of this principle in the lives of African American women demands greater commitment by all members of the legal profession.

SUMMARY OF IMPLICATIONS FROM
NARRATIVES, DATA, AND LEGAL TRENDS

The overrepresentation of African American women in the prodigious women's prison population warrants closer attention to the specific circumstances of their lives, the conditions of their imprisonment, and their needs upon returning to society. While the concerns of incarcerated women often transcend race, African American women's unique circumstances are generally overlooked within the population of incarcerated women. For example, while most incarcerated women come from impoverished backgrounds, with personal health already compromised upon entering prison, this is particularly true for African American women. Thus, all incarcerated women require proper screening and treatment for any gynecological and obstetrical problems, as well as female-specific cancers, such as breast, ovarian, or cervical. As attorney-activist Ellen Barry observes:

> [T]here is a higher prevalence of depression, HIV, and hepatitis C in women prisoners than in the general adult female population. . . . [B]ecause of these risk factors, it would be logical and prudent public policy to expect that the medical care provided to women prisoners would be at the least adequate and, perhaps, preventive. Instead, there remain widespread deficiencies that have resulted in serious injury and, sometimes, death.[4]

Yet, as Barry further notes, "because women of color are dramatically overrepresented in this population, there is a disproportionate prevalence of certain types of illnesses, such as diabetes, high blood pressure, sickle cell anemia, and a higher instance of undetected breast cancer."[5] As incarcerated women of color present with a higher incidence of HIV infection and AIDS-related illnesses, adequate attention to these medical conditions must also be paid. Jo Lydia Sabur, coordinator of a counseling program for former female offenders in New York City, observes: "There is a sense of helplessness and lack of control, even over little things. There is no say in your medical care or nutritional needs. . . . HIV-positive women are further isolated when they are placed in special units. They are treated like lepers by the regular staff and the medical staff. Considering the special needs of a person who has HIV, prison is the worst place that they can be."[6]

Moreover, as the overall prison population continues to age, greater attention to the special needs of older inmates is required, including special concerns of older women. Thus, the numerous and unique health concerns of African American women and other women of color must be addressed.

Recent reports by national and international organizations shed light on some of the disparate and deplorable conditions in women's prisons and the treatment of women incarcerated therein. These reports documented that women are vulnerable to further sexual violation while incarcerated. In 1996, Human Rights Watch reported on the prevalence of sexual abuse against women in prison. The report highlighted the problems of sexual misconduct and cross-gender supervision in U.S. prisons. Based on its investigation, Human Rights Watch concluded that "being a woman prisoner in U.S. state prisons can be a terrifying experience," and that few effective means of redress existed for women's complaints.[7]

Shortly after the Human Rights Watch report, Amnesty International released *"Not Part of My Sentence": Violations of the Human Rights of Women in Custody*, in 1999. In its report, Amnesty International also identified sexual abuse as a particular problem facing women in prison. In 1999, the GAO also studied the matter of sexual abuse of female inmates by correctional staff in U.S. prisons.[8] The GAO found that the jurisdictions under review—Texas, the Federal Bureau of Prisons, California, and the District of Columbia—were woefully inadequate in recording complaints and maintaining systematic data collection in order to respond to incidents of sexual abuse.[9] Clearly, then, U.S. prisons must adopt effective measures to prevent and punish sexual misconduct by corrections authorities against incarcerated women.

In addition, the high incidence of sexual abuse in the women's lives prior to incarceration demands the availability of adequate psychological counseling, as it often relates to their criminality. Addressing these traumas through counseling is critical to the women's physical and emotional well-being and ultimate rehabilitation. In this regard, drug and alcohol abuse counseling that pays particular attention to women's gender, racial and cultural backgrounds, and experiences also is necessary. In her research on correlations between women's criminality and experiences of prior sexual abuse, psychologist Cathy McDaniels Wilson notes that prison "[p]rogram development needs to incorporate into its foundation the understanding of the socio-historical context under which many African Americans have lived and continue to live. Facilitators should be focused on ways in which to validate, empower, and educate this subpopulation."[10] Instead, a 1997 survey of fifty-two departments of correction found that "only twenty-seven departments reported that they provide substance abuse programs developed specifically for women; only nineteen departments provided domestic violence programs developed specifically for women; only nine departments offered programs for victims of sexual assault; and only nine departments provided special programs to address women's health education."[11]

Moreover, an *Inner Lives* survey of administrators at women's correctional institutions suggests that culturally specific programming for African American women and other women of color is nonexistent or rare.[12] Administrators at ten female correctional institutions across the

Northeast, Midwest, South, and West were asked about the availability of programs or components of programs that addressed the specific concerns of women of color. None of the ten randomly selected institutions offered culturally specific programs for African American women inmates. Explanations varied, as some respondents did not perceive a need for such programs and felt that African American women's needs were sufficiently addressed through general programs. In contrast, other respondents attempted informally to incorporate culturally specific aspects of educational or counseling programs that are directed to African American and other women of color. While conclusions regarding the existence or extent of programs that address African American women's particular experiences and needs are tentative and require further systematic study, the initial responses are not encouraging.

Just as correctional facilities have recognized that women inmates have needs that are distinguishable from male inmates, so too, are racially engendered experiences of African American women worthy of particularized attention. More research on the programming possibilities in this area is warranted due to the positive effects they would have on African American women's self-awareness and rehabilitation. One step in this direction is suggested in Appendix A, which presents a course on African American women's history. As a self-study course, women can complete the suggested readings individually or in study groups with others. In addition, institutions may consider providing courses on African American women's history within their range of educational offerings. As the majority of *Inner Lives* participants expressed, their educational experiences prior to incarceration were often desultory, as their academic needs and potential were largely ignored or underestimated, even when the women exhibited intellectual interest and capability.[13]

In another significant area, incarcerated women's roles as the primary caretakers of minor children also require special attention. Long sentences for relatively minor offenses affect the lives of the women and their children. Furthermore, under circumstances where correctional institutions are located far from women's families, it is extremely difficult to maintain family bonds during prolonged incarceration periods.[14] These circumstances are detrimental to all involved, as women may become despondent and children may lose their connection to their primary parent. The great distances to correctional institutions also jeopardize other important personal ties, making it difficult for women to maintain positive community connections. Therefore, it is vital that prison policies adopt flexible means to facilitate visits by women inmates' family members and make other support systems available. Furthermore, counseling for the particular emotional and material needs of children and substitute caretakers stemming from a mother's incarceration must be addressed as well.[15]

Further, overreliance on incarceration must end. Most women in prison, including most African American women, are excellent candidates for alternatives to imprisonment. They generally are nonviolent offenders who would benefit from drug treatment and educational and employment opportunities.[16] Prisons must provide the necessary resources or training programs that will improve incarcerated women's chances of later sustaining themselves and their families with marketable skills and a living wage. Community alternatives to prison and transitional programs upon release from prison will give the women opportunities to become productive and independent.

Finally, and perhaps most importantly, greater attention must be paid to preventive efforts that reduce women's incarceration altogether. In one respect, prevention must address the safety of African American girls so that they are free from physical and sexual abuse in their homes and elsewhere. The strong correlation between women's histories of physical and sexual abuse and subsequent criminality demands that families, communities, and societal institutions fulfill their roles in protecting African American youth from such harms and guiding their progress toward healthy adulthood. Similarly, where abuse in women's lives originates in adulthood, serious responses to these painful and unlawful acts must be accorded to African American women within their communities, and by social services agencies and legal institutions.[17]

Another instance in which prevention must occur lies within the structure of the criminal justice system itself. Harsh mandatory minimum sentences primarily for low-level drug offenders are indisputably counterproductive and patently destructive of many young people's lives. American society is unjustified in extinguishing the life potential of great numbers of people of color in this manner. Moreover, these laws defy proportionality mandates for criminal punishment and do little to promote public safety. They demand immediate repeal. RAND Institute researchers found that drug treatment is far more effective in addressing direct and ancillary offenses related to drug use.[18]

Notably, such reconsideration is occurring in states where the most stringent application of such measures originated. Increasing financial constraints are forcing reconsideration in several states.[19] In California, notable for its three-strikes and mandatory minimum provisions, voters recently challenged a bond issue for further prison construction and also approved a referendum requiring treatment rather than imprisonment for first-time nonviolent drug offenders.[20] Similarly, in New York State, extensive discussions across the political spectrum are underway to dismantle the notorious Rockefeller drug laws.[21] The fundamental flaw in many state and federal mandatory sentences for drug offenses is that punishment is based on the weight of the substance rather than the individual's involvement in the offense.[22] Therefore, any efforts to reform laws must properly focus on individual culpability rather than be based arbitrarily on the weight of the substance.

African American women's incarceration is not solely due to drug offenses, however. In this regard, more pervasive systemic changes must occur to rid the criminal justice system of all vestiges of race, gender, and class bias that affect the charging decision and the chance for fair disposition of criminal allegations.[23]

A third area of prevention involves judicial oversight of prisons. As Judge Edmund Spaeth, Jr., noted three decades ago, "[I]f the courts are to serve with honor, they must say what they expect the prisons to do, and try to make them do it."[24] Yet, as Judge Spaeth further noted, "The courts' responses to prisoners' suits have proceeded from indifference to confusion, or . . . uncertainty."[25] More recently, Chief Judge Jon Newman of the Second Circuit Court of Appeals, observed that "[a] concerted effort to disparage the vindication of prisoners' rights and to limit opportunities for legal redress"[26] existed within the United States. As Chief Judge Newman recognized, accounts of frivolous prisoner lawsuits are often misleading.[27] Primarily based on misconceptions and misrepresentations about the legitimacy of inmate complaints, Congress's recently enacted Prison Litigation Reform Act severely limits inmates' access to the courts.[28] Thus, legislatures and courts are ceding to prison authorities near total control of inmate access to legal redress and public awareness of prison conditions. At a time of unparalleled prison construction and inmate population growth,[29] it is more important than ever to ensure judicial oversight regarding correctional policies, institutional conditions, and the treatment of inmates.[30]

One hundred years ago, W. E. B. Du Bois remarked about the unrealized promise of Reconstruction era reforms, "Despite compromise, war, and struggle, the Negro is not free. In well-nigh the whole rural South the black farmers are peons, bound by law and custom to an economic slavery from which the only escape is death or the penitentiary."[31] As the French say, *plus ça change, plus c'est la même chose* (the more things change, the more they remain the same). Regretfully, this aphorism renders Du Bois' commentary as true today as a century ago with respect to the appalling proportion of African Americans in U.S. prisons and jails. These trends can be reversed, however, beginning in this new century. Thus, in the end, I hope that this book, through its data, analyses, narratives, and photographs will prompt greater recognition of the value of African American girls' and women's lives. More broadly, I hope that U.S. society will pursue more effective solutions than imprisonment to address social problems and criminality. This requires fundamental changes in our society, not just changes in the women who directly experience incarceration. It is imperative that inequality in society and law finally be eradicated. American society must actualize the principles of fairness that it so often espouses. If we commit to a vision that encompasses African American women's experiences and perspectives within the concept of justice, we will learn to our great benefit that everyone can contribute to society given the opportunity and means to do so.

Afterword

Angela J. Davis, Professor,
American University Washington College of Law

AFRICAN AMERICAN WOMEN are the fastest-growing and arguably worst-treated segment of the American prison population. They receive much more severe sentences and harsher overall treatment than their similarly situated White counterparts. Yet although there has been significant focus on the plight of African American men in the criminal justice system in the scholarly literature and media, African American women have been relatively invisible despite their growing numbers and severe problems in America's prisons. In *Inner Lives*, Professor Paula Johnson discovers these women for us all and reveals their pain, struggles, and triumphs.

I was a public defender in the District of Columbia for twelve years before becoming a law professor. The racial disparities in the criminal justice system (in the District of Columbia and nationwide) were always obvious to me, as were the unique problems and disparate treatment of women. The vast majority of my male clients and all of my female clients were African American. The men who were incarcerated in the District of Columbia received little to no rehabilitative treatment, very little education, and inadequate health care. The women received even less of everything, and almost all of them suffered from abuse and lack of a basic education and health care. It seemed as if no one paid attention to these women, perhaps because their numbers were relatively small at that time. This was before Professor Brenda Smith's groundbreaking litigation and advocacy on behalf of D.C. women prisoners.

Since my days as a public defender in the 1980s, the number of African American women in the criminal justice and prison systems has grown exponentially. The proliferation of mandatory minimum sentencing laws, the expansion of prosecutorial discretion, and the discriminatory treatment of African Americans at every stage of the criminal process seem to have taken their toll on African American women more than on any other segment of the prison population. Yet, with a few notable exceptions, very little has been written about the deplorable, unimaginable conditions under which these women have lived—before and after their imprisonment. Professor Johnson fills this void.

In *Inner Lives*, Professor Johnson makes an extremely important contribution to criminal justice and prison literature, to the criminal justice and prison systems, and to the lives of African American women. In part 1, Professor Johnson provided a thorough summary and analysis of the treatment of African American women in the criminal justice and prison systems. This part of the book provides important historical context and demonstrates how racial, socio-economic, and gender disparities have plagued African American women in the criminal justice system from slavery times to the present day. Professor Johnson's presentation of critical data and her analysis of historical and contemporary legal phenomena are both substantive and accessible to a broad audience.

Part 2 consisted of Professor Johnson's powerful presentation of the narratives of African American women who are currently incarcerated or have previously served prison time. This part also contains the stories of women who work with African American women in the criminal justice and prison systems in a variety of capacities. The power and passion of these women's stories gives the book its unique strength. It is through these narratives that the many injustices Professor Johnson discusses in part 1 are illustrated so clearly. Certain themes resonate throughout many of the stories: unfair treatment by law enforcement, inadequate and uncaring defense counsel, extremely harsh sentences for nonviolent offenses, and racially discriminatory treatment in the court system and in prison facilities. There are the unthinkable cases of innocent women serving many years of hard time before being released and others maintaining innocence who may never be released. There are also the stories of women who admit wrongdoing but received extremely harsh sentences for nonviolent offenses or for minimal involvement in a violent offense. The other consistent themes that predominate the narratives of those who admit guilt as well as those who maintain innocence: incredibly difficult lives as children and adults;

sexual, physical, and emotional abuse as children and adults; lack of nurturing and demonstrations of affection from their mothers; and substance abuse as a way to forget the pain.

It is very difficult to come away from these narratives without empathy for these women, an appreciation of their gifts and values as human beings, and an understanding of how good and loving people might do bad things if the circumstances are bad enough. And this is the power and uniqueness of this book. It provides critical information about the plight of African American women in the criminal justice and prison systems. But unlike other works about injustice in these systems, it compels the reader to care by putting a human face on the cold, hard facts. The facts about the harshness of mandatory minimum drug laws come to life through Elizabeth's fifty-year sentence and Rae Ann's two life sentences for drug distribution. Consistent physical violence and emotional abuse in these women's lives become all too real through the painful childhood memories of Betty Tyson, Mamie, and Cynthia.

The narratives of the criminal justice officials and advocates are inspiring. Judge Newton's firm nurturing of a young woman who appeared before her and her connection to the young woman's mother remind us why diversity on the bench is so important. Professor Smith's advocacy, Rhodessa Jones's theater project, and the work of the women at Grace House and AIM give us hope. Gerald Clay's decision to start a gospel choir at the Franklin Pre-Release Center show us how these women can inspire us all to do a little more.

Inner Lives should be required reading for every person who works in the criminal justice and prison systems—police officers, prosecutors, defense attorneys, judges, probation and parole officers, and corrections officials. It will open the eyes of those who continue to deny the obvious race and class disparities and blame the victims for their circumstances. For those who know the injustices exist but feel hopeless, *Inner Lives* will inspire them to redouble their efforts. Perhaps the prosecutor and judge will exercise their discretion to promote fairness and provide rehabilitative treatment when needed. Hopefully, the defense attorney will work harder to provide the best defense possible in every case, regardless of the client's income or circumstance. Maybe the prison official will treat the women in her care with dignity and compassion.

Those of us who believe in justice and humane treatment for all should work to implement Professor Johnson's recommendations. All human beings deserve a nurturing and loving childhood and access to education and health care. No one should have to endure a life of abuse and pain. We must all work to demand that resources be provided for preventive measures, indigent defense, and rehabilitative treatment. We should advocate for the elimination of mandatory minimum laws that result in the unfair and racially discriminatory treatment of African American women. *Inner Lives* provides the motivation and inspiration to renew and continue the struggle.

Appendix A

Self-Study Course on
African American Women's History

Your time is now, my sisters. . . . New goals and new priorities, not only for this country, but for all of mankind must be set. Formal education will not help us do that. We must therefore depend upon informal learning. We can do that by confronting people with their humanity and their own inhumanity—confronting them wherever we meet them: in the church, in the classroom, on the floor of the Congress and the state legislatures, in the bars, and on the streets. We must reject not only the stereotypes that others hold of us, but also the stereotypes that we hold of ourselves.

—Shirley Chisholm

THIS RECOMMENDED READING LIST is the basis for a course on African American women's history. It grows out of my belief that self-awareness and education are essential to African American women's empowerment and self-sufficiency. While no one was paid for participating in *Inner Lives*, I wanted to leave something meaningful with the incarcerated women I interviewed. Therefore, I gave them copies of *A Shining Thread of Hope: The History of Black Women in America* by Darlene Clark Hine and Kathleen Thompson. Several women wrote back to say that they appreciated the book and that they learned much from it. This more extensive reading list, then, is designed to introduce or reintroduce the rich and diverse experiences of African American women to those who need it most—African American women. While this reading list is by no means definitive, it does provide a starting point for information and critical evaluation of the historical, social, political, legal, artistic, and cultural dimensions of African American women's lives.

As a self-study course, these materials can be studied individually or in discussion groups by incarcerated women and other readers. Moreover, readers can construct their own courses by selecting readings within particular subject areas that interest them. Through these readings, I hope that African American women will find their connection to others who have faced and surmounted major challenges, and will thereby find resonance and application in their own lives. I hope that readers will share their experiences with the books with me so that the course will continue to develop in a dynamic way: Which readings did you like or not like and why? What did you learn from the different books? Were there books, individuals, or characters that were especially relevant to you? How will you incorporate what you have learned from the books into your life? Are there other books or topics that you would recommend for a course on African American women's history and experiences?

Also, I hope that readers who have greater resources will contribute books on the list to women's prisons and jails. Often prisons require that books be forwarded directly from the publisher; therefore, readers should check with prison administrators about such procedures. Also, in Appendix B you will note listings for organizations that provide books to inmates. You may contact them to donate books on this list.

Those who have time to donate might consider contributing to literacy efforts and discussion groups for women in prison. If you contribute in any of these or in other ways, I hope that you will drop a note to let me know about your experiences as well.

SELF-STUDY COURSE READING LIST

Herstory

Paula Giddings, *When and Where I Enter: The Impact of Black Women on Race and Sex in America* (Bantam Books, 1998).

Darlene Clark Hine and Kathleen Thompson, *A Shining Thread of Hope: The History of Black Women in America* (Broadway Books, 1998).

Darlene Clark Hine, Elsa Barkley Brown, and Rosalyn Terborg-Penn (eds.), *Black Women in America: An Historical Encyclopedia Vol. I (A-L) and Vol. II (M-Z)* (Indiana University Press, 1993).

Deborah Gray White, *Ar'n't I a Woman* (Norton, 1985).

Deborah Gray White, *Too Heavy a Load: Black Women in Defense of Themselves, 1894–1994* (Norton, 1999).

Autobiography and Biography

Amy Alexander, *Fifty Black Women Who Changed America* (Citadel Press, 1999).

Joyce A. Brown, *Justice Denied* (Noble Press, 1990).

Michelle Cliff, *Claiming an Identity They Taught Me to Despise* (Persephone, 1980).

Leon Dash, *Rosa Lee: A Mother and Her Family in Urban America* (Plume, 1996).

Sarah L. Delany and A. Elizabeth Delany (with Amy Hearth), *Having Our Say: The Delany Sisters' First 100 Years* (Dell, 1993).

Patrice Gaines, *Laughing in the Dark: From Colored Girl to Woman of Color—A Journey from Prison to Power* (Anchor, 1995).

Joanne Grant, *Ella Baker: Freedom Bound* (John Wiley/Sons, 1999).

Chana Kai Lee, *For Freedom's Sake: The Life of Fannie Lou Hamer* (University of Illinois Press, 2000).

Audre Lorde, *Zami, A New Spelling of My Name: A Biomythography* (Crossing Press, 1982).

Nell Irvin Painter, *Sojourner Truth: A Life, A Symbol* (Norton, 1996).

Assata Shakur, *Assata: An Autobiography* (Lawrence Hill, 1980).

Literature and Poetry

Toni Cade Bambara, *The Salt Eaters* (Random House, 1980).

Margaret Busby (ed.), *Daughters of Africa: An International Anthology of Words and Writings by Women of African Descent from the Ancient Egyptians to the Present* (Ballantine, 1992).

Lucille Clifton, *Good Woman: Poems and a Memoir, 1969–1980* (BOA Editions, 1987).

Toni Morrison, *Beloved* (Plume, 1987).

Sonia Sanchez, *Shake Loose My Skin: New and Selected Poems* (Beacon, 1999).

Lalita Tademy, *Cane River* (Warner, 2001).

Social and Political Thought

Patricia Hill Collins, *Fighting Words: Black Women and the Search for Justice* (University of Minnesota Press, 1998).

Joy James (ed.), *The Angela Y. Davis Reader* (Blackwell, 1984).

Audre Lorde, *Sister Outsider: Essays and Speeches* (Crossing Press, 1984).

Beth E. Richie, *Compelled to Crime: The Gender Entrapment of Battered Black Women* (Routledge, 1996).

Barbara Smith, *The Truth That Never Hurts: Writings on Race, Gender, and Freedom* (Rutgers University Press, 1998).

Alice Walker, *Anything We Love Can Be Saved* (Random House, 1997).

Health

Julia A. Boyd, *Can I Get a Witness? Black Women and Depression* (Plume, 1998).

bell hooks, *Sisters of the Yam: Black Women and Self-Recovery* (South End, 1993).

Charlotte Pierce-Baker, *Surviving the Silence: Black Women's Stories of Rape* (Norton, 1998).

Evelyn C. White, *The Black Woman's Health Book: Speaking for Ourselves* (Seal, 1990).

Evelyn C. White, *Chain, Chain, Change: For Black Women in Abusive Relationships* (Seal, 1994).

Beverly Yates, *Heart Health for Black Women: A Natural Approach to Healing and Preventing Heart Disease* (Marlowe, 2000).

Art and Culture

Angela Y. Davis, *Blues Legacies and Black Feminism* (Vintage, 1998).

Rena Fraden, *Imagining Medea: Rhodessa Jones and Theater for Incarcerated Women* (University of North Carolina Press, 2001).

Chester Higgins, *Elder Grace: The Nobility of Aging* (Bulfinch, 2000).

Kathleen Thompson and Hilary MacAustin, *The Face of Our Past: Images of Black Women from Colonial America to the Present* (Indiana University Press, 1999).

Jacqueline L. Tobin and Raymond G. Dobard, *Hidden in Plain View: A Secret Story of Quilts and the Underground Railroad* (Anchor, 1999).

Spirituality

Akasha Gloria Hull, *The New Spirituality of African American Women* (Inner Traditions, 2001).

Iyanla Vanzant, *Acts of Faith: Daily Meditations for People of Color* (Fireside, 1993).

James Melvin Washington, *Conversations with God: Two Centuries of Prayers by African Americans* (Harper, 1994).

Films

Julie Dash, *Daughters of the Dust* (Kino Int'l, 800-562-3330, www.kino.com).

Karina Epperlein, *Voices from Inside: Women Prisoners and Their Children Speak Out* (New Day Films, 888-367-9154, www.newday.com).

Appendix B

Resource Directory

I GRATEFULLY ACKNOWLEDGE the ACLU National Prison Project and the Prisoner Activist Resource Center for their generous permission to reprint listings from their manuals for this resource directory. This list of resources provides currently or formerly incarcerated women and their families with information on a variety of issues. Please consult these organizations if you have any questions about resources, programs, or services available to those involved in the correctional system.

As it is not possible to print every resource available, I strongly encourage you to consult the three organizations listed immediately below. The Websites for these organizations provide information about many more organizations and resources for female inmates.

American Civil Liberties Union (ACLU)—National Prison Project
733 15th Street, NW, Suite 620
Washington, DC 20005
Phone: 202-393-4930; Fax: 202-393-4931
Website: www.aclu.org/issues/prisons
Description: Seeks to create constitutional conditions of confinement and strengthen prisoners' rights through class-action litigation and public education.

Prison Activist Resource Center
P.O. Box 339
Berkeley, CA 94701
Phone: 510-893-4648; Fax: 510-893-4607
Website: www.prisonactivist.org
Email: parc@prisonactivist.org

Description: Provides support for educators, activists, prisoners, and prisoners' families. Works to build networks for action and produces materials that expose human rights violations while challenging the rapid expansion of the prison industrial complex.

Texas Woman's University—Women in Criminal Justice
Dr. Jim Williams
Department of Sociology and Social Work
Denton, TX 76204
Website: www.twu.edu/as/wcrim/PRISN.HTM
Description: Directory of resources for inmates and their families, and of scholars and students of criminal law.

ADVOCACY GROUPS

CURE (Citizens United for the Rehabilitation of Errants)
P.O. Box 2310
Washington, DC 20013-2310
Phone: 202-789-2126; Fax: 413-845-9787
Website: www.curenational.org
Description: Organizes currently and formerly incarcerated individuals, their familes, and concerned citizens in order to work for reform of sentencing procedures and promote the use of rehabilitation programs.

California Coalition for Women Prisoners
100 McAllister St.
San Francisco, CA 94102
Phone: 415-255-7036, ext. 4; Fax: 415-552-3150
Website: http://womenprisoners.org
Email: cccp@igc.org
Description: CCWP raises awareness about the cruel and inhumate conditions under which women in prison live. Advocates change and promotes leadership of women prisoners, and gives a voice to currently and formerly incarcerated women and their families.

Families Against Mandatory Minimums (FAMM)
1612 K St., NW, Suite 1400
Washington, D.C. 20006
Phone: 202-822-6700; Fax: 202-822-6704
Website: www.famm.org
Email: famm@famm.org
Description: Promotes sentencing policy reform. Advocates sentencing procedures that result in sentences that are proportional to the crime committed.

Human Rights Watch: Prison Conditions and the Treatment of Prisoners
Website: www.hrw.org/prisons
Email: hrwnyc@hrw.org
Description: Advocacy organization. Raises awareness about prison conditions in countries all over the world. Publishes articles and statistics concerning prison conditions.

Rights for All, Amnesty International's Campaign on the United States
Amnesty International
322 8th Avenue
New York, New York 10001
Phone: 212-807-8400; Fax: 212-463-9193
Website: www.rightsforall-usa.org
Email: admin-us@aiusa.org
Description: Prisoner rights advocate, worldwide. Monitors prison conditions and prison policy.

Stop Prisoner Rape, Inc.
6304 Wilshire Blvd., Suite 205
Los Angeles, CA 90048
Phone: 323-653-7867; Fax: 323-653-7870
Website: www.spr.org
Email: info@spr.org
Description: Seeks to end sexual violence against all inmates in all types of detention. SPR works nationally to shed light on the dangers of sexual abuse in prison and to help survivors access resources and support one another.

HEALTH ISSUES

The Correctional HIV Consortium
San Francisco, CA
Email: chc@silcom.com
Description: Nationally oriented nonprofit organization providing programs and services to county, state, and federal prisoners, the recently released and their family members, and correctional systems on HIV/AIDS, TB, hepatitis, and other infectious diseases.

The National Gains Center for People with Co-Occuring Disorders in the Justice System
c/o Policy Research Associates
345 Delaware Avenue
Delmar, NY 12054
Phone: 1-800-311-4246; Fax: 518-439-7612
Description: Partnership between the Subtance Abuse and Mental Health Services Administration (SAMHSA), a federal agency, and Policy Research Associates, a private-sector research firm. The National GAINS Center conducts research, educates the public, and works to improve mental health care within the correctional system for individuals who have mental disorders.

Bazelon Center for Mental Health Law
1101 15th Street, NW, Suite 1212
Washington, DC 20005-5002
Phone: 202-467-5730; Fax: 202-223-0409
TDD: 202-467-4232
Email: webmaster@bazelon.org
Description: National Mental Health Law Center. Advocates for persons with mental health issues/disorders. Publishes information concerning mental health treatment, policy, and education. Provides list of resources. Cannot assist individuals.

LESBIAN/BISEXUAL

Gay and Lesbian Prisoner Project

Bromfield Street Educational Foundation
29 Stanhope Street
Boston, MA 02116
Phone: 617-262-6969
Description: Provides printed material and other sources of sup-
    port to gay and lesbian prisoners. Prisoners receive complimen-
    tary subscriptions to *Gay Community News*, health information,
    and reading material.

Gay and Lesbian Rights Project of the ACLU
125 Broad Street, 17th Floor
New York, NY 10004
Phone: 212-549-2690
Website: www.aclu.org/issues/gay/hmgl.html
Description: Goal of this project is equal treatment and equal dig-
    nity for lesbians, gay men, and bisexuals. Address civil rights
    issues of G/L/B inmates. Files impact litigation.

National Gay and Lesbian Task Force
1700 Kalorama Road, NW
Washington, DC 20009-2624
Phone: 202-332-6483; TTY 202-332-6219; Fax: 202-332-0207
Website: www.ngltf.org
Description: National, progressive organization working for the
    civil rights of gay, lesbian, bisexual, and transgendered people,
    with the vision and commitment to building a powerful politi-
    cal movement.

EDUCATION, ART, AND LITERATURE FOR INMATES

Art Behind Bars, Inc.
P.O. Box 2034
Key West, FL 33040
Phone/Fax: 305-294-7345
Website: www.artbehindbars.org
Email: artbhndbrs@aol.com
Description: Facilitates art programs for incarcerated inmates. Col-
    lects and sells inmate art for fund-raisers for charities.

Books through Bars
4722 Baltimore Avenue
Philadelphia, PA 19143
Phone: 215-727-0882, ext. 2
Website: www.booksthroughbars.org
Email: info@booksthroughbars.org
Description: Works to empower prisoners by providing them
    with tools for self-education. Supplies free educational and
    progressive political reading materials; offers particular sup-
    port to those prisoners engaged in political education study
    groups.

Books to Prisoners
c/o Left Bank Books
92 Pike Street, Box A
Seattle, WA 98101
Phone: 206-622-0195
Website: http://bp.tao.ca
Description: Provides free books to inmates all across the USA.
    Requests should be made in writing. Donations are greatly ap-
    preciated (even postage stamps). Requests may take time to fill.
    Patience is greatly appreciated.

Prison Book Program
92 Green Street
Jamaica Plain, MA 02130
Phone: 617-884-5132
Description: Dedicated to promoting prisoner literacy nationwide.
    Provide free books to prisoners. Some publications in Spanish.
    Inmates may request specific titles or books on general topics.

Prison Library Project
915 West Foothill Blvd., Suite C128
Claremont, CA 91711
Website: www.inmate.com/prislibr.htm
Description: Provides books and cassette tapes to individual pris-
    oners, study groups, prison libraries, and prison chaplains free
    of charge. Also publishes a resource list for inmates.

Women's Prison Book Project
c/o Arise Bookstore
2441 Lyndale Avenue, South
Minneapolis, MN 55405
Voicemail: 952-837-1762
Email: wpbp@prisonactivist.org
Website: www.prisonactivist.org/wpbp
Description: Provides women in prison with free reading materials covering a wide range of topics from law and education (dictionaries, GED, etc.) to politics, history, and women's health. Seeks to meet the specific needs of women in prison.

LEGAL AND SOCIAL RESOURCES

Aid to Children of Imprisoned Mothers, Inc. (AIM)
1514 Cleveland Avenue, Suite 115
East Point, GA 30344
Phone: 404-762-5433; Fax: 404-762-7664
Website: www.takingaim.org
Description: Provides emotional and financial support for imprisoned mothers, their children, and families. Programs include transportation for visits, educational assistance, counseling, after-school programs for kids, and support groups for inmates and caregivers.

Aid to Inmate Mothers (AIM, Inc.)
P.O. Box 986
Montgomery, AL 36101-0986
Phone: 334-262-2245; 1-800-679-0246
Website: www.inmatemoms.org
Email: inmatemoms@mindspring.com
Description: Assists incarcerated women and their families to maintain a relationship. Facilitates visitations and encourages participation of inmate moms in their childrens' lives.

The Center for Children of Incarcerated Parents
P.O. Box 41-286

Eagle Rock, CA 90041
Phone: 626-449-8796
Website: www.e-ccip.org
Email: ccip@earthlink.net
Description: Conducts research and provides information concerning incarcerated parent-child relationships. Provides programs and therapy for incarcerated parents and their children.

Center for Community Alternatives: Crossroads: An Alternative for Women Offenders
39 West 19th Street
New York, NY 10011
Phone: 212-675-0825; Fax: 212-675-0825
Website: www.centerforcommunityalternatives.org
Description: A day drug treatment program specifically designed as an alternative for women offenders. Helps women conquer their drug addictions and acquire the economic, emotional, and social tools they need to lead law-abiding lives. Also helps women reclaim their lives and the lives of their children.

Center for Women in Transition
2647 Ohio Street, Suite 302
St. Louis, MO 63118
Phone: 314-771-5207; Fax: 314-771-0066
Website: www.geocities.com/cwitstl
Email: cwit@cwit
Description: Works with and on behalf of currently and formerly incarcerated women. Helps inmates make the transition between prison and society. Works to increase public awareness of criminal justice issues. Advocates rehabilitation instead of punishment of inmates.

Chicago Legal Advocacy to Incarcerated Mothers (CLAIM)
220 South State Street, Suite 830
Chicago, IL 60604
Phone: 312-332-5537; Fax: 312-332-2570
Website: www.c-l-a-i-m.org
Email: info@c-l-a-i-m.org

Description: Provides legal and educational services to incarcerated women and their families in an effort to preserve families.

Count the Cost, Inc.
P.O. Box 1447
Decatur, GA 30031
Phone: 404-523-2178
Website: www.countthecost.org
Description: Conducts workshops on criminal justice issues, including individual and human rights, stress, anger, and conflict resolution. Provides support networks and programs for youth and adults.

Families with a Future
c/o LSPC
100 McAllister St., Suite 200
San Francisco, CA 94102
Phone: 415-255-7036, ext. 320; Fax: 415-552-3150
Website: www.fwaf.net
Email: fwaf@aol.com
Description: Network of advocates dedicated to keeping incarcerated women united with their children. Founded by former political prisoner Ida P. McCray in 1996.

Family and Corrections Network
32 Oak Grove Road
Palmyra, Va 22963
Phone: 434-589-3036; Fax: 434-589-6520
Website: www.fcnetwork.org
Email: fcn@fcnetwork.org
Description: Provides information on programs serving families involved in the correctional system. Offers consultation, technical assistance and program development.

The Fortune Society
53 West 23rd Street, 8th Floor
New York, NY 10010
Phone: 212-691-7554; Fax: 212-255-4948
Website: www.fortunesociety.org

Email: info@fortunesociety.org

Description: Community-based organization dedicated to educating the public about prisons, criminal justice issues, and the root causes of crime. Helps ex-offenders and at-risk youth break the cycle of crime and incarceration through a broad range of services.

Legal Services for Prisoners with Children
100 McAllister St.
San Francisco, CA 94102
Phone: 415-255-7036; Fax: 415-552-3150
Website: http://prisonerswithchildren.org
Email: info@prisonerswithchildren.org

Description: LSPC advocates for the civil rights and empowerment of incarcerated parents, children, family members, and people at risk for incarceration through response to requests for information, education, technical assistance, litgation, and community activism.

Lydia's Place, Inc.
711 Penn Avenue, Suite 706
Pittsburgh, PA 15222
Phone: 412-471-3410
Website: www.lydiasplace.org
Email: alydiasplace@cs.com

Description: Interdenominational, interracial, Christian agency dedicated to servicing the holistic needs of women offenders. Helps women rebuild their lives, reunite with their children, and learn to live crime-free lives.

M.A.S.S. (Mothers-Fathers for the Advancement of Social Systems, Inc.
P.O. Box 225067
Dallas, TX 75222-5067
Phone: 214-821-8810; Fax: 214-824-6891

Description: Provides support to inmates who have been falsely accused and incarcerated. Also provides counseling, skills training, and mentorship programs in First Offender Return to

Society Program, and Youth Programs for children of incarcerated caregivers.

National Clearinghouse for the Defense of Battered Women
125 South 9th Street, Suite 302
Philadelphia, PA 19107
Phone: 215-351-0010; Fax: 215-315-0779
Description: Helps battered women who, faced with life-threatening violence from their abusers, are forced to defend themselves. Provides technical assistance, support, resources, networking, and training nationwide.

Prison Fellowship International
P.O. Box 17434
Washington, DC 20041
Phone: 703-481-0000; Fax: 703-481-0003
Website: www.pfi.org
Email: info@pfi.org
Description: Through ministries in eighty-three countries, this organization responds to the needs of prisoners, ex-prisoners, victims, and those affected by crime.

Project Return
Robert E. Roberts
2703 General de Gaulle Drive
New Orleans, LA 70144-6222
Phone: 504-988-1000; Fax: 504-263-8976
Website: www.projectreturn.com
Email: bob@projectreturn.com
Description: Provides an integrated delivery network aimed at reducing the high rate of recidivism of former offenders, which includes substance abuse and alcohol treatment, family counseling, GED classes, conflict resolution training, job training, and placement assistance.

Revelation S.E.E.D.
P.O. Box 56623
Atlanta, GA 30343

Phone: 404-753-6159

Description: Provides prison ministry, parenting workshops for incarcerated mothers, support groups for formerly incarcerated women and survivors of domestic violence, HIV/AIDS, addiction, and homelessness. Also provides employment assessment and training.

Step by Step of Rochester, Inc.
2229 Clifford Avenue
Rochester, NY 14609
Phone: 585-224-0763; Fax: 716-288-8026
Website: www.stepbysteprochester.org
Email: sbys@frontiernet.net
Description: Mission is to assist women who have been incarcerated, to reclaim their gifts and strengths as the foundation on which to rebuild their lives.

Women's Advocacy Project
P.O. Box 833
Austin, TX 78767-0833
Phone: 512-476-5377, 800-777-3427 (toll free); Fax: 512-476-5773
Website: www.women-law.org
Email: vwing@women-law.org
Description: Offers free legal services for any domestic violence survivor in Texas, without qualification. Through toll-free hotlines, women can receive legal advice on any matter involving family violence.

Women's Project
2224 S. Main
Little Rock, AR 72206
Phone: 501-372-5113; Fax: 501-372-0009
Website: http://members.aol/com/wproject/
Description: Mission is to achieve social justice for women. Programs include newsletter publication, information and referral services, AIDS education, technical assistance, producing cultural activities.

Notes

NOTES TO THE PREFACE

1. Deborah Gray White, *Too Heavy a Load: Black Women in Defense of Themselves: 1894–1994*, at 11 (1999).

NOTES TO THE INTRODUCTION

1. Sharon McQuaide and John H. Ehrenreich, "Women in Prison: Approaches to Understanding the Lives of a Forgotten Population," 13 *Affilia* 233, 234 (1998).

2. bell hooks, *Ain't I a Woman* 120–21 (1981).

3. Patricia Hill Collins, *Black Feminist Thought: Knowledge, Consciousness and the Politics of Empowerment* 22 (1990). See also Kimberle Crenshaw, "Demarginalizing the Intersection of Race and Sex: A Black Feminist Critique of Antidiscrimination Doctrine, Feminist Theory and Antiracist Politics," *University of Chicago Legal Forum* 139 (1989); and Kimberle Crenshaw, "Mapping the Margins: Intersectionality, Identity Politics, and Violence against Women of Color," 43 *Stanford Law Review* 1241 (1991).

4. Patricia Hill Collins, *Black Feminist Thought: Knowledge, Consciousness and the Politics of Empowerment* 22 (1990).

5. Ibid. at 37.

6. See U.S. Department of Justice, Sourcebook of Criminal Justice Statistics 2000, "Persons under Correctional Supervision," table 6.1, at 488 (2000).

7. At roughly 16 percent, women remain a much smaller fraction of the total prison population. Nevertheless, women's increases have been much faster and more numerous than increases in the male prison population. See U.S. General Accounting Office, "Women in Prison: Issues and Challenges Confronting U.S. Correctional Systems" 18 (1999).

8. U.S. Department of Justice, Bureau of Justice Statistics, "Special Report: Women Offenders" 6 (1999).

9. U.S. Department of Justice, Bureau of Justice Statistics, "Women in Prison: Survey of State Prison Inmates" 1, 2 (1991).

10. Ibid.

11. Ibid.

12. U.S. Department of Justice, Federal Bureau of Prisons, "A Profile of Female Offenders" 3 (1998).

13. U.S. Department of Justice, Bureau of Justice Statistics, "Special Report: Women Offenders" 6–7 (1999).

14. Ibid. at 10, table 24 (emphasis added).

15. U.S. General Accounting Office, "Women in Prison: Issues and Challenges Confronting U.S. Correctional Systems" 20 (1999).

16. Mark Mauer and Tracy Huling, "Young Black Americans and the Criminal Justice System: Five Years Later," Sentencing Project 1 (1995).

17. U.S. Department of Justice, Bureau of Justice Statistics, "Women in Prison: Survey of State Prison Inmates" 2 (1991).

18. See U.S. Department of Justice, Bureau of Justice Statistics," Additional Crime Facts at a Glance" (2001) (noting substantial decreases, as much as 22 percent in some categories, in violent crime rates since 1994, including homicide, rape, robbery, and assault, and similar declines in property crimes, including burglary, theft, and motor vehicle theft. The bureau noted that some crime decreases in 2000 were "the lowest level ever recorded").

19. Charlotte Pierce-Baker, *Surviving the Silence: Black Women's Stories of Rape* 83 (1998) (emphasis added).

20. U.S. General Accounting Office, "Women in Prison: Issues and Challenges Confronting U.S. Correctional Systems" 24, 33 (1999).

21. U.S. Department of Justice, Bureau of Justice Statistics, "Special Report: Women Offenders" 8 (1999).

22. U.S. Department of Justice, National Institute of Justice, "Full Report of the Prevalence, Incidence, and Consequences of Violence against Women" 59 (2000).

23. Ibid.

24. Ibid.

25. Charlotte Pierce-Baker, *Surviving the Silence: Black Women's Stories of Rape* 84 (1998).

26. Emma Coleman Jordan, "Images of Black Women in the Legal Academy: An Introduction," 6 *Berkeley Women's Law Journal* 1, 3–4 (1990–91) (footnotes omitted). See also, Margaret (H.R.) Chon, "On the Need for Asian American Narratives in Law: Ethnic Specimens, Native Informants, Storytelling and Silences," 3 *Asian Pacific American Law Journal* 4 (1995); Jerome M. Culp, "Autobiography and Legal Scholarship and Teaching: Finding the Me in the Legal Academy," 77 *Virginia Law Review* 539 (1991); William N. Eskridge, Jr., "Gaylegal Narratives," 46 *Stanford Law Rev.* 607 (1994); and Alex M. Johnson, "De-

fending the Use of Narrative and Giving Content to the Voice of Color: Rejecting the Imposition of Process in Legal Scholarship," 79 *Iowa Law Review* 803, 817 (1994).

27. Mary Frances Berry, *The Pig Farmer's Daughter* 20 (1999).

28. Chester Higgins quoted in Jimmie Briggs, "Whiteout: How the Media Ignores the Perspectives of Minority Photographers," *Photo District News*, November 2000, at 38.

29. Laura Wexler, "Seeing Sentiment, Photography, Race and the Innocent Eye," in Elizabeth Abel et al., eds., *Feminism* 159, 164 (1997).

30. Katheryn K. Russell, *The Color of Crime: Racial Hoaxes, White Fear, Protectionism, Police Harrassment and Other Macroaggressions* xiii (1998).

31. Laura Wexler, "Seeing Sentiment, Photography, Race and the Innocent Eye," in Elizabeth Abel et al., eds., *Feminism* 159, 166–67 (1997).

32. Karen Croft, "Using Her Body," *Salon.com*, February 22, 2001, www.salon.com/sex/feature/2001/renee_cox/. See also Elisabeth Bumiller, "Affronted by Nude 'Last Supper,' Guiliani Calls for Decency Panel," *New York Times*, February 6, 2001, at A1 (the mayor described the depiction as "disgusting," "outrageous," and "anti-Catholic").

33. Chester Higgins quoted in Jimmie Briggs, "Whiteout: How the Media Ignores the Perspectives of Minority Photographers," *Photo District News*, November 2000, at 38.

34. Darlene Clark Hine, in Hillary MacAustin and Kathleen Thompson, *Faces of Our Past: Images of Black Women from Colonial America to the Present* ix (1999).

35. For an extensive survey of his work, see *Roy DeCarava: A Retrospective* (1996).

36. Howard Zehr, *Doing Life: Reflections of Men and Women Serving Life Sentences* 3 (1996).

37. Sharon McQuaide and John H. Ehrenreich, "Women in Prison: Approaches to Understanding the Lives of a Forgotten Population," 13 *Affilia* 243 (1998).

38. See Andrea L. Cole and J. Gary Knowles, eds., *Lives in Context: The Art of Life History Research* (2001).

39. Beth E. Richie, *Compelled to Crime: The Gender Entrapment of Battered Black Women* 16–18 (1996). See also Pauline Polkey, ed., *Women's Lives into Print* (1999); and Eleanor Miller, *Street Women* (1986).

40. Gwendolyn Etter-Lewis, "Black Women's Life Stories: Reclaiming Self in Narrative Texts," in Sherna Berger Gluck and Daphne Patai, eds., *Women's Words: The Feminist Practice of Oral History* 43 (1991).

41. Ibid. at 52.

42. Beth E. Richie, *Compelled to Crime: The Gender Entrapment of Battered Black Women* 2 (1996).

NOTES TO PART I

1. Lawrence M. Friedman, *Crime and Punishment in American History* 23 (1993).

2. Winthrop D. Jordan, *White over Black: American Attitudes toward the Negro, 1550–1812*, at 45–48 (1968).

3. Orlando Patterson, *Slavery and Social Death: A Comparative Study* 7 (1982). Along these lines, Paul Finkelman also notes that enslaved African Americans and White indentured servants worked together in Virginia during the advent of slavery. In 1661, however, the Virginia legislature passed a fraternization law that delineated punishments for running away from servitude. The penalty for White indentured servants was increased if they ran away with an enslaved African American. See Paul Finkelman, "The Crime of Color," 67 *Tulane Law Review* 2063, 2080–81 (1993).

4. A. Leon Higginbotham, Jr., *In the Matter of Color: Race and the American Legal Processes: The Colonial Period* 395 (1978). For an informative discussion of the differences between indentured servitude and slavery, see ibid. at 392–95.

5. See Philip J. Schwartz, *Twice Condemned: Slaves and the Criminal Laws of Virginia, 1705–1865*, at ix (1988); and Lawrence M. Friedman, *Crime and Punishment in American History* 37, 40–41, 44 (1993).

6. See, e.g., Philip J. Schwartz, *Twice Condemned: Slaves and the Criminal Laws of Virginia, 1705–1865*, at ix, xi (1988) (noting that the severest punishments were reserved for enslaved persons in Virginia, which was the largest slaveholding society in North America between 1705 and 1865); and Lawrence M. Friedman, *Crime and Punishment in American History* 44 (1993) (noting that one of the most extreme incidents of capital punishment during the colonial era occurred in New York, in 1741, in which over 150 enslaved persons and twenty Whites were accused of an insurrection conspiracy. Over thirty of the enslaved insurrectionists were hanged or burned alive, while four of the accused Whites were hanged for their roles in the offense). See also Paul Finkelman, "The Crime of Color," 67 *Tulane Law Review* 2100–2105 (1993) (citing racially specific criminal laws in Massachusetts, Pennsylvania, New York, New Jersey, and Delaware, in which race defined criminal conduct or was the basis for harsher punishment).

7. Paul Finkelman, "The Crime of Color," 67 *Tulane Law Review* 2063–69 (1993).

8. See Estelle Freedman, "Their Sister's Keepers: A Historical Perspective of Female Correctional Institutes in the U.S., 1870–1900," 2 *Feminist Studies* 77–94 (1974); and Clarice Feinman, "An Historical Overview of the Treatment of Incarcerated Women: Myths and Realities of Rehabilitation," 63 *Prison Journal* 12–26 (1984), cited in Catherine Fisher Collins, *The Imprisonment of African American Women* 5 (1997).

9. Paula Giddings, *When and Where I Enter: The Impact of Black Women on Race and Sex in America* 37 (1984); see also Paul Finkelman, "The Crime of Color," 67 *Tulane Law Review* 2081 (1993). Notably, antimiscegenation laws remained in force in the United States until 1967, when the Supreme Court struck such laws in its opinion in *Loving v. Virginia*, 388 U.S. 1 (1967). After a public referendum, the state of Alabama repealed its antimiscegenation statute as late as November 2000. See Ala. Const. Art. IV § 102; and Mike Gadd, "Views on Mixed Marriage Are Stuck in the Past," *San Francisco Chronicle*, January 7, 2001, at S6.

10. See discussion in Paula Giddings, *When and Where I Enter: The Impact of Black Women on Race and Sex in America* 36–37 (1984).

11. Paul Finkelman, "The Color of Crime," 67 *Tulane Law Review* 2081 (1993).

12. Brenda E. Stevenson, "Slavery," in Darlene Clark Hine et al., eds., 2 *Black Women in America* 1054–55 (1993) (quoting Elizabeth Sparks, in Charles Perdue et al., eds., *Weavils in the Wheat: Interviews with Virginia Ex-Slaves* (1976).

13. See discussion in Katheryn K. Russell, *The Color of Crime* 15 (1998).

14. *United States v. Amy*, 24 F. Cas. 792 (Va. 1859).

15. Ibid. at 810. Notably, Chief Justice Taney also authored the U.S. Supreme Court's infamous *Dred Scott v. Sandford* opinion, 60 U.S. 393 (1857), holding that slaves had no recognizable rights as citizens. See also discussion in Paula C. Johnson, "At the Intersection of Injustice: Experiences of African American Women in Crime and Sentencing," 4 *American University Journal of Gender and Law* 16–18 (1995).

16. See discussion in Katheryn K. Russell, *The Color of Crime* 16 (1998).

17. Ibid.

18. Ibid. at 16–17.

19. Miss. 316 (1859).

20. The most noteworthy legal reforms of the Reconstruction era were "Reconstruction Amendments" to the U.S. Constitution: the Thirteenth Amendment (ratified in 1865, ending slavery and involuntary servitude); the Fourteenth Amendment (ratified in 1868, conferring citizenship upon formerly enslaved Africans, and guaranteeing recognition of privileges and immunities, due process, and equal protection of the laws of the states); and the Fifteenth Amendment (ratified in 1870, conferring voting rights on African American men). In addition to these constitutional measures, federal civil rights statutes were enacted during this time to ensure federal enforcement of the former slaves' newly acquired citizenship rights. These included the Civil Rights of 1866 and the Civil Rights Act of 1870. Congress reenacted the 1866 statute as part of the Enforcement Act of 1870, which is now codified in Title 42 of the U.S. Code. 42 U.S.C. § 1981 gives Blacks equal rights to make contracts and participate in judicial proceedings, and 42 U.S.C. § 1982 gives Blacks equal rights to own property. Recurring problems regarding the Reconstruction statutes

concern whether or not they prohibit private acts or discrimination, or whether state action is required to advance such claims. In addition, § 2 of the 1866 Civil Rights is now codified as 42 U.S.C. § 1983, which prohibits state officials from using their authority to harass, intimidate or otherwise discriminate against African Amer:cans, as occurred under the Black Codes. Further, the provisions were designed to provide federal court jurisdiction over civil rights claims brought under these statutory provisions. For more detailed analysis of the Reconstruction statutes and U.S. Supreme Court cases interpreting them, see Girardeau A. Spann, *Race against the Court: The Supreme Court and Minorities in Contemporary America* 42–50 (1993); and A. Leon Higginbotham, Jr., *Shades of Freedom: Racial Politics and Presumptions of the American Legal Process* 75–88 (1996).

21. See Lawrence M. Friedman, *Crime and Punishment in American History* 94 (1993); John Hope Franklin and Alfred A. Moss, Jr., *From Slavery to Freedom: A History of African Americans* 225 (7th ed., 1994).

22. See John Hope Franklin and Alfred A. Moss, Jr., *From Slavery to Freedom* 223–37 (7th ed., 1994); and Delores D. Jones-Brown, "Race as a Legal Construct: The Implications for American Justice," in *Race as a Legal Construct: The Implications for American Justice, in* Michael W. Markowitz and Delores D. Jones-Brown, eds., *The System in Black and White: Exploring the Connections between Race, Crime, and Justice* 139, 142–43 (2000).

23. W. E. B. Du Bois, "Reconstruction and Its Benefits," 15 *American Historical Review* 781–99 (1910).

24. See, generally, C. Vann Woodward, *The Strange Career of Jim Crow* (1966); and Leon F. Litwack, *North of Slavery* (1961). The U.S. Supreme Court emboldened White extremism by its notorious decision in *Dred Scott v. Sandford* (1896), in which segregation was upheld by the highest legal authority in the nation. See discussion of the analysis and impact of the Dred Scott opinion in Girardeau A. Spann, *Race against the Court: The Supreme Court and Minorities in Contemporary America* 139 (1993); and A. Leon Higginbotham, Jr., *Shades of Freedom* 104, 112, 117 (1996).

25. Katheryn K. Russell, *The Color of Crime* 21 (1998) (citing U.S. Census, *Historical Statistics of the United States, Colonial Times to 1970, Bicentennial Edition*, part 2, at 422 (1975).

26. Barbara Holden-Smith, "Lynching, Federalism, and the Intersection of Race and Gender in the Progressive Era," 8 *Yale Journal of Law and Feminism* 31 (1996).

27. See Randall Kennedy, *Race, Crime and the Law* 45–46 (1997) (stating, "The alleged need to deter and avenge rapes perpetrated by black men against white women became the *principal* rationale for lynching").

28. Barbara Bair, "Though Justice Sleeps, 1880–1900," in Robin D. G. Kelley and Earl Lewis, eds., *To Make Our World Anew: A History of African Americans*

281, 306 (2000). In addition, Reconstruction and post-Reconstruction era cruelty against Black women included repeated episodes of rape by individual White males and groups of White racist marauders. See Dorothy Sterling, ed., *The Trouble They Seen: The Story of Reconstruction in the Words of African Americans* 48–50, 91–98, 391–93 (1994).

29. *New York Tribune*, February 8, 1904, quoted in Randall Kennedy, *Race, Crime and the Law* 44 & n.65 (1997).

30. *The Crisis*, July 1911, quoted in Randall Kennedy, *Race, Crime and the Law* 44 & n.68 (1997).

31. Randall Kennedy, *Race, Crime and the Law* 49 (1997). For a useful list of historical and research sources regarding lynching, see ibid. at 42n.57.

32. In 1884, Ida B. Wells was forcibly removed from a train after refusing to comply with Jim Crow laws in Tennessee. Wells had purchased a first-class ticket and refused to be relegated to the second-class smoking section. After her removal from the train, Wells sued the railroad. While the local court ruled in her favor in 1884, the decision was reversed by Tennessee Supreme Court in 1887. The episode prompted Wells to write in her diary, "I felt so disappointed. I had hoped such great things from my suit for my people generally. I have firmly believed all along that the law was on our side and would, when we appealed to it, give us justice." Although disillusioned by the appellate court defeat, Wells nevertheless recounted the train incident as a turning point in her life, which led her to champion many civil rights causes throughout her life, including the fight against lynching. Barbara Bair, "Though Justice Sleeps, 1880–1900," in Robin D. G. Kelley and Earl Lewis, eds., *To Make Our World Anew: A History of African Americans* 301 (2000).

33. Colin A. Palmer, "The First Passage: 1502–1619," in Robin D. G. Kelley and Earl Lewis, eds., *To Make Our World Anew: A History of African Americans* 38–49, 90–95 (2000). See also Cedric J. Robinson, *Black Movements in America* (1997).

34. Angela Y. Davis, *Women, Race and Class* 5 (1981).

35. Deborah Gray White, "Let My People Go: 1804–1860," in Robin D. G. Kelley and Earl Lewis eds., *To Make Our World Anew: A History of African Americans* 169, 193 (2000).

36. Paula Giddings, *When and Where I Enter: The Impact of Black Women on Race and Sex in America* 39–46 (1984).

37. Deborah Gray White, "Let My People Go: 1804–1860," in Robin D. G. Kelley and Earl Lewis eds., *To Make Our World Anew: A History of African Americans* 195 (2000).

38. Ibid. at 195–96.

39. Barbara Bair, "Though Justice Sleeps, 1880–1900," in Robin D. G. Kelley and Earl Lewis, eds., *To Make Our World Anew: A History of African Americans* 293 (2000).

40. See Paula Giddings, *When and Where I Enter: The Impact of Black Women on Race and Sex in America* 46–55 (1984).

41. Suzanne Lebsock, *The Free Women of Petersburg: Status and Culture in a Southern Town, 1784–1860*, at 87–88 (1984), cited in Paula C. Johnson, "At the Intersection of Injustice: Experiences of African American Women in Crime and Sentencing," 4 *American University Journal of Gender and Law* 24 (1995) (emphasis added).

42. See K. Sue Jewell, *From Mammy to Miss America and Beyond: Cultural Images and the Shaping of U.S. Social Policy* 35–54 (1993) (noting that "[r]esearch on cultural images of African American women has revealed that, until the 1980s, there were essentially four categories in which African American women have been portrayed. They are mammy, Aunt Jemima, Sapphire, and Jezebel or the bad-black-girl").

43. See, e.g., Patricia Hill Collins, *Black Feminist Thought: Knowledge, Consciousness, and the Politics of Empowerment* 92 (noting, "Most African American women simply do not define ourselves as mammies, matriarchs, welfare mothers, mules or sexually denigrated women. The ideology of domination in which these controlling images are embedded is much less cohesive or uniform than imagined").

44. See, e.g., Adam Fairclough, *Better Day Coming: Blacks and Equality, 1890–2000* (discussing African American resistance movements).

45. See Deborah Gray White, *Too Heavy a Load: Black Women in Defense of Themselves: 1894–1994* (1999); and Cheryl Townsend Gilkes, "If It Wasn't for the Women . . .": African American Women, Community Work, and Social Change," in Maxine Baca Zinn and Bonnie Thornton Dill, eds., *Women of Color in U.S. Society* 229–46 (1994).

46. See, e.g., Adam Jay Hirsch, *The Rise of the Penitentiary: Prisons and Punishment in Early America* xi (1992).

47. Norval Morris and David J. Rothman, "Introduction," in Norval Morris and David J. Rothman, eds., *The Oxford History of the Prison: The Practice of Punishment in Western Society* vii (1998). See also Lawrence M. Friedman, *Crime and Punishment in American History* 48–50 (1993) (noting that in the colonial era, imprisonment took two forms: jails and workhouses. Jails were primarily for debtors and criminal defendants awaiting trial, while workhouses were reserved for vagrants and paupers).

48. David J. Rothman, "Perfecting the Prison: United States, 1789–1865," in Norval Morris and David J. Rothman, eds., *The Oxford History of the Prison: The Practice of Punishment in Western Society* 100, 103 (1998).

49. The movement for greater use of prisons between 1796 to 1800 was led by Pennsylvania, New York, New Jersey, Virginia, Kentucky, and Massachusetts, with Vermont, New Hampshire, and Maryland following suit shortly thereafter. See ibid. at vii.

50. Ibid. at 106.

51. Ibid.

52. Ibid. at 112.

53. Ibid. at 157.

54. See H. Bruce Franklin, ed., *Introduction, Prison Writing in 20th Century America* 4–5 (1998).

55. For example, the death rate among leased Alabama Black convicts in 1869 was 41 percent. H. Bruce Franklin, *Prison Writing in 20th Century America* 5 & n.5 (1998). See also, David M. Oshinsky, *"Worse than Slavery": Parchman Farm and the Ordeal of Jim Crow Justice* 35–36 (1996) (noting, "[B]efore convict leasing officially ended, a generation of black prisoners would suffer and die under conditions far worse than anything they had ever experienced as slaves").

56. Edgardo Rotman, "The Failure of Reform, United States, 1865–1965," in Norval Morris and David J. Rothman, eds., *The Oxford History of the Prison: The Practice of Punishment in Western Society* 159 (1998).

57. Ibid. at 170.

58. Standard Minimum Rules for the Treatment of Prisoners, adopted by the First United Nations Congress on the Prevention of Crime and the Treatment of Offenders, reprinted in United Nations, *A Compilation of International Instruments: Volume I (First Part) Universal Instruments* (United Nations, 1993), E.93.XIV.1, at 243–63.

59. Norval Morris, "The Contemporary Prison: 1965–Present," in Norval Morris and David J. Rothman, eds., *The Oxford History of the Prison: The Practice of Punishment in Western Society* 202 (1998).

60. Norval Morris and David J. Rothman, "Introduction," in Norval Morris and David J. Rothman, eds., *The Oxford History of the Prison: The Practice of Punishment in Western Society* xii (1998).

61. Lucia Zedner, "Wayward Sisters: The Prison for Women," in Norval Morris and David J. Rothman, eds., *The Oxford History of the Prison: The Practice of Punishment in Western Society* 295, 297 (1998) (further noting that women inmates were provided individualized cells at a much later date than male inmates. Even where women were provided separate accommodations within male prisons, they were placed with vulnerable male inmates such as informants or insane persons. Prison staff and fellow inmates sexually exploited girls and women who were incarcerated in these facilities).

62. Nicole Hahn Rafter, *Partial Justice* 16–21 (1990). Federal prisons for women also lagged behind their male counterparts. The first federal prison was built in 1891, in Leavenworth, Kansas. However, the first female federal prison was built in Alderson, West Virginia, in 1928. It followed the reformatory model of women's prisons, as cottages were located around the unfenced grounds.

63. Nicole Hahn Rafter, *Partial Justice* 16 (1990).

64. Lucia Zedner, "Wayward Sisters: The Prison for Women," in Norval Morris and David J. Rothman, eds., *The Oxford History of the Prison: The Practice of Punishment in Western Society* 316 (1998).

65. Nicole Hahn Rafter, *Partial Justice* 21 (1990).

66. Ibid. at xxviii.

67. See Kathryn Watterson, *Women in Prison: Inside the Concrete Womb* 196 (1996).

68. Nicole Hahn Rafter, *Partial Justice* xxviii (1990).

69. Ibid.

70. See Lucia Zedner, "Wayward Sisters: The Prison for Women," in Norval Morris and David J. Rothman, eds., *The Oxford History of the Prison: The Practice of Punishment in Western Society* 321 (1998); and Nicole Hahn Rafter, *Partial Justice* xxix (1990).

71. Nicole Hahn Rafter, *Partial Justice* xii (1990).

72. See Paula C. Johnson, "At the Intersection of Injustice: Experiences of African American Women in Crime and Sentencing," 4 *American University Journal of Gender and Law* 29–31 (1995).

73. David M. Oshinsky, *"Worse than Slavery": Parchman Farm and the Ordeal of Jim Crow Justice* 79 (1996).

74. Ibid. at 125 & n.40 (1996).

75. Ibid.

76. See also Catherine Fisher Collins, *The Imprisonment of African American Women* 15–17 (1997), for a compelling discussion of the Texas prison lessee system as well.

77. David M. Oshinsky, *"Worse than Slavery": Parchman Farm and the Ordeal of Jim Crow Justice* 174–75 (1996).

78. Ibid.

79. Ibid. at 176–77.

80. *Gates v. Collier*, 501 F.2d 1291 (5th Cir. 1982); *Gates v. Collier*, 371 F. Supp. 1368 (D.C. Miss. 1973); and *Gates v. Collier*, 349 F. Supp. 881 (D.C. Miss. 1972). See also David M. Oshinsky, *"Worse than Slavery": Parchman Farm and the Ordeal of Jim Crow Justice* 241–55 (1996); and Sheldon Krantz, *Corrections and Prisoners' Rights in a Nutshell* 200, 301, 311 (1988).

81. Most notably, sociologists Freda Adler and Rita Simon sought to determine the impact of the women's liberation movement on female criminality. Both researchers believed the women's newly found freedoms and participation in the workforce would provide impetus and opportunity for criminal conduct. Beyond this, Adler argued that African American women's overrepresentation in the criminal justice system was due to their long-standing "liberation" from White women's domestic confines. See Catherine Fisher Collins, *The Imprisonment of African American Women* 30–31 (1997; and Kathryn Watterson, *Women in Prison: Inside the Concrete Womb* 39 (1996).

82. As Myrna Raeder notes, "It is the absence, rather than the availability of employment opportunity for women [that] seems to lead to increases in female crime." Myrna S. Raeder, "Gender and Sentencing: Single Moms, Battered Women and Other Sex-Based Anomalies in the Gender-Free World of the Federal Sentencing Guidelines," 20 *Pepperdine Law Review* 905 (1993).

83. Symposium, "Developments in Law: Alternatives to Incarceration," 111 *Harvard Law Review* 1921, 1927 (1998).

84. Norval Morris, "The Contemporary Prison: 1865–Present," in Norval Morris and David J. Rothman, eds., *The Oxford History of the Prison* 202 (1998).

85. For discussion of the impact of drug law disparities with regard to African American women, see Paula C. Johnson, "At the Intersection of Injustice: Experiences of African American Women in Crime and Sentencing," 4 *American University Journal of Gender and Law* 41–45 (1995).

86. See David Rudovsky, "Law Enforcement by Stereotypes and Serendipity: Racial Profiling and Stops and Searches without Cause," 3 *University of Pennsylvania Journal of Constitutional Law* 296 (2001); and Angela J. Davis, "Benign Neglect of Racism in the Criminal Justice System," 94 *Michigan Law Review* 1660 (1995).

87. *Dateline NBC*, "Color Blind? Disproportionate Number of Black Women are Strip-Searched by U.S. Customs Agents," April 27, 1999, program transcript.

88. African American women recounting their customs search experiences on WMAQ-NBC News, Chicago, in 1998, quoted on *Dateline NBC*, "Color Blind? Disproportionate Number of Black Women are Strip-Searched by U.S. Customs Agents," April 27, 1999, program transcript.

89. Statement of Janneral Denson, Testimony before the Subcommittee on Oversight, of the House Committee on Ways and Means, Hearing on the U.S. Customs Service Passenger Inspection Operations, May 20, 1999, www.house.gov/ways_means/oversight/106cong/5-20-99/5-20dens.htm.

90. Ibid.

91. *Dateline NBC*, "Color Blind? Disproportionate Number of Black Women are Strip-Searched by U.S. Customs Agents," April 27, 1999, program transcript.

92. Ibid.

93. Statement of Edward M. Fox, Esq., Testimony before the Subcommittee on Oversight, of the House Committee on Ways and Means, Hearing on the U.S. Customs Service Passenger Inspection Operations, May 20, 1999, www.house.gov/ways_means/oversight/106cong/5-20-99/5-20fox.htm. By comparison, White females were searched 23 percent of the time and White males were searched 11 percent of the time. Ibid.

94. Ibid.

95. *Dateline NBC*, "Color Blind? Disproportionate Number of Black

Women are Strip-Searched by U.S. Customs Agents," April 27, 1999, program transcript.

96. See *Sharon Anderson et al. v. Mario Cornejo et al.*, 199 F.R.D. 228 (N.D.Ill. 2000) (granting plaintiffs' motion for class certification in lawsuit for purposes of injunctive relief against the U.S. Customs Service). As of March 2002, discovery was largely completed in the case, with a trial date anticipated later in 2002. Personal correspondence with Attorney Ed Fox, Ed Fox and Associates, March 4, 2002, on file with author.

97. *Harvard Law Review* 1419 (1991). Professor Roberts has written extensively and quite cogently on the denial of African American women's reproductive rights within criminal law regimes. Among her works, see also *Killing the Black Body: Race, Reproduction, and the Meaning of Liberty* (1997); "Mothers Who Fail to Protect Their Children: Accounting for Private and Public Responsibility," in Julia Hanigsberg and Sara Ruddick, eds., *Mother Troubles: Rethinking Contemporary Maternal Dilemmas* 31–49; (1999); and "Racism and Patriarchy in the Meaning of Motherhood," 1 *American University Journal of Gender and Law* 1(1993).

98. Dorothy Roberts, "Punishing Drug Addicts Who Have Babies: Women of Color, Equality, and the Right of Privacy," 104 *Harvard Law Review* at 1424.

99. Vivian Berger, "No Way to Treat a Baby," *National Law Journal*, November 13, 2000, at A21.

100. Forty-two women were arrested and incarcerated based on the detection of cocaine from urine samples. Forty-one of the forty-two were African American. Notably, only women who were suspected of crack or powder cocaine use were tested without their knowledge or consent although the protocol was directed at "all drug use." Vivian Berger, "No Way to Treat a Baby," *National Law Journal*, November 13, 2000, at A21. See also 121 S.Ct. 1281, 1284–86.

101. S.Ct. 1281 (2001).

102. The women were charged with drug possession, child neglect, and distributing drugs to a minor, offenses which carried penalties of two to twenty years. Rachel Roth, "Policing Pregnancy: Civil Rights of Pregnant Drug Users," *The Nation*, October 16, 2000, at 6.

103. Vivian Berger, "No Way to Treat a Baby," *National Law Journal*, November 13, 2000, at A21. As Professor Roberts describes, "[L]ori Griffin was transported weekly from the jail to the hospital in handcuffs and leg irons for prenatal care. Three weeks after her arrest, she went into labor and was taken, still in handcuffs and shackles, to MUSC. Once at the hospital, she was kept handcuffed to her bed *during the entire delivery*." Dorothy Roberts, *Killing the Black Body* 166 (1997) (emphasis in original).

104. Vivian Berger, "No Way to Treat a Baby," *National Law Journal*, November 13, 2000, at A21.

105. See, e.g., Terry A. Adirim and Nandini Sen Gupta, "A National Survey of the State Maternal and Newborn Drug Testing and Reporting Policies," U.S. Department of Health and Human Services Public Health Report 292–96 (1991) (estimating that at least 10 percent of all babies were exposed to drugs while in the womb). But see Deborah A. Frank et al., "Growth, Development, and Behavior in Early Childhood Following Prenatal Cocaine Exposure: A Systematic Review," 285 *Journal of the American Medical Association* 1613–25 (2001); and Jacquelyn Litt and Maureen McNeill, "Biological Markers and Social Differentiation: Crack Babies and the Construction of the Dangerous Mother," 18 *Health Care for Women International* 31–41 (1997) (noting that previous estimates and harmful effects were exaggerated).

106. Rachel Roth, "Policing Pregnancy: Civil Rights of Pregnant Drug Users," *The Nation*, October 16, 2000, at 6. See also 121 S.Ct. at 1290 (noting, "Respondents argue in essence that their ultimate purpose—namely, protecting the health of both mother and child—is a beneficent one").

107. This point was made by Judge Blake in her dissent in the Fourth Circuit's opinion: "[I]t . . . is clear from the record that an initial and continuing focus of the policy was on the arrest and prosecution of drug-abusing mothers" (186 F.3d 469, 484 (1999) *quoted with approval in* 121 S.Ct. at 1290.

108. In testimony before Congress, Commissioner Kelly assured the subcommittee members, "In response to these shortcomings, we've undertaken a variety of important measures, [including] the formation of internal and external committees to review our search procedures; immediate reforms to certain steps in the personal search such as strengthening the role of supervisors; and far-reaching changes to our passenger processing environment that focus on improved information, training, and technology." Statement of Raymond W. Kelly, Commissioner, U.S. Customs Service, Testimony before the Subcommittee on Oversight, of the House Committee on Ways and Means, Hearing on the U.S. Customs Service Passenger Inspection Operations, May 20, 1999, www.house.gov/ways_means/oversight/106cong/5-20-99/5-20kell.htm. See Sanford Cloud, Jr., "Independent Advisor's Report to Commissioner Kelly on the U.S. Customs Service's Personal Search Review Commission's Findings and Recommendations," June 21, 2000. The Customs Service significantly revised its search procedures after findings and recommendations by the Personal Search Review Commission and the Independent Advisor.

109. With respect to the MUSC program, the Civil Rights Division of the Department of Health and Human Services (HHS) had investigated possible violations of African American women patients' civil rights. In 1994, at the risk of losing millions of dollars in federal funding, MUSC suspended the "test-arrest" program as part of a settlement agreement with HHS. See Dorothy Roberts, *Killing the Black Body* 168 (1997).

110. See Henry Weinstein, "Racial Profiling Gains Support as Search Tactic," *Los Angeles Times.Com,* www.latimes.com/news/nationworld/nation/la-092401racial.story, September 24, 2001.

111. See Aviation and Security Act, 49 U.S.C. § 114 (2001) (enacting greater passenger screening and other security measures at U.S. airports).

112. See N.Y. PENAL LAW § 70.00(2) (a), 70.00(3) (a) (I) (McKinney 1998); see also Paula C. Johnson, "At the Intersection of Injustice," 4 *American University Journal of Gender and Law* 1 (1995).

113. See Paula C. Johnson, "At the Intersection of Injustice: Experiences of African American Women in Crime and Sentencing," 4 *American University Journal of Gender and Law* 1 (1995).

114. Pub. L. No. 104-38, § 2, 3 (1997); and U.S. Sentencing Commission, "Special Report to Congress: Cocaine and Federal Sentencing" (1995).

115. As David Cole cites, African Americans comprise 90 percent of those found guilty of crack cocaine crimes, but only 20 percent of those found guilty of powder cocaine crimes. David Cole, *No Equal Justice* 8 (1999). Cole further notes that "Black defendants have challenged the crack/powder disparity on constitutional grounds, but every federal challenge has failed. . . . Even though black cocaine offenders in the federal system serve sentences on average five years longer than white cocaine offenders, the courts see no constitutional problem." Ibid. at 141–46. See also *U.S. v. Armstrong,* 517 U.S. 456 (1996); and *U.S. v. Clary,* 846 F. Supp. 768 (E.D. Mo. 1993), *rev'd* , 34 F.3d 709 (8th Cir. 1994), *cert. denied,* 115 S.Ct. 1172 (1995).

116. William Spade, Jr., "Beyond the 100:1 Ratio: Towards a Rational Cocaine Sentencing Policy," 38 *Arizona Law Review* 1233, 1254–55 (1996). Eric Sterling, a former staff member of the House Judiciary Committee, described the passage of the legislation as "this frenzied panic atmosphere. . . . It was the crassest political poker game." Ibid. at 1255. See also *U.S. v. Clary,* 846 F. Supp. 768, 784–87 (1994) (discussing the lack of congressional deliberation on the cocaine sentencing laws).

117. U.S. Sentencing Comm'n, "Special Report to the Congress: Cocaine and Federal Sentencing Policy," 198 (1995).

118. This majority consisted of Chairman Richard Conaboy, Commissioners Wayne Budd and Michael Gelacak, and Judge David Mazzone. The majority recognized that the sentencing scheme resulted in more lenient sentencing of higher-level powder-cocaine dealers than the crack dealers whom they supplied. The racial disparities in the sentencing ratio led this group to advocate a one-to-one ratio. U.S. Sentencing Commission, "Materials Concerning Sentencing for Crack Cocaine Offenses," 57 *Criminal Law Reporter* 2129 (1995). See also William Spade, Jr., "Beyond the 100:1 Ratio: Towards a Rational Cocaine Sentencing Policy," 38 *Arizona Law Review* 1235 (1996).

119. U.S. Sentencing Commission, "Materials Concerning Sentencing for Crack Cocaine Offenses," 57 *Criminal Law Reporter* 2131 (1995).

120. Ibid.

121. F. Supp. 768 (E.D. Mo. 1994), *rev'd*, 34 F.3d 709 (8th Cir. 1994), *cert. denied*, 115 S.Ct. 1172 (1995).

122. F. Supp. at 778–79.

123. U.S. 456 (1996).

124. Ibid.

125. Katheryn K. Russell, *The Color of Crime* 32, 133 (1998).

126. Mark Mauer and Tracy Huling, "Young Black Americans and the Criminal Justice System: Five Years Later," *The Sentencing Project* 19 (1995).

127. See, generally, Paula C. Johnson, "A Legal and Qualitative Study of the Relationships between Incarcerated African American Mothers and Their Children" (unpublished, on file with author).

128. *See* Myrna Raeder, "Gender and Sentencing: Single Moms, Battered Women, and Other Sex-Based Anomalies in the Gender-Free World of the Federal Sentencing Guidelines," 20 *Pepperdine Law Review* 938 (1993) (noting "African American women received nearly ten percent fewer family departures than their percentage in the sentenced female population").

129. See Paula C. Johnson, "A Legal and Qualitative Study of the Relationships between Incarcerated African American Mothers and Their Children" (unpublished, on file with author) (discussing impact of ASFA on incarcerated African American women and their children); see also Steven R. Donziger, ed., *The Real War on Crime* 154–55 (1996).

130. David Rudovsky, "The Impact of the War on Drugs on Procedural Fairness and Racial Equality," 1994 *University of Chicago Legal Forum* 237 (1994).

131. Ibid.

132. Paul Finkelman, "The Second Casualty of War: Civil Liberties and the War on Drugs," 66 *Southern California Law Review* 1389, 1406 (1993). See also *Employment Division, Department of Human Resources of Oregon v. Smith*, 494 U.S. 872 (1990) (*aff'g* Oregon's right to punish members of a Native American church who took the hallucinogen peyote as part of their religious practice). And see Garrett Epps, *To an Unknown God: Religious Freedom on Trial* (2000) (discussing the Smith case).

133. David Rudovsky, "The Impact of the War on Drugs on Procedural Fairness and Racial Equality," 1994 *University of Chicago Legal Forum* 237 & n.89 (1994).

134. Paul Finkelman, "The Second Casualty of War: Civil Liberties and the War on Drugs," 66 *Southern California Law Review* 1451 (1993).

135. 18 U.S.C. § 3141 et seq. See also Marc Miller and Martin Guggenheim, "Pretrial Detention and Punishment," 75 *Minnesota Law Review* 335 (1990).

136. Paul Finkelman, "The Second Casualty of War: Civil Liberties and the War on Drugs," 66 *Southern California Law Review* at 1452. See also john a. powell and Eileen B. Hershenov, "Hostage to the Drug War: The National Purse, the Constitution and the Black Community," 24 *University of California-Davis Law Review* 557 (1991).

NOTES TO PART II

Chapter 8

1. Sandeep Kaushik, "Hard Times: Ohio Is Spending Hundreds of Millions on 15,000 Prisoners Who Should be Paroled," February 20, 2002, p. 10.

Chapter 10

1. F.Supp. 1265 (D.C.Tex. 1980), *stay granted by* 650 F.2d 555 (5th Cir. 1981), *and aff'd in part, rev'd in part by* 679 F.2d 1115 (5th Cir. 1982), *amended in part, vacated in part by* 688 F.2d 266 (5th Cir. 1982).

Chapter 12

1. See U.S. v. Walls, 841 F.Supp. 24 (D.D.C. 1994), *aff'd in part, remanded in part* 70 F.3d 1323 (D.C.Cir. 1995), *cert. denied* Campbell v. U.S., 517 U.S. 1147 (1996), *and cert. denied* Jackson v. U.S., 519 U.S. 827 (1996), *and cert. denied* Walls v. U.S., 519 U.S. 827 (1996), *and on remand to sub. nom.* U.S. v. Campbell, 959 F.Supp. 20 (D.D.C. 1997), *and appeal after remand sub. nom.* U.S. v. Blakney, 132 F.3d 1482 (D.C.Cir. 1997), *and on remand to sub. nom.* U.S. v. Campbell, 985 F.Supp. 158 (D.D.C. 1997), *aff'd by* 172 F.3d 921 (D.C.Cir. 1998).

Chapter 13

1. H. Rap Brown, now known as Jamil Abdullah Al-Amin, was former minister of justice for the Black Panther Party. He later became an imam of a Muslim community in Atlanta, Georgia. In 2002, he was convicted of killing one Fulton County, Georgia, deputy and wounding another.

2. In the 1960s, the FBI began a counterintelligence program—COINTELPRO—that targeted leftist and progressive political organizations in African American, Native American, and Latino communities, in addition to student and youth groups that opposed the Vietnam War. See Ward Churchill and Jim Vander, *The COINTELPRO Papers: Documents from the FBI's Secret Wars against Dissent in the United States* (South End Press, 2002).

Chapter 15

1. F.Supp. 1265 (D.C.Tex. 1980), *stay granted by* 650 F.2d 555 (5th Cir. 1981),

and aff'd in part, rev'd in part by 679 F.2d 1115 (5th Cir. 1982), *amended in part, vacated in part by* 688 F.2d 266 (5th Cir. 1982).

Chapter 17

1. People v. Thompson, 190 A.D.2d 162 (N.Y.App.Div. 1993), *leave to appeal granted by* 81 N.Y.2d 1022 (N.Y. 1993), *and leave to appeal granted denied by* 82 N.Y.2d 727 (N.Y. 1993), *and order rev'd by* 83 N.Y.1994).

2. People v. Broadie, 332 N.E.2d (N.Y. 1975).

3. Gideon v. Wainwright, 372 U.S. 335 (1963).

Chapter 22

1. Women Prisoners of the D.C. Dep't of Corrections v. District of Columbia, 899 F.Supp. 659 (D.D.C.), *vacated, in part, remanded* 93 F.3d 910 (1996).

2. Amnesty International, *"Not Part of My Sentence": Violations of Human Rights of Women in Custody* (1999).

NOTES TO PART III

1. Michael Tonry, "Why Are U.S. Incarceration Rates So High?" 10 *Overcrowded Times* 1, 8 (1999) (noting increased procedural protections for criminal defendants in the European Union, in contrast to reductions of such protections in the United States).

2. See Charles R. Lawrence, "The Id, the Ego, and Equal Protection: Reckoning with Unconscious Racism," 39 *Stanford Law Review* 317 (1987).

3. New York v. Thompson, 596 N.Y.S.2d at 422–23 (Judge Newton ruled that "sentencing her to 15 years to life without wiping out the possibility of Angela Thompson . . . would be . . . an unconstitutional sentence"). At the time of the trial, Thompson was an eighteen-year-old African American women, a first offender who was a minor player in her uncle's drug operation. She lived with her uncle after being passed to various relatives after losing both of her parents. See extensive discussion of *New York v. Thompson* in Paula C. Johnson, "At the Intersection of Injustice: Experiences of African American Women in Crime and Sentencing," 4 *American University Journal of Gender and Law* 1 (1995).

4. Ellen M. Barry, "Health Care Inadequacies in Women's Prisons," *A.B.A.* 39, 40 (Spring 2001). See also D. S. Young, "Contributing Factors to Poor Health among Incarcerated Women: A Conceptual Model," 11 *Affilia* 440 (1996).

5. Ellen M. Barry, "Health Care Inadequacies in Women's Prisons," *A.B.A.* 39, 40 (Spring 2001).

6. Jo Lydia Sabur, Coordinator, Center for Community Alternatives Women's Choices Program, interview on file with author.

7. Human Rights Watch, *All Too Familiar: Sexual Abuse of Women in U.S. State Prisons* 1–2 (1996).

8. See U.S. General Accounting Office, "Women in Prison: Sexual Misconduct by Correctional Staff" (1999).

9. Ibid.

10. Cathy McDaniels Wilson, "The Relation of Sexual Abuse History to the MMPI-2 Profiles and Criminal Involvement of Incarcerated Women," unpublished dissertation, Ohio State University, 1998. See also Brenda V. Smith, "Sexual Abuse against Women in Prison," *A.B.A.* 31 (Spring 2001).

11. Amnesty International, "'Not Part of My Sentence:' Violations of Human Rights of Women in Custody," 25 and n. 72 (1999).

12. This research was conducted by telephone during October and November 2000. Admittedly, this was not an extensive study and further inquiry along these lines is planned. Initially, however, it was conducted informally in order to gain an impression as to whether or not prison programming recognized and addressed the particular needs of the overwhelmingly African American female inmate population. The survey questionnaire is on file with the author.

13. See Linda Grant, "Helpers, Enforcers, and Go-Betweens: Black Females in Elementary School Classrooms," in Maxine Baca Zinn and Bonnie Thornton Dill, eds., *Women of Color in U.S. Society* 43 (1994) (noting that stereotyped role casting of African American girls in primary schools may emphasize their social development at the expense of their academic development, which may be a disadvantage to them in the long run).

14. See Paula C. Johnson, "A Qualitative Study of the Relationships between African American Incarcerated Mothers and Their Children" (unpublished paper, 2001).

15. See Katherine Gabel and Denise Johnston, eds., *Children of Incarcerated Parents* (1995); see also Paula C. Johnson, "A Qualitative Study of the Relationships between African American Incarcerated Mothers and Their Children" (unpublished paper, 2001).

16. See Symposium, "Alternatives to Incarceration," 111 *Harvard Law Review* 1898–1919, 1921–44 (1998); Morris and Tonry, *Between Prison and Probation* (1990); and Patricia O'Brien, *Making It in the "Free World": Women in Transition from Prison* (2001).

17. See Paula C. Johnson, "Danger in the Diaspora: Law, Culture and Violence against Women of African Descent in the United States and South Africa," 1 *Iowa Journal of Gender, Race and Justice* 471 (1998); Beth E. Richie, *Compelled to Crime: The Gender Entrapment of Battered Black Women* (1996); and Linda Ammons, "Mules, Madonnas, Babies, Bathwater, Racial Imagery and Stereotypes: The African-American Woman and the Battered Woman's Syndrome," 1995 *Wisconsin Law Review* 1003.

18. Jonathan P. Caulkins et al., "Mandatory Minimum Drug Sentences: Throwing Away the Key or the Taxpayers' Money?" *RAND* (1997).

19. See Fox Butterfield, "Tight Budgets Force States to Reconsider Crime and Penalties," *New York Times,* January 21, 2002, at A1 (noting prison closures and staff lay-offs in California, Ohio, Michigan, and Illinois; in addition to re-consideration of the number of offenses falling under the three-strikes provi-sion in California).

20. See Evelyn Nieves, "Storm Raised by Plan for a California Prison," *New York Times,* August 27, 2000, at 16 (noting that a broad coalition of groups sued to stop prison construction despite vigorous lobbying by the economically de-pressed farm town of Delano, Department of Corrections and California Peace Officers Assn., for another maximum security prison. Groups argued that a ref-erendum requiring alternatives to incarceration for nonviolent drug offenders, an eight-year crime drop, and a reduced prison population made a proposed new prison superfluous). See also Proposition 36, adopted by California voters on November 7, 2000; codified as the Substance Abuse and Crime Prevention Act of 2000, Cal. Health & Saf. Code § 11999.4 (2001). California noted the ben-efits of the Drug Medicalization, Prevention, and Control Act of Arizona (1996), as reported by the Arizona Supreme Court, which found "the Arizona law 're-sulting in safer communities and more substance abusing probationers in re-covery,' has already saved state taxpayers millions of dollars, and is helping more than 75 percent of program participants to remain drug free." And see Michael Isikoff, "A New Front in the Drug War," *Newsweek,* August 28, 2000, at 29.

21. Over 95 percent of drug offenders in New York prisons are African American or Hispanic, although they comprise less than one-third of the state's population. First enacted in 1973, these laws have accounted for a prison popu-lation that soared from 12,500 in 1973 to more than 71,400 in 2000; the drug-in-mate population was less than 2,000 in 1980, and grew to 22,000 in 2000. See Terry Tang, "New York's Busted Drug Laws," *Rolling Stone,* October 12, 2000, at 55.

22. The Rockefeller drug laws impose a fifteen to life sentence for posses-sion of more than four ounces of cocaine or heroin, or for sale of two ounces or more of those substances. N.Y. Penal Law § 70.00(2) (a).

23. See Sentencing Project, *Reducing Racial Disparity in the Criminal Justice System: A Manual for Practitioners and Policymakers* (2000).

24. Edmund B. Spaeth, Jr., "The Courts' Responsibility for Prison Reform," 16 *Villanova Law Review* 1029, 1031 (1971).

25. Ibid.

26. Jon O. Newman, "Commencement Address to Brooklyn Law School," in Daniel Burton-Rose et al., eds., *The Celling of America: An Inside Look at the U.S. Prison Industry* 55 (1998).

27. Ibid. at 55–57 (providing the underlying facts of several prisoner claims that attorneys general of four states described as frivolous).

28. Pub. L. No. 104-134, §§ 801–10 (1996).

29. See, e.g., Eric Schlosser, "The Prison-Industrial Complex," *Atlantic Monthly*, December 1998 (discussing employment creation and economic profiteering generated by prison overcrowding, especially noting the growth in private for-profit prison construction).

30. See Cassandra Shaylor, "'It's Like Living in a Black Hole': Women of Color and Solitary Confinement in the Prison Industrial Complex," 24 *New England Journal on Criminal and Civil Confinement* 385 (1998) (questioning the increased use of control units in women's prisons, disproportionately applied against women of color).

31. W. E. B. Du Bois, quoted in Dorothy Sterling, ed., *The Trouble They Seen: The Story of Reconstruction in the Words of African Americans* 67 (1994). Obviously, the lives of African Americans have improved greatly since the Reconstruction era; nevertheless, as the Urban League's recent report states, "Today, as a result of struggle, the rights and privileges of African Americans have changed. . . . [t]here is much left to be done." Urban League, "The State of Black America" (1999).

Bibliography

Addis, Adeno. "'Hell Man, They Did Invent Us': The Mass Media, Law and African Americans." *Buffalo Law Review* 41 (Spring 1993): 523–626.

Adleman, Jeanne, and Gloria M. Enguidanos-Clark. *Racism in the Lives of Women: Testimony, Theory and Guides to Antiracist Practice.* New York: Haworth Press, 1995.

Adler, Freda. *Sisters in Crime: The Rise of the New Female Criminal.* New York: McGraw-Hill, 1975.

American Correctional Association (ACA). *The Female Offender: What Does the Future Hold?* Washington, D.C.: St. Mary's, 1990.

Armour, Jody. "Race Ipsa Loquitur: Of Reasonable Racists, Intelligent Bayesians, and Involuntary Negrophobes." *Stanford Law Review* 46 (April 1994): 781–816.

Arnold, Regina. "Process of Victimization and Criminalization of Black Women." In Barbara Price and Natalie J. Sokoloff, eds., *The Criminal Justice System and Women Offenders, Victims and Workers.* New York: McGraw-Hill, 1995.

Atwood, Jane Evelyn. *Too Much Time: Women in Prison.* London: Phaidon, 2000.

Austin, James. *America's Growing Correctional-Industrial Complex.* San Francisco: National Council on Crime and Delinquency, 1990.

Austin, James, Barbara Bloom, and Trish Donahue. *Female Offenders in the Community: An Analysis of Innovative Strategies and Programs.* National Council on Crime and Delinquency. Washington, D.C.: National Institute of Corrections, 1992.

Austin, Regina. "'The Black Community', Its Lawbreakers, and a Politics of Identification." *Southern California Law Review* 65 (May 1992): 1769–1817.

Avery, Byllye. "The Health Status of Black Women." In R. Braithwaite and S. E. Taylor, eds., *Health Issues in the Black Community.* San Francisco: Jossey-Bass, 1992.

Baldus, David, George Woodworth, and Charles A. Pulaski, Jr. *Equal Justice and the Death Penalty.* Boston: Northeastern University Press, 1990.

Barry, Ellen. "Pregnant, Addicted and Sentenced." *ABA Criminal Justice Journal* 5 (Winter 1991): 22(6).

———. "Pregnant Prisoners." *Harvard Women's Law Journal* 12 (1989): 189–205.

————. "Women Prisoners and Health Care: Locked Up and Locked Out." In Kary Moss, ed., *Manmade Medicine: Women's Health, Public Policy and Reform*. Durham, N.C.: Duke University Press, 1995.

Barry, Ellen, River Ginchild, and Doreen Lee. "Legal Issues for Prisoners with Children." In Katherine Gabel and Denise Johnston, eds., *Children of Incarcerated Parents*. Lexington, Mass: Lexington Books, 1995.

Baunach, Phyllis Jo. *Mothers in Prison*. New Brunswick, N.J.: Transaction Books, 1985.

Beardsley, Edward. "Race as a Factor in Health." In Rima Apple, ed., *Women, Health and Medicine in America: A Historical Handbook*. New York: Garland, 1990.

Bell, Derrick. *And We Are Not Saved: The Elusive Quest for Racial Justice*. New York: Basic Books, 1987.

————. *Faces at the Bottom of the Well: The Permanence of Racism*. New York: Basic Books, 1992.

————. *Race, Racism, and American Law*. Boston: Little, Brown, 1992.

Bennett, Lerone. *Before the Mayflower: A History of Black America*. New York: Penquin, 1993.

Bloom, Barbara, Meda Chesney-Lind, and Barbara Owen. *Women in California Prisons: Hidden Victims of the War on Drugs*. San Francisco: Center on Juvenile and Criminal Justice, 1994.

Boudouris, James. *Parents in Prison: Address the Needs of Families*. Lanham, Md.: American Correctional Association, 1996.

Branham, Lynn S., and Sheldon Krantz. *The Law of Sentencing, Corrections, and Prisoners' Rights*. 5th ed.. St. Paul, Minn.: West Publishing, 1997.

Bresler, Lewis, and Diane K. Lewis. "Black and White Women Prisoners: Differences in Family Ties and Their Programmatic Implications." *Prison Journal* 63 (Autumn–Winter 1983): 116–23.

Brown, Joyce Ann, and Jay Gaines. *Joyce Ann Brown: Justice Denied*. Chicago: The Noble Press, 1990.

Bullough, Vern L. *The History of Prostitution*. New Hyde Park, N.Y.: University Books, 1964.

Burke, Peggy, and Linda Adams. *Classification of Women Offenders in State Correctional Facilities: A Handbook for Practitioners*. Washington, D.C.: Cosmos Corp. for the National Institute of Corrections, 1991.

Calhoun-Stuber, Susan. *Women Arrested for Domestic Violence: Views of Self, Definitions of Abuse, and Use of Violence*. Denver: University of Denver, 1995.

Carlen, Pat. *Alternatives to Women's Imprisonment*. Philadelphia: Open University Press, 1990.

Chapman, Jane Roberts. *Economic Realities and the Female Offender*. Lexington, Mass.: Lexington Books, 1980.

Chesney-Lind, Meda. "Chivalry Reexamined: Women and the Criminal Justice System." In Lee H. Bowker and Meda Chesney-Lind, eds., *Women, Crime, and the Criminal Justice System*. Lexington, Mass.: Lexington Books, 1978.

———. "Girls, Delinquency, and Juvenile Justice: Toward a Feminist Theory of Young Women's Crime." In Barbara Raffel Price and Natalie Sokoloff, eds., *The Criminal Justice System and Women*. New York: McGraw-Hill, 1995.

———. "Patriarchy, Prisons, and Jails: A Critical Look at Trends in Women's Incarceration." *Prison Journal* 71 (Spring–Summer 1991): 51–67.

Collins, Catherine Fisher. *The Imprisonment of African American Women: Causes, Conditions, and Future Implications*. Jefferson, N.C.: McFarland and Company, 1997.

Cose, Ellis. *The Rage of a Privileged Class*. New York: HarperCollins, 1993.

Crockett, George W. "The Role of the Black Judge." In *The Criminal Justice System and Blacks*. New York: Clark Boardman, 1984.

Daly, Kathleen. "Criminal Law and Justice System Practices as Racist, White and Racialized." *Washington and Lee Law Review* 51 (Spring 1994): 431–64.

Davis, Angela J. "Benign Neglect of Racism in the Criminal Justice System." *Michigan Law Review* 94 (May 1996): 1660–86.

Davis, Angela Y., et al. *If They Come in the Morning*. New York: Signet Books, 1971.

Davis, Peggy. "Law as Microaggression." *Yale Law Journal* 98 (June 1989): 1559–77.

Diaz-Cotto, Juanita. "Women and Crime in the United States." In Chandra Talpade Mohanty, Ann Russo, and Lourdes Torres, eds., *Third World Women and the Politics of Feminism*. Bloomington: Indiana University Press, 1991.

Ellison, Ralph. *The Invisible Man*. New York: Vintage, 1947.

Enos, Sandra. *Mothering from the Inside: Parenting in a Women's Prison*. Albany: State University of New York Press, 2001.

Erikson, Erik H. *Childhood and Society*. New York: Norton, 1964.

Ethridge, Philip, and James Marquart. "Private Prisons in Texas: The New Penology for Profit." *Justice Quarterly* 10 (March 1993): 29.

Families of Prisoners. San Francisco: Nurturing Press, 1988.

Feinman, Clarice. "An Historical Overview of the Treatment of Incarcerated Women: Myths and Realities of Rehabilitation." *Prison Journal* 63 (Autumn–Winter 1983): 12–26.

———. *Women in the Criminal Justice System*. New York: Praeger, 1980.

———. *Women in the Criminal Justice System*. 2d ed. New York: Praeger, 1986.

Finkelman, Paul. "The Crime of Color." *Tulane Law Review* 67 (1993): 2063–2112.

———, ed. *Race Law and American History 1700–1990: The African American Experience*. New York: Garland, 1992.

Fletcher, Beverly R., Lynda Dixon Shaver, and Dreama G. Moon, eds. *Women Prisoners. A Forgotten Population*. Westport, Conn.: Praeger, 1993.

Flowers, B. Ronald. *Minorities and Criminality*. Westport, Conn.: Greenwood, 1990.

———. *Women and Criminality: The Woman as Victim, Offender and Practitioner*. Westport, Conn.: Greenwood, 1987.

Foner, Eric. *Reconstruction: America's Unfinished Revolution, 1863–1877*. Harper and Row, 1988.

Forer, Lois G. *Criminals and Victims*. New York: Norton, 1980.

———. *A Rage to Punish: The Unintended Consequences of Mandatory Sentencing*. New York: Norton, 1994.

Freedman, Estelle. *Their Sister's Keepers: Women's Prison Reforms in America, 1870–1930*. Ann Arbor: University of Michigan Press, 1981.

French, Laurence. "An Assessment of the Black Female Prisoner in the South." *Signs: Journal of Women in Culture and Society* 3 (Winter 1977): 483–88.

———. "Incarcerated Black Female—The Case of Social Double Jeopardy." *Journal of Black Studies* 8 (March 1978): 321–35.

———. "A Profile of the Incarcerated Black Female Offender." *Prison Journal* 63 (Autumn–Winter 1983): 80–87.

Friedman, Lawrence M. *Crime and Punishment in American History*. New York: Basic Books, 1993.

Gabel, Katherine. *Legal Issues of Female Inmates*. Washington, D.C.: National Institute of Corrections, U.S. Department of Justice, 1982.

Gabel, Katherine, and Denise Johnston. *Children of Incarcerated Parents*. New York: Lexington Books, 1995.

Genty, Philip M. "Procedural Due Process Rights of Incarcerated Parents in Termination of Parental Rights Proceedings: A Fifty-State Analysis." *Journal of Family Law* 30 (August 1992): 757–846.

———. "Protecting the Parental Rights of Incarcerated Mothers Whose Children Are in Foster Care: Proposed Changes to New York's Termination of Parental Rights Law." *Fordham Urban Law Journal* 17 (Winter 1989): 1–26.

Gillmer, Jason. "*U.S. v. Clary:* Equal Protection and the Crack Statute." *American University Law Review* 45 (December 1995): 497–565.

Glick, Ruth, and Virginia Neto. *National Study of Women's Correctional Programs*. Washington, D.C.: National Institute of Law Enforcement and Criminal Justice, Law Enforcement Assistance Administration, U.S. Department of Justice, June 1977.

Hacker, Andrew. *Two Nations: Black and White, Separate, Hostile, Unequal*. New York: Ballantine, 1992.

Harden, Judy, and Marcia Hill. *Breaking the Rules: Women in Prison and Feminist Therapy*. Binghamton, N.Y.: Haworth Press, 1998.

Harris, Jean. *Marking Time: Letters from Jean Harris to Shana Alexander*. New York: Scribner's, 1991.

————. *They Always Call Us Ladies: Stories from Prison*. New York: Scribner's, 1988.

Harris, Trudier. *Exorcising Blackness: Historical and Literary Lynching and Burning Rituals*. Bloomington: Indiana University Press, 1984.

Henriques, Zelma Weston. *Imprisoned Mothers and Their Children: A Descriptive and Analytical Study*. Washington, D.C.: University Press of America, 1982.

Herman, Judith. *Trauma and Recovery*. New York: Basic Books, 1992.

Higginbotham, A. Leon, Jr. *In the Matter of Color: Race and the American Legal Process*. New York: Oxford University Press, 1978.

————. *Shades of Freedom: Racial Politics and Presumption of the American Legal Process*. New York: Oxford University Press, 1996.

Higginbotham, A. Leon, Jr., and Anne F. Jacobs. "The 'Law Only as an Enemy': The Legitimization of Racial Powerlessness through the Colonial and Ante-Bellum Criminal Laws of Virginia." *North Carolina Law Review* 70 (April 1992): 969–1070.

Hill, Gary D., and Elizabeth M. Crawford. "Women, Race and Crime." *Criminology* 28 (November 1990): 601–26.

Immarigeon, Russ, and Meda Chesney-Lind. *Women's Prisons: Overcrowded and Overused*. San Francisco: National Council on Crime and Delinquency, 1992.

Jackson, George. *Soledad Brother: The Prison Letters of George Jackson*. New York: Bantam Books, 1970.

James, Jennifer. *The Prostitute as Victim: Criminal Justice System and Women*. New York: Clark Boardman, 1982.

Johnson, Byron R., and Paul P. Ross. "The Privatization of Correctional Management: A Review." *Journal of Criminal Justice* 18 (July–August 1990): 351–58.

Johnson, Paula C. "At the Intersection of Injustice: Experiences of African American Women in Crime and Sentencing." *American University Journal of Gender and the Law* 4 (Fall 1995): 1–76.

————. "Danger in the Diaspora: Law, Culture and Violence against Women of African Descent in the United States and South Africa." *Journal of Gender, Race and Justice* 1 (Spring 1998): 471–527.

————. "Silence Equals Death: The Response to AIDS within Communities of Color." *University of Illinois Law Review* 1992 (Fall 1992): 1075–83.

Johnson, Sheri L. "Black Innocence and the White Jury." *Michigan Law Review* 83 (June 1985): 1611–1708.

————. "Racial Imagery in Criminal Cases." *Tulane Law Review* 67 (June 1993): 1739–1805.

————. "Unconscious Racism and the Criminal Law." *Cornell Law Review* 73 (September 1988): 1016–37.

Jones, Ann. *Women Who Kill*. New York: Fawcett, 1980.

Kairys, David. *The Politics of Law.* New York: Pantheon, 1990.

———. *With Liberty and Justice for Some.* New York: New Press, 1993.

Kennedy, Randall. *Race, Crime, and the Law.* New York: Pantheon Books, 1997.

Kruttschnitt, Candace. "Respectable Women and the Law." *Sociological Quarterly* 23 (Spring 1982): 221–34.

Lawrence, Charles R., III. "The Id, the Ego, and Equal Protection: Reckoning with Unconscious Racism." *Stanford Law Review* 39 (1987): 317–88.

Lekkerkerker, Eugenia. *Reformatories for Women in the United States.* Groningen, Netherlands: J. B. Wolters, 1931.

Levy, Howard, and David Miller. *Going to Jail: The Political Prisoner.* New York: Grove Press, 1971.

Lewis, Diane, and L. Bresler. "Black Women Offenders and Criminal Justice—Some Theoretical Considerations." In Marguerite Q. Warren, ed., *Comparing Female and Male Offenders.* Beverly Hills, Calif.: Sage, 1981.

Lombroso, Cesare, and William Ferrero. *The Female Offender* (1895). Reprints. New York: D. Appleton, 1915, 1920.

Lord, Elaine. "A Prison Superintendent's Perspective on Women in Prison." *Prison Journal* 75 (June 1995): 257.

Mann, Coramae Richey. "Women of Color and the Justice System." In Barbara Price and Natalie Sokoloff, eds., *The Criminal Justice System and Women Offenders, Victims and Workers.* New York: McGraw-Hill, 1995.

———. *Unequal Justice: A Question of Color.* Bloomington: Indiana University Press, 1993.

Mauer, Marc. "Intended and Unintended Consequences: State Racial Disparities in Imprisonment." Washington, D.C.: The Sentencing Project, 1997.

Mauer, Marc, and Tracy Huling. "Young Black Americans and the Criminal Justice System: Five Years Later." Washington, D.C.: The Sentencing Project, 1995.

Mauer, Marc, Cathy Potler, and Richard Wolf. *Gender and Justice: Women, Drugs, and Sentencing Policy.* Washington, D.C.: The Sentencing Project, 1999.

McConahay, John B., Courtney J. Mullin, and Jeffrey T. Fredrick. *The Uses of Social Science in Trials with Political and Racial Overtones: The Trial of JoAnn Little.* Durham, N.C.: Center for Policy Analysis, Institute of Policy Sciences and Public Affairs, Duke University, 1976.

Menninger, Karl. *The Crime of Punishment.* New York: Viking Press, 1968.

Merlo, Alida V., and Joycelyn M. Pollock. *Women, Law, and Social Control.* Boston: Allyn and Bacon, 1995.

Morrison, Toni, ed. *Race-ing Justice, En-gendering Power: Essays on Anita Hill, Clarence Thomas, and the Construction of Social Reality.* New York: Pantheon Books, 1992.

Moyer, Imogene L. *The Changing Roles of Women in the Criminal Justice System:*

Offenders, Victims and Professionals. Prospect Heights, Ill.: Waveland Press, 1992.

Myrdal, Gunnar. *An American Dilemma: The Negro Problem and Modern Democracy.* New York: Harper, 1944.

National Criminal Justice Commission. *The Real War on Crime: The Report of the National Criminal Justice Commission.* Ed. Steven R. Donziger. New York: Harper Perennial, 1996.

National Criminal Justice Reference Service (U.S.) and National Institute of Justice (U.S.). *Topical Search: Inmates and Their Families.* Rockville, Md.: U.S. Dept. of Justice, Office of Justice Programs, National Institute of Justice, 1995.

Norman-Eady, Sandra, and George Coppolo. *Cross-gender Body Searches in Correctional Institutions.* Hartford: Connecticut General Assembly, Office of Legislative Research, 2001.

O'Brien, Patricia. *Making It in the "Free World": Women in Transition from Prison.* Albany: State University of New York Press, 2001.

O'Shea, Kathleen A. *Women and the Death Penalty in the United States, 1900–1998.* Westport, Conn.: Praeger, 1999.

Owen, Barbara, and Barbara Bloom. "Profiling Women Prisoners: Findings from National Surveys and a California Sample." *Prison Journal* 75 (June 1995): 165.

Owens, Charles E. *Mental Health and Black Offenders.* Lexington, Mass.: D. C. Heath, 1980.

Pollak, Otto. *The Criminality of Women.* Philadelphia: University of Pennsylvania Press, 1950.

Pollock, Joy. "Early Theories of Female Criminality." In Lee H. Browker, ed., *Women, Crime and the Criminal Justice System.* Lexington, Mass.: Lexington Books, 1978.

Pollock-Byrne, Joycelyn M. *Women, Prison and Crime.* Pacific Grove, Calif.: Brooks/Cole Publishing, 1990.

Rafter, Nicole. *Partial Justice: State Prisons and Their Inmates, 1800–1935.* Boston: Northeastern University Press, 1990.

Roberts, Dorothy. *Killing the Black Body: Race, Reproduction, and the Meaning of Liberty.* New York: Pantheon Books, 1997.

———. "Punishing Drug Addicts Who Have Babies: Women of Color, Equality, and the Right of Privacy." *Harvard Law Review* 104 (May 1991): 1419–82.

———. "Racism and Patriarchy in the Meaning of Motherhood." *American University Journal of Gender and the Law* 1 (1993): 1–38.

Rogers, Helen Worthington. "A Digest of Laws Establishing Women's Reformatories in the United States." *Journal of the American Institute of Criminal Law and Criminology* 13 (November 1922): 382–437.

Rudovsky, David. *The Rights of Prisoners*. Revised ed. Carbondale: Southern Illinois University Press, 1988.

Russell, Katheryn. *The Color of Crime: Racial Hoaxes, White Fear, Black Protectionism, Police Harassment, and Other Macroaggressions*. New York: New York University Press, 1998.

Sellin, J. T. *Slavery in the Penal System, 1896–1930*. New York: Elsevier, 1976.

Seymour, Cynthia, and Creasie Finney Hairston. *Children with Parents in Prison*. Washington, D.C.: Child Welfare League of America, 1998.

Simon, Rita, and Jean Landes. *The Crimes Women Commit, the Punishments They Receive*. Lexington, Mass.: Lexington Books, 1991.

Smith, Brenda V. *An End to Silence: Women Prisoners' Handbook on Identifying and Addressing Sexual Misconduct*. Washington, D.C.: National Women's Law Center, 1998.

Smith, J. Clay. "Justice and Jurisprudence and the Black Lawyer." *Notre Dame Law Review* 69 (July 1994): 1077–1113.

Spade, William, Jr. "Beyond the 100:1 Ratio: Towards a Rational Cocaine Sentencing Policy." *Arizona Law Review* 38 (Winter 1996): 1233–89.

Stampp, Kenneth. *The Peculiar Institution: Slavery in the Antebellum South*. New York: Knopf, 1956.

Swan, L. Alex. *Families of Black Prisoners: Survival and Prayers*. Boston: G. K. Hall, 1981.

Thomas, Dorothy Q. *All Too Familiar: Sexual Abuse of Women in U.S. State Prisons*. New York: Human Rights Watch, 1996.

Thomas, Jim. *Prisoner Litigation: The Paradox of the Jailhouse Lawyer*. Totowa, N.J.: Rowman and Littlefield, 1988.

Tidwell, Mike. *In the Shadow of the White House: Drugs, Death, and Redemption on the Streets of the Nation's Capital*. Rocklin, Calif.: Prima, 1992.

Tilbor, Karen. *Prisoners as Parents: Building Parent Skills on the Inside*. Portland: Edmund S. Muskie Institute of Public Affairs, University of Southern Maine, 1998.

Tonry, Michael. *Malign Neglect: Race, Crime and Punishment in America*. New York: Oxford University Press, 1995.

U.S. Department of Health and Human Services, National Institute of Health. *Substance Abuse among Blacks in the U.S.* Washington, D.C., February 1990.

U.S. Department of Justice, Bureau of Justice Statistics Special Report. (Tracy Snell.) *Survey of State Prison Inmates, 1991: Women in Prison*. Washington, D.C., 1991.

U.S. Department of Justice, Bureau of Justice Statistics. (Lawrence A. Greenfield and Tracy Snell.) *Women Offenders*. Washington, D.C., 1999.

U.S. Department of Justice, Federal Bureau of Prisons. "Race of Females in Federal Prison Facilities as of January 1, 1996." Correspondence with Denise Golvbaski.

U.S. Department of Labor, Office of Policy Planning and Research. (Daniel P. Moynihan.) *The Negro Family: The Case for National Action.* Washington, D.C.: Government Printing Office, 1965.

U.S. Federal Bureau of Prisons. (Sue Kline and Patty Garretti.) *Research Report: Black Females in Bureau of Prison Facilities.* Washington, D.C., October 13, 1991.

U.S. General Accounting Office. *Foster Care, Parental Drug Abuse Has Alarming Impact on Young Children.* Washington, D.C.: GAO/HEHS-94-89, April 1994.

U.S. Sentencing Commission. *Cocaine and Federal Sentencing Policy.* Washington, D.C.: Government Printing Office, 1995.

Van Anterwerp, Kathleen. *"I can't go to school today—my Mom's in prison and I don't have a ride": A Collection of Stories.* Ventura, Calif.: Quiet Thunder Publishing, 1998.

Watterson, Kathryn. *Women in Prison: Inside the Concrete Womb.* Boston: Northeastern University Press, 1996.

Wells-Barnett, Ida B. *On Lynchings: Southern Horrors, a Red Record, Mob Rule in New Orleans.* New York: Arno Press, 1969.

West, Cornel. *Race Matters.* Boston: Beacon Press, 1992.

Wicker, Tom. *A Time to Die: The Attica Prison Revolt.* Lincoln: University of Nebraska Press, 1994.

Wilson, James Q. "Crime, Race and Values." *Society* 30 (November/December 1992): 90–93.

Wilson, William J. *The Truly Disadvantaged: The Inner City, the Underclass, and Public Policy.* Chicago: University of Chicago Press, 1987.

Wolfgang, Marvin E. *Crime and Justice.* New York: Basic Books, 1977.

———. "Making the Criminal Justice System Accountable." *Crime and Delinquency* 18 (January 1972): 15–22.

Women's Press Collective. *Save JoAnn Little.* Oakland, Calif.: Women's Press Collective, 1976.

Index

About the Author

PAULA C. JOHNSON is professor of law at Syracuse University College of Law, in New York. She received her B.A. from the University of Maryland, College Park, her J.D. from Temple University Law School, and her LL.M. from Georgetown University Law Center. At Syracuse University, she teaches criminal law, criminal procedure, voting rights, professional responsibility, and a seminar on women in the criminal justice system. She also has taught at the University of Arizona, the University of Baltimore and Northern Illinois University.

Her legal writings include "Danger in the Diaspora: Law, Culture and Violence against Women of African Descent in the United States and South Africa," 1 *University of Iowa Journal of Gender, Race and Justice* 471 (1998); "The Social Construction of Identity in Criminal Cases: Cinema Verité and the Pedagogy of Vincent Chin," 1 *Michigan Journal of Race and Law* 347 (1996); "At the Intersection of Injustice: Experiences of African American Women in Crime and Sentencing," 4 *American University Journal of Gender and Law* 1 (1995); and "Silence Equals Death: The Response to AIDS within Communities of Color," *University of Illinois Law Review* 1075 (1992).

Her photographs, particularly of African peoples and landscapes, have been widely exhibited.

She was raised in Washington, D.C., and Maryland, and currently resides in New York. Her email address is pcjohnso@law.syr.edu.